COMPOSITION: MODELS AND EXERCISES

John E. Warriner
General Editor

FIFTH COURSE

HARCOURT BRACE JOVANOVICH, PUBLISHERS
Orlando   New York   Chicago   San Diego   Atlanta   Dallas

JOHN E. WARRINER taught English for thirty-two years in junior and senior high schools and in college. He is the general editor of the *Composition: Models and Exercises* series, the chief author of the *English Grammar and Composition* series, a coauthor of the *English Workshop* series, and editor of *Short Stories: Characters in Conflict.*

Printed in the United States of America

ISBN 0-15-310959-9

ACKNOWLEDGMENTS; *For permission to reprint copyrighted material, grateful acknowledgment is made to the following sources:*
ASSOCIATED BOOK PUBLISHERS LTD.: From *The English Language* by C. L. Wrenn. Published by Methuen & Co. Ltd.
GEORGE BORCHARDT, INC.: From *Charles Dickens: His Tragedy and Triumph* by Edgar Johnson, © 1952 by Edgar Johnson.
CURTIS BROWN, LTD.: "History on the Silver Screen" in *Talents and Geniuses* by Gilbert Highet. Copyright © 1957 by Gilbert Highet. "One of the Best" from *A Pocketful of Pebbles* by Jan Struther. Copyright 1936, 1943, 1944, 1945, 1946 by Jan Struther; copyright renewed © 1973 by Adolf Kurt Placzek.
SHIRLEY COLLIER AGENCY: From *Miners Hill* by Michael O'Malley, published by Harper & Row, Publishers, Inc., © by Michael O'Malley 1962.
THE DIAL PRESS and JAMES BALDWIN: From *Another Country* by James Baldwin, copyright © 1960, 1962 by James Baldwin.
DODD, MEAD & COMPANY, INC.: From *The Lost Woods* by Edwin Way Teale, copyright 1945 by Edwin Way Teale, copyright renewed 1973 by Edwin Way Teale.
DOUBLEDAY & COMPANY, INC.: From *Crusade in Europe* by Dwight D. Eisenhower. Copyright 1948 by Doubleday & Company, Inc.
DOUBLEDAY & COMPANY, INC. and VICTOR GOLLANCZ LTD.: Excerpts from *This Hallowed Ground* by Bruce Catton. Copyright © 1955, 1956 by Bruce Catton.
E. P. DUTTON & CO., INC.: From *Shakespeare of London* by Marchette Chute, copyright 1949 by E. P. Dutton & Co., Inc.
W. H. FREEMAN AND COMPANY: From "The Spider and the Wasp" by Alexander Petrunkevitch, copyright 1952 by Scientific American, Inc. All rights reserved.
HARCOURT BRACE JOVANOVICH, INC.: From "The Patented Gate and the Mean Hamburger" by Robert Penn Warren. Copyright 1947, 1975 by Robert Penn Warren. Reprinted from his volume, *The Circus in the Attic and Other Stories.* From *A Walker in the City* by Alfred Kazin. Copyright 1951 by Alfred Kazin.
HARCOURT BRACE JOVANOVICH, INC. and GEORGE ALLEN & UNWIN LTD.: From "How Dictionaries Are Made" in *Language in Thought and Action,* Second Edition by S. I. Hayakawa. Copyright 1941, 1949, © 1963, 1964 by Harcourt Brace Jovanovich, Inc.

Contents

SECTION THREE: NARRATION

SECTION SIX: WRITING ABOUT LITERATURE

The Paragraph

LESSON **1**
Unity in Paragraphs

An effective paragraph is unified, which is another way of saying that every sentence in it contributes to a common goal. This lesson illustrates how unity is achieved in three different types of paragraphs: descriptive, narrative, and expository.

UNITY IN A DESCRIPTIVE PARAGRAPH   The following paragraph, from Virginia Woolf's novel *To the Lighthouse*, describes a deserted dwelling. In doing so, it conveys a single vivid impression.

1   Virginia Woolf in *To the Lighthouse*

The house was left; the house was deserted. It was left like a shell on a sandhill to fill with dry salt grains now that life had left it. The long night seemed to have set in; the trifling airs, nibbling, the clammy breaths, fumbling, seemed to have triumphed. The saucepan had rusted and the mat decayed. Toads had nosed their way in. Idly, aimlessly, the swaying shawl swung to and fro. A thistle thrust itself between the tiles in the larder. The swallows nested in the drawing room; the floor was strewn with straw; the plaster fell in shovelfuls; rafters were laid bare; rats carried off this and that to gnaw behind the wainscots. Tortoise-shell butterflies burst from the chrysalis and pattered their life out on the windowpane. Poppies sowed themselves among the dahlias; the lawn waved with long grass; giant artichokes towered among roses; a fringed carnation flowered among the cabbages; while the gentle tapping of a weed at the window had become, on winters' nights, a drumming from sturdy trees and thorned briars which made the whole room green in summer.

The Writer's Craft

1. The desolation of an abandoned dwelling is the *unifying idea* of this paragraph of description. Does every sentence help the reader visualize the house and feel its atmosphere?

2. In writing description the writer should avoid irrelevant details — extraneous bits of information (however interesting in themselves) that have no connection with the unifying idea of the paragraph. Consider the italicized sentence below:

> The swallows nested in the drawing room; the floor was strewn with straw; the plaster fell in shovelfuls; rafters were laid bare; rats carried off this and that to gnaw behind the wainscots. *One object the rats removed was a high-button, patent-leather shoe.* Tortoise-shell butterflies burst from the chrysalis and pattered their life out on the windowpane.

Does the italicized sentence have anything to do with the appearance or condition of the house? How does it affect the unity of the paragraph?

Now You Try It

Choose one of the following assignments:

1. Write a paragraph describing one of the places or objects listed below. Be sure that all your sentences help create a vivid impression of the subject chosen.

    a. A carefully restored antique car
    b. A fashionable new dress
    c. A site where a building is being erected
    d. A lake in the woods
    e. A house that is said to be haunted

2. Use one of the following sentences as the introductory statement in a paragraph of description. Make sure that every detail you mention supports the introductory statement, which in this case will be the unifying idea.

a. Although nearly forty, he still looked like a teddy bear.
b. Everything about his face proclaimed one emotion: anger!
c. He tried to be stern, but all his features spoke of gentleness and kindness.
d. Obviously little Jennifer had been playing in the mud.

UNITY IN A NARRATIVE PARAGRAPH   In the following model the author remembers a childhood story which tells of Lo Bun Sun who gets shipwrecked on an uninhabited island. One day he discovers a human footprint on the beach.

2   Maxine Hong Kingston in *China Men*

One day while patrolling the beach, where the crabs rolled seaweed bubbles across the sand, Lo Bun Sun saw something that sent a burning fear up his spine— a human footprint. He ran to one of his fortifications. He chattered, "It can't be. It can't be." After starving for human company for twelve years, he did not shout, "Where are you? Who are you? Hey, where are you? Come on out. Welcome. Welcome. I'm here. I'm over here." Instead, he became scared and henceforth timid on his island. His eyelid began to twitch. He took up the musket, which he always kept loaded anyway, and never again walked abroad without it. He stuck loaded pistols and rifles in gunports in his walls. For days he shivered in his cave, peeked through cracks in every direction, jumped at noises of winds and animals. He had another look at the print. Perhaps he had construed a human foot rather than paw or hoof or claw because of his loneliness. In need of human company, he had imagined the five toes and a heel. But, no, there it was —unmistakably the imprint of a naked human foot.

The Writer's Craft

1. What incident is depicted in the paragraph? Are all the sentences in the paragraph related to that incident? Is the paragraph unified?

2. Suppose the author had added this sentence to the conclusion of the paragraph:

> Lo Bun Sun thought of the shipwreck, when all of his fellow sailors perished in the storm-swept surf.

How would this sentence affect the unity of the paragraph?

Now You Try It

Choose a simple incident — one with a clear beginning, middle, and end — and tell about it in a single paragraph. Be sure that all the sentences in the paragraph relate directly to the incident. Use one of the ideas suggested below, or devise one of your own.

    a. A student finds ten dollars at school, hesitates, then decides to turn it in.

    b. The end drops a key pass in an important football game.

    c. A student opens a letter from a college and learns that she (he) has been accepted.

    d. A student hurries into class late and sits down.

UNITY IN AN EXPOSITORY PARAGRAPH The next paragraph is expository. Identify the unifying idea and notice whether each sentence helps support it.

3   Rachel Carson in *The Sea Around Us*

Perhaps the most striking differences are in the range of tide, which varies tremendously in different parts of the world, so that what the inhabitants of one place might consider disastrously high water might be regarded as no tide at all by coastal communities only a hundred miles distant. The highest tides in the world occur in the Bay of Fundy, with a rise of about 50 feet in

Minas Basin near the head of the Bay at the spring tides.* At least half a dozen other places scattered around the world have a tidal range of more than 30 feet—Puerto Gallegos in Argentina and Cook Inlet in Alaska, Frobisher Bay in Davis Strait, the Koksoak River emptying into Hudson Strait, and the Bay of St. Malo in France come to mind. At many other places 'high tide' may mean a rise of only a foot or so, perhaps only a few inches. The tides of Tahiti rise and fall in a gentle movement, with a difference of no more than a foot between high water and low.

* **spring tides:** tides that occur at the new and the full moon, producing the highest flood tide and the lowest ebb tide of each month.

The Writer's Craft

1. The unifying idea in Carson's paragraph is that the change in the water level from high to low tide varies greatly from place to place. In some places the water level rises and falls more than thirty feet, and in others only a foot or so. Do all of the sentences support the paragraph's unifying idea?

2. If the italicized sentence below were added, what effect would it have on the unity of the paragraph?

> *The highest tides of the month occur when the sun, the moon, and the earth are directly in line.*

Now You Try It

Use one of the following as the first sentence of an expository paragraph. Develop or support the idea expressed in the opening sentence with relevant facts and examples.

  a. The American is, on the whole, _____. (Supply an appropriate adjective or adjectives.)
  b. The best teen-age books are those not written specifically for teen-agers.
  c. The United States has regained (or lost) its worldwide supremacy in sports.
  d. Ideas about education are changing in the United States.

LESSON **2**
The Topic Sentence

A unified paragraph develops a single clear idea. But how is that idea conveyed? Does a writer repeat it in every sentence of the paragraph? Or does the writer merely hint at the idea, hoping the reader will guess what it is? A look at a typical expository paragraph will provide the answer.

4   Lesley Byrd Simpson in *Many Mexicos*

Rainfall is of such transcendental importance in the life of Mexico that we must follow the map around in order to understand it. Beginning with the extreme northwest we find the long tongue of Lower California spanning the belt of greatest aridity. Its northern end, on the Pacific coast at least, comes in for a small share of the rains brought by the cyclonic storms, but the next 700 miles of it are a scorched and almost uninhabited desert, until its southern tip intrudes a little way into the fringe of the tropical rain belt. Crossing over to the east side of the Gulf of California, we come to the Sonora Desert, which for 500 miles south of the border is one of the most fearfully arid wastes on the surface of the globe, where the temperature rises to such heights as to make the desert impassable save in the relatively cool months of winter. But south of Guaymas the aspect of the coastal plain gradually changes, becoming greener and more habitable in Sinaloa, and, finally, going to the opposite extreme, becomes a dense tropical jungle north of Cape Corrientes.

The Writer's Craft

1. The paragraph includes many factual details: among them, that cyclonic storms bring rain to the northern end of Lower California, that much of the rest of Lower California is uninhabited, that the Sonora Desert is 500 miles across and one of the most fearfully arid wastes on the surface of the globe, and that the area in Mexico north of Cape Corrientes is a dense tropical jungle. Does the presence of so many different facts mean that the paragraph lacks unity? Or is there one unifying idea that ties together all the separate details?

2. The author expresses the unifying idea of the paragraph in a single sentence, called the *topic sentence*. Which sentence is it?

THE TOPIC SENTENCE AT THE BEGINNING OF A PARAGRAPH   A topic sentence directly expresses the main idea of a paragraph. Very often the topic sentence comes first, as in Model 4 and also in the paragraph below.

5   Barbara W. Tuchman in *A Distant Mirror*

The crossbow, made of wood, steel, and sinew, and pulled by aid of the archer's foot in a stirrup and a hook or winding handle attached to his belt, or by a complicated arrangement of winches and pulleys, shot a bolt of great penetrating power, but the bow was slow and cumbersome to wield and heavy to carry. The crossbowman usually carried about fifty bolts with him into action, and his equipment en route had to be transported by wagon. Owing to the long wind-up, the crossbow was in fact more useful in static situations such as clearing ramparts in sieges than in open battle. A charge of knights willing to take some losses could generally shatter the crossbowmen's line. Although its mechanical power when first invented had been frightening so that it was banned by the Church in 1139, the crossbow had continued in use for 200 years without threatening the knights' mailed* dominion.

> * **mailed:** armored (from **chain mail:** flexible armor made from overlapping metal rings or scales)

The Writer's Craft

1. Tuchman's paragraph discusses the advantages and the disadvantages of the crossbow. Are its advantages and disadvantages treated equally? Does discussing both aspects of the crossbow destroy the unity of the paragraph?

2. How does the first sentence—the topic sentence—help unify the paragraph? Would it be equally effective as the last sentence of the paragraph? Why, or why not?

Now You Try It

Select one of the topics listed below; then write a topic sentence that makes a specific statement about it and develop it into a complete paragraph. Make sure the paragraph you write is unified.

a. The first step in applying to college
b. The chief advantage of extracurricular activities
c. The main ingredient in teen-age popularity
d. Our city's major attraction
e. The quality I most admire in a teacher
f. One way in which American society has changed during the past year
g. The biggest effect inflation has had on your daily life
h. The most promising career opportunities now available to graduates

THE TOPIC SENTENCE AT THE END OF A PARAGRAPH Although commonly found at the beginning, the topic sentence may appear anywhere within the paragraph, or be omitted entirely when what unifies the paragraph is perfectly clear. In the following model the topic sentence occurs at the end.

6 Edgar Allan Poe in "The Fall of the House of Usher"

The room in which I found myself was very large and lofty. The windows were long, narrow, and pointed, and at so vast a distance from the black oaken floor as to be altogether inaccessible from within. Feeble gleams of encrimsoned light made their way through the trellised panes, and served to render sufficiently distinct the more prominent objects around. The eye, however, struggled in vain to reach the remoter angles of the chamber, or the recesses of the vaulted and fretted ceiling. Dark draperies hung upon the walls. The general furniture was profuse, comfortless, antique, and tattered. Many books and musical instruments lay scattered about, but failed to give any vitality to the scene. I felt that I breathed an atmosphere of sorrow. An air of stern, deep, and irredeemable gloom hung over and pervaded all.

The Writer's Craft

1. If Poe had chosen to put the topic sentence first, the paragraph might have begun:

> An air of stern, deep, and irredeemable gloom hung over the room in which I found myself. It was a very large and lofty room. The windows were long. . . .

Does placing the topic sentence at the beginning make the paragraph less effective than the original? Explain.

2. A paragraph like Poe's may be said to move inductively. Evidence is presented piece by piece; then the unifying idea is stated in the last sentence. Under what circumstances might placing a topic sentence at the end of a paragraph be effective?

Write a paragraph using one of the following as the concluding topic sentence.

a. As such movies show, Hollywood can ruin a good book.
b. Each morning brings a new crisis that our family just barely survives.
c. All these attributes are important in a faculty adviser.
d. The popularity of teen-age idols is short-lived.
e. For those reasons, it may not be wise to sell a used car to a friend.

THE CLINCHER SENTENCE   Occasionally a writer, having stated the main idea in the first sentence, will restate it — in slightly different words — in the last sentence of the paragraph. The following model shows why such a summarizing device, called the *clincher sentence*, is especially useful in long, complex paragraphs.

7   Brooks Atkinson in "An Introduction to Thoreau's Writings"

As a writer Thoreau embraced so many subjects that it is still difficult to catalogue him. He was "poet-naturalist," as Channing described him; but he was also philosopher, historian, economist, rebel, revolutionary, reporter. Apart from its poetic record of an idyllic adventure, *Walden* is the practical philosophy of rebellion against the world's cowardly habits of living. Most formless of his books and yet most winning and lighthearted, *The Week* is a compound of thought, scholarship, speculation, and narrative. *The Maine Woods* is the most pungent and profound study of woods and camping that has ever been written. *On the Duty of Civil Disobedience* is an eloquent declaration of the principles that make revolution inevitable in times of political dishonor. The John Brown papers are political pamphleteering. Large portions of the journals are character studies of the people in Concord whom Thoreau most admired. Although he rarely left Concord and seldom read the newspapers, he was well informed about the life of his times and had fiery opinions about slavery and justice. His achievements in those fields have somewhat overshadowed the range of his scholarship and the brilliance of his detached portraits of people. Almost nothing escaped the keen eyes and mind of this tireless writer; there is a bewildering variety in his work.

The Writer's Craft

1. What idea unifies the paragraph? Which sentence is the topic sentence? Which is the clincher sentence? Why do you think the author used a clincher sentence in this instance?

2. The clincher sentence is not a word-for-word repetition of the topic sentence. Why is it desirable to vary the wording?

3. Sometimes the clincher sentence is stated more emphatically than the topic sentence. Why might that be?

Now You Try It

Select one of the following as a topic sentence. Put it first, develop a paragraph based on it, and end the paragraph with an effective clincher sentence.

a. Young people influence the quality of American life.

b. Shoes can be instruments of torture.

c. Slang has a vividness that is missing in formal usage.

d. The best mystery stories have believable characters as well as a distinctive atmosphere.

e. Proverbs don't always give sound advice.

LESSON **3**

Paragraph Development

A topic sentence, which states a unifying idea, almost never constitutes the entire substance of a paragraph. Nevertheless, inexperienced writers often create paragraphs simply by repeating over and over in different words the statement made in the topic sentence. The result is inevitably poor. Effective development requires the use of specific details, of which three kinds are examples, incidents, and reasons. To be sure, many paragraphs use a combination of these devices, but in this lesson each of the three will be examined separately.

DEVELOPMENT WITH EXAMPLES   Often the unifying idea of a paragraph can be effectively supported or clarified by means of specific examples, either of facts or opinions. Hard facts are used in the following model.

8   Shirley Foster Hartley
in *Population: Quantity vs. Quality*

Although we have witnessed an unprecedented decline in death rates, physicians are not miracle workers; they are human beings who are still learning about many of the afflictions of the human system. They are limited in numbers and especially scarce in the less developed countries. In those areas, public health administrators with mass campaigns, vaccines, and residual insecticides have served large areas well. Yet Dr. M. G. Candau, Director-General of the World Health Organization, points out that nearly 380 million human beings in the malarious areas of the world are still without the protection of eradication schemes. There are probably even now around ten million sufferers from leprosy, and more than 4.5 million from yaws. There are possibly 400 million who suffer from trachoma, 200 million from bilharziasis (a debilitating intestinal disease), and 20 million from onchocerciasis (a parasitic disease that sometimes causes blindness). It is estimated that in certain countries bilharziasis affects 30– 40 percent of the population at one time or another in their lives. Even more astonishing to those who take their own advantages for granted are estimates that about 70 percent of the *world's* population lacks an adequate safe water supply and 85 percent has to depend on the most primitive methods for the disposal of excreta and refuse. All of these problems would be within the realm of health and medical control if only there were adequate numbers of medical workers and auxiliary services.

The Writer's Craft

1. The first two sentences in this paragraph state the general ideas that doctors are not miracle workers and that there is a shortage of medical workers. How does Hartley develop those ideas? What effect do you think her method of development was intended to have on readers?

2. After Hartley gives statistics on diseases and on lack of sanitation in less-developed countries, she writes a final sentence for her paragraph. What purpose does that sentence serve? Do you feel it's necessary? Explain.

Model 8 was developed with statistics, which are factual. Model 9 is another paragraph in which the topic sentence is developed with examples, though in this case they are not statistics.

9   Ruth Kirk in *Snow*

Wild animals have certain safeguards for the snow they are sure to encounter. Polar bears' eyes, for instance, are equipped with a nictitating* membrane that passes sideways across the eyeball and clears slush, which blinds prairie cattle and arctic sled dogs. At the onset of winter, sables outside Moscow grow forty-four fine underhairs for each longer bristle hair, twice the number of underhairs they have in summer and marvelous protection against cold and wind-driven snow. Martens achieve the same effect in a different way. The underhairs of their fur nearly double in length, and the new bristle hairs grow in one-third longer than those of the summer coat. This means more air trapped within the double winter coat and, therefore, increased insulation. Arctic foxes turn white in winter, as camouflage, and the shafts of the new hairs hold minute dead-air spaces for insulation. The soles of their feet become furry, which simultaneously helps keep the paws warm and acts as built-in "snowshoes."

* **nictitating:** the action of an inner eyelid winking or blinking to clean the eye.

The Writer's Craft

1. How many examples does the author give to support her topic sentence? Would fewer examples have been just as effective? How does an author decide how many examples to use?

2. When a unifying idea of a paragraph is supported by specific examples sometimes a distinction is drawn between examples which are facts and examples which are reasons. In practice the distinction is often hard to maintain. Facts *prove*, and reasons *illustrate*. Are the examples used in the paragraph facts or reasons? Why, or why not?

The examples that develop a paragraph may take many forms, including those of opinions, of statistics (as in Model 8), and of factual statements (as in Model 9). The following passage illustrates yet another form that examples may assume.

10   H. L. Mencken in *The American Language*

The settlement of the continent, once the Eastern coast ranges were crossed, proceeded with unparalleled speed, and so the naming of the new rivers, lakes, peaks and valleys, and of the new towns and districts, strained the inventiveness of the pioneers. The result is the vast duplication of names that shows itself in the Postal Guide. No less than eighteen imitative *Bostons* and *New Bostons* still appear, and there are nineteen *Bristols*, twenty-eight *Newports*, and twenty-two *Londons* and *New Londons*. Argonauts starting out from an older settlement on the coast would take its name with them, and so we find *Philadelphias* in Illinois, Mississippi, Missouri, and Tennessee; *Richmonds* in Iowa, Kansas, and nine other Western States, and *Princetons* in fifteen. Even when a new name was hit upon, it seems to have been hit upon simultaneously by scores of scattered bands of settlers; thus we find the whole land bespattered with *Washingtons*, *Lafayettes*, *Jeffersons*, and *Jacksons*, and with names suggested by common and obvious natural objects, e.g., *Bear Creek*, *Bald Knob*, and *Buffalo*. The Geographic Board, in its fourth report, made a belated protest against this excessive duplication. "The names *Elk*, *Beaver*, *Cottonwood*, and *Bald*," it said, "are altogether too numerous." Of post offices alone there are fully a hundred embodying *Elk;* counting in rivers, lakes, creeks, mountains, and valleys, the map of the United States probably shows at least twice as many such names.

The Writer's Craft

1. Examples in the model are place-names, and they make up the substance of the paragraph. Yet even so, examples are not enough; a statement of the topic is essential. Where does the author state the topic? How many sentences does he use to make the statement?

2. Reconsider the paragraph with the statement of the topic omitted. What is the effect of constructing the paragraph with examples alone?

3. Could the author have supported his statement about "the vast duplication of names" in American geography without giving examples? Does his use of the word *vast* control, to some extent, the number of examples he must give? Do you think Mencken gives more examples than are necessary to prove his point?

Consider one more paragraph developed with examples.

11   Edith Hamilton in *Mythology*

The terrifying irrational has no place in classical mythology. Magic, so powerful in the world before and after Greece, is almost nonexistent. There are no men and only two women with dreadful, supernatural powers. The demoniac wizards and the hideous old witches who haunted Europe and America, too, up to quite recent years, play no part at all in the stories. Circe and Medea* are the only witches and they are young and of surpassing beauty—delightful, not horrible. Astrology, which has flourished from the days of ancient Babylon down to today, is completely absent from classical Greece. There are many stories about the stars, but not a trace of the idea that they influence

* **Circe . . . Medea:** the sorceress-goddess who transformed Odysseus' men into swine . . . the beautiful princess, skilled in magic, who helped Jason obtain the Golden Fleece.

men's lives. Astronomy is what the Greek mind finally made out of the stars. Not a single story has a magical priest who is terribly to be feared because he knows ways of winning over the gods or alienating them. The priest* is rarely seen and is never of importance. In the *Odyssey* when a priest and a poet fall on their knees before Odysseus, praying him to spare their lives, the hero kills the priest without a thought, but saves the poet. Homer says that he felt awe to slay a man who had been taught his divine art by the gods. Not the priest, but the poet, had influence with heaven—and no one was ever afraid of a poet. Ghosts, too, which have played so large and so fearsome a part in other lands, never appear on earth in any Greek story. The Greeks were not afraid of the dead—"the piteous dead," the *Odyssey* calls them.

* **priest:** high priest; to the ancient Greeks a kind of sorcerer.

The Writer's Craft

1. What idea unifies the paragraph? Is it stated in a single topic sentence? If not, in how many sentences is it stated?
2. The author says that the "irrational had no place in classical mythology," and that magic was almost nonexistent in classical Greece. Does the author provide enough examples to support her idea convincingly?
3. Compare Hamilton's paragraph with the preceding one (Model 10). What differences do you notice in the kinds of examples used in the two models?

Now You Try It

Select one of the following topics and develop it into a paragraph by means of examples—statistical or otherwise.

a. Average life expectancy in the United States is increasing.
b. Many English words are derived from the names of places or persons. (Look up, for example, *maudlin, sandwich, hector, mentor, macadam, bedlam, boycott.*)
c. Styles in clothes change every year.

d. A knowledge of history makes us realize that our problems are not unique.

e. Frequently modern fiction portrays the unheroic hero.

DEVELOPMENT WITH AN INCIDENT   Another way to develop a paragraph is by means of one or more incidents that illustrate the idea expressed in the topic sentence.

12   Margaret Mead in "Living with the Natives of Melanesia"

The endless tabus upon mentioning the names of any relative-in-law in a person's presence make it necessary to know the social organization of the village by heart, all the past marriages, the present marriages, the contemplated marriages. In addition it is necessary to know each person's three or four names. Even then one is continually trespassing, as when I inadvertently sneezed in the presence of a woman whose daughter was engaged to a youth named "Sneeze." There are relatives-in-law who may not look at each other, and it was necessary to construct a house with several exits, so that mothers-in-law could depart as sons-in-law entered, for it is always the women who have to do the running away. On one occasion, when I was alone in the village and had added to my household of six small boys and two girls, a man and his wife, there were so many complicated relationships that the only place where Ngaoli, my seventeen-year-old girl, could eat, without transgressing, was huddled in a corner behind the bed. And the linguistic confusion which resulted from getting a new cook boy who was the brother-in-law of three of the other boys was terrifying. One could not say his name in front of them but must refer to him grandiloquently as "the husband of Pondramet" (their sister); if he were also in the room, even this would not serve, as his wife's name could not be mentioned in his presence.

The paragraph begins with a statement of the social situation that the anthropologist-writer found on a South Pacific island. (It should be noted that she wrote this piece in 1931.) As the paragraph continues, Mead discusses not only the tabus against mentioning the names of relatives-in-law but also the tabus against looking at certain relatives-in-law. Throughout the paragraph, Mead uses incidents to illustrate the general statements she makes. What three incidents does she cite as support for her statements about the complex tabus?

Here is another paragraph in which an incident is used to develop a topic sentence.

13   Bruce Catton in *This Hallowed Ground*

In the Shenandoah Valley, Union soldiers were learning that southern civilians could be exactly like the folks at home and that there could be a touch of friendship now and then between the invaders and the invaded. The 13th Massachusetts was appealed to by a valley farmer for protection against foragers, and the colonel detailed four men to guard the place. The farmer insisted that they stay in the house and make themselves comfortable; he would go about his duties and would call them if any prowlers appeared. His wife would not let them bunk down in the yard when night came, but put them in bedrooms with soft mattresses and clean white sheets, told them to sleep until they were called in the morning, served breakfast at eight-thirty — hominy and bacon, potatoes and fried chicken, hot biscuits and coffee, all they could eat. When the regiment finally had to move on and the detail was called away, the farmer went to the colonel to testify what fine young men these soldiers were, and his wife sent a huge basket of biscuits and cakes for them to take with them. All the rest of the war the 13th Massachusetts nursed this memory.

The Writer's Craft

1. Everyone likes a story; accordingly, an incident has a built-in appeal. But incidents vary, of course, in their interest. Do you find the one Catton relates interesting? What idea does it illustrate? Why do you think an author like Bruce Catton, whose writings about history are intended for the general reader rather than the scholar, makes frequent use of incidents in developing paragraphs?

2. In developing paragraphs with incidents, where would you place the topic sentence? Is one position more effective than another? Explain.

Now You Try It

Select one of the topic sentences below, or devise one of your own, and develop it into a paragraph by means of a brief incident.

a. Many city dwellers are indifferent to their neighbors.
b. Some people have an infuriating habit of saying things at the wrong time.
c. Practical jokes are not always funny.
d. An election is sometimes won or lost because of a single event.
e. I had a few hair-raising experiences where I worked last summer.

DEVELOPMENT WITH REASONS Paragraphs in which the topic sentence states an opinion may be developed with reasons, which in turn may be either examples, incidents, or additional supporting opinions. Reasons support the opening statement of opinion in the following paragraph.

14 Edgar Johnson
in *Charles Dickens: His Tragedy and Triumph*

Of all Dickens' novels, *David Copperfield* is the most enchanting. Few novelists have ever captured more poignantly the feeling of childhood, the brightness and magic and terror of the world as seen through the eyes of a child and colored by his dawning emotions. Dickens renders all the vividness and flavor of those early days when the grass is unbelievably green and fruit "riper and richer than fruit has ever been since." He mirrors the tenderness of reposing safely in the assurance of maternal love, the heart-quaking mystery of a sudden harshness or frightening anger in grown-ups, the disjointed strangeness of a universe discovered to contain such wonders as geese and crocodiles and graveyards and cathedrals. *David* has, too, the savagery and brutality of boyhood, its boyish hero worship, and its luminous blur of shining aspiration. And, following on these, come the widening though still confused horizons of adolescence and its endeavors to grasp the world, the problems of embarking upon a career, the tremulous silliness and ecstasy of youthful love.

The Writer's Craft

1. What is the topic sentence in this paragraph, and what opinion does it express? Do the author's reasons adequately support the broad generalization of the topic sentence? Are his reasons factual, or are they statements of specific opinions that support his overall opinion?

2. Would a clincher sentence make the paragraph even more effective? Why, or why not?

Here is another paragraph developed with reasons. Notice how they help answer the unstated question raised by the topic sentence — "Why?"

15   Margaret Mead in "What Women Want"

Women in our society complain of the lack of stimulation, of the loneliness, of the dullness of staying at home. Little babies are poor conversationalists, husbands come home tired and sit reading the paper, and women who used to pride themselves on their ability to talk find on the rare evening they can go out that their words clot on their tongues. As the children go to school, the mother is left to the companionship of the Frigidaire and the washing machine. Yet she can't go out because the delivery man might come, or a child might be sent home sick from school. The boredom of long hours of solitary one-sided communication with things, no matter how shining and streamlined and new, descends upon her. Moreover, the conditions of modern life, apartment living, and especially the enormous amount of moving about, all serve to rob women of neighborhood ties. The better her electric equipment, the better she organizes her ordering, the less reason she has to run out for a bit of gossipy shopping at the corner store. The department stores and the moving-picture houses cater to women — alone — on their few hours out. Meanwhile efficient mending services and cheap ready-made clothes have taken most sensible busy work out of women's hands and left women — still at home — listening to the radio, watching television.

The Writer's Craft

1. What are some of the reasons given to explain why women are bored with their home life? Do the reasons support the topic sentence?

2. The writer's topic sentence might be developed by means of an incident or incidents. What specific incidents would you use in developing such a paragraph?

Now You Try It

Develop one of the following topic sentences into a paragraph by means of reasons that are clear and fully explained.

    a. Not everybody should go to college.
    b. Every high school student should learn to type.
    c. _____ is not much of a movie.
    d. Congress should (or should not) subsidize a national theater.

LESSON **4**

Arrangement of Details

1. order of location
2. chronological order in a narrative
*   "   "   " exposition*
3. order of importance
4. order of comparison or contrast

Details in a paragraph may be arranged in a number of ways, four of which are considered in this lesson. The organizational method you choose for a particular paragraph will depend on your purpose, the nature of the subject, and the kinds of details that are used.

ORDER OF LOCATION   Details in descriptive paragraphs are usually presented according to their location in space and their relationship to one another. The following model is illustrative.

16   Winston Churchill in "The Battle of Britain"

The Group Operations Room was like a small theatre, about sixty feet across, and with two storeys. We took our seats in the Dress Circle.* Below us was the large-scale map table, around which perhaps twenty highly trained young men and women, with their telephone assistants, were assembled. Opposite to us, covering the entire wall, where the theatre curtain would be, was a gigantic blackboard divided into six columns with electric bulbs for the six fighter stations, each of their squadrons having a sub-column of its own, and also divided by lateral lines. Thus the lowest

* **Dress Circle:** a theater balcony.

row of bulbs showed as they were lighted the squadrons which were "Standing By" at two minutes' notice, the next row those at "Readiness," five minutes, then at "Available," 20 minutes, then those which had taken off, the next row those which had reported having seen the enemy, the next — with red lights — those which were in action, and the top row those which were returning home. On the left-hand side, in a kind of glass stage box, were the four or five officers whose duty it was to weigh and measure the information received from our Observer Corps, which at this time numbered upwards of 50,000 men, women, and youths. Radar was still in its infancy, but it gave warning of raids approaching our coast, and the observers, with field glasses and portable telephones, were our main source of information about raiders flying overland. Several roomfuls of experienced people in other parts of the underground headquarters sifted them with great rapidity, and transmitted the results from minute to minute directly to the plotters seated around the table on the floor and to the officers supervising from the glass stage box.

The Writer's Craft

1. Churchill is describing a complex scene — the Group Operations Room that he visited at the height of the Battle of Britain. Personally involved in the scene, he describes it from his vantage point: "Below us," "Opposite to us," and so on. He explains the blackboard signaling system in considerable detail. How does he make the system clear to the reader?

2. Throughout the description a comparison is suggested. To what is the Group Operations Room being compared? What words and phrases indicate the comparison? Why do you think Churchill makes the comparison?

Now You Try It

Write a descriptive paragraph based on one of the following topic sentences. Present details in an order determined by their location.

a. Even the simple daisy is quite a complicated flower.
b. The room was in disarray.
c. From the top of the hill, I could see the town spread out beneath me.
d. With the decorations in place, the gym was hard to recognize.
e. One look at that alley would have depressed even the most cheerful spirit.
f. After the game, the field was a scene of bedlam.
g. It was the most beautiful building I had ever seen.

(circle "Location" words.)

CHRONOLOGICAL ORDER IN A NARRATIVE PARAGRAPH Most narrative paragraphs are arranged in chronological order; that is, the events are presented in the sequence in which they occurred, as in the following example.

17 James Baldwin in *Another Country*

The sun struck, on steel, on bronze, on stone, on glass, on the gray water far beneath them, on the turret tops and the flashing windshields of crawling cars, on the incredible highways, stretching and snarling and turning for mile upon mile, on the houses, square and high, low and gabled, and on their howling antennae, on the sparse, weak trees, and on those towers, in the distance, of the city of New York. The plane tilted, dropped and rose, and the whole earth slanted, now leaning against the windows of the plane, now dropping out of sight. The sky was hot, blank blue, and the static light invested everything with its own lack of motion. Only things could be seen from here, the work of people's hands: but the people did not exist. The plane rose up, up, as though loath to descend from this high tranquillity; tilted, and Yves looked down, hoping to see the Statue of Liberty, though he had been warned that it could not be seen from here; then the plane began, like a stone, to drop, the water rushed up at them, the motors groaned, the wings trembled, resisting the awful, downward pull.

Then, when the water was at their feet, the white strip of the landing flashed into place beneath them. The wheels struck the ground with a brief and heavy thud, and wires and lights and towers went screaming by. The hostess' voice came over the speaker, congratulating them on their journey, and hoping to see them soon again.

The Writer's Craft

1. Events in this paragraph, from the early sight of New York to the completed landing, are presented in the order in which they happened. What words help you keep that order clear?

2. On occasion an author will emphasize one event by presenting it out of chronological order. If Baldwin had done so, the result might have read something like this:

> The wheels struck the ground with a brief and heavy thud. For some minutes before that instant, Yves had watched from the plane window as the sun glared down on steel, on bronze, on stone, on glass, on the gray water far beneath them. . . .

Why do you think the author in this instance adhered to strict chronological order?

CHRONOLOGICAL ORDER IN AN EXPOSITORY PARAGRAPH Often a paragraph that explains how to do something, or how something is done, is organized chronologically, as in the following model, which presents a step-by-step explanation of how a fresco is painted.

18 Joshua Taylor in *Learning to Look*

Preliminary to painting a fresco, the wall, which must be sound and free from dampness, is given one or more coats of plaster made from lime and sand. Often the artist then transfers his cartoon to the wall to judge the effect of his design before proceeding. When the artist is ready to paint, a very fine layer of smooth plaster is applied over that portion of the surface that the artist intends to finish in one working period. This smooth coating, called the intonaco, is made from very fine sand, lime, and sometimes marble dust. Onto this surface the artist transfers his final design and proceeds to paint with his water-ground pigments while the plaster is still damp. If a portion of the final intonaco coat remains unpainted at the end of the working period, it is scraped away before it dries, since true fresco must be painted on fresh plaster. A large fresco is completed, then, in small sections at a time, often carefully predetermined so that their joinings correspond with contours in the painting and are thus less conspicuous.

The Writer's Craft

1. The paragraph presents steps in fresco painting in the order in which they occur. What words and phrases help make the sequence clear?

2. Is the paragraph intended for someone who wants to paint a fresco, or simply for the person who wants to know how a fresco is painted? How can you tell?

3. The paragraph has no topic sentence, though it does, of course, have a unifying idea. In other words, the topic sentence is *implied*. What is there about the development of the paragraph that makes a stated topic sentence unnecessary? You could put an appropriate topic sentence at the beginning of the paragraph. If you did, how would you word it?

Now You Try It

Select one of the following as the topic sentence for a narrative or an expository paragraph that you will develop by giving details in chronological order.

a. In interviewing for a job you can make a good impression by following certain steps.

b. Planning and going out on a first date is a ritual with clearly established procedures.

c. The events of that tragic day are still a nightmare to me.
d. For me, getting up in the morning is a long and involved process.
e. An actor putting on make-up proceeds one step at a time.
f. Repainting an old car is no simple matter.
g. I remember every mistake I made in that game.
h. The crowd was about to get out of hand.

① list consequence of postponing D-day
② list own order of importance for your pa

ORDER OF IMPORTANCE The writer of an expository paragraph often arranges supporting details in the order of their importance. Usually the most effective order is from least to most important, so that the result builds toward a climax. On the other hand, a writer will sometimes reverse the order and put the most important details first. In reading the following paragraph about the possible results of postponing D-day in World War II, notice the order in which details are presented.

19 Dwight D. Eisenhower in *Crusade in Europe*

If none of these three days should prove satisfactory from the standpoint of weather, consequences would ensue that were almost terrifying to contemplate. Secrecy would be lost. Assault troops would be unloaded and crowded back into assembly areas enclosed in barbed wire, where their original places would already have been taken by those to follow in subsequent waves. Complicated movement tables would be scrapped. Morale would drop. A wait of at least fourteen days, possibly twenty-eight, would be necessary — a sort of suspended animation involving more than 2,000,000 men! The good weather period available for major campaigning would become still shorter and the enemy's defenses would become still stronger! The whole of the United Kingdom would become quickly aware that something had gone wrong and national discouragement there and in America could lead to unforeseen results. Finally, always lurking in the background was the knowledge that the enemy was developing new, and presumably effective, secret weapons on the French coast. What the effect of these would be on our crowded harbors, especially at Plymouth and Portsmouth, we could not even guess.

The Writer's Craft

1. What is the topic sentence of the paragraph? Does every other sentence help support it?

2. Which consequences of the postponement of D-day do you think General Eisenhower regarded as most important, in the sense of being potentially the most serious or dangerous? Which consequences did he probably consider as being of lesser importance? In what general order, then, are the supporting details arranged: from least to most important or from most to least important? Why is that an effective arrangement for the paragraph?

Now You Try It

Develop one of the following topic sentences in a paragraph in which details are organized according to order of importance.

a. _____ (name a city, state, or country) is known chiefly for three things.
b. Young people should have part-time jobs for a number of reasons.
c. The President of the United States has many responsibilities.
d. Educational television has by no means reached its fullest potential.
e. The Vietnam War resulted in changes in American attitudes.
f. Overemphasizing interscholastic sports can cause problems for a school.
g. A student should prepare for an important test in _____ stages. (You decide on the number.)

ORDER OF COMPARISON OR CONTRAST Sometimes an expository paragraph can be developed effectively by means of *comparisons* (to show similarities) and *contrasts* (to show differences). Usually an author will choose one of two variations on a special organizational pattern. Occasionally an author will mix the two organizational patterns when doing so helps to achieve a desirable effect. In the following model, a foreword to *A Night to Remember,* the author compares the ironic similarities between two seemingly unrelated events.

20   Walter Lord in *A Night To Remember*

In 1898 a struggling author named Morgan Robertson concocted a novel about a fabulous Atlantic liner, far larger than any that had ever been built. Robertson loaded his ship with rich and complacent people and then wrecked it one cold April night on an 5 iceberg. This somehow showed the futility of everything, and in fact, the book was called *Futility* when it appeared that year, published by the firm of M. F. Mansfield. Fourteen years later a British shipping company named the White Star Line built a steamer 10 remarkably like the one in Robertson's novel. The new liner was 66,000 tons displacement; Robertson's was 70,000 tons. The real ship was 882.5 feet long; the fictional one was 800 feet. Both vessels were triple screw and could make 24-25 knots. Both could carry 15 about 3000 people, and both had enough lifeboats for only a fraction of this number. But, then, this didn't seem to matter because both were labeled "unsinkable." On April 10, 1912, the real ship left Southampton on her maiden voyage to New York. 20 Her cargo included a priceless copy of the Rubáiyát of Omar Khayyám and a list of passengers collectively worth $250 million dollars. On her way over she too struck an iceberg and went down on a cold

April night. Robertson called his ship the *Titan;* the [25]
White Star Line called its ship the *Titanic.* This is
the story of her last night.

The Writer's Craft

1. In this paragraph the author has mixed the two types of
organizational patterns used when making comparisons. First
(lines 3–5) he discusses details pertaining only to the fictional
ship, and later (lines 12–14) he discusses details pertaining only
to the real ship. In the rest of the paragraph he uses the alternative
type of organizational pattern. How does this alternative type of
organization differ from discussing each ship separately?

2. Does mixing the two types of organization achieve a desirable effect? Would it have been wiser to apply only one type of
organization to the comparison?

Now You Try It

Select one of the topic sentences below, or devise one of your
own, to develop in a paragraph organized according to the pattern used in Model 20.

a. The United States Congress and the British Parliament
differ in several important ways.

b. More than just age makes seniors different from sophomores.

c. Pop art and realism are worlds apart.

d. Although they sprang from the same roots, jazz and the blues
have taken different forms.

e. Soccer and football call for quite different skills.

f. There are sharp differences between urban and suburban
living conditions in the United States.

LESSON **5**

Coherence in Paragraphs

A paragraph is coherent when the sentences that compose it are logically linked so that the reader can follow the sequence of ideas without confusion. Unity means that all the sentences relate to a single idea; coherence means that the sentences occur in a logical order. This lesson considers some ways in which writers achieve coherence by making relationships between sentences clear.

COHERENCE THROUGH TRANSITIONAL EXPRESSIONS   Certain words are particularly useful in showing relationships. *Afterward, moreover, finally, therefore, however, for example* — these and similar words and phrases, called *transitional expressions,* help make writing coherent by indicating precisely how ideas in paragraphs are related to each other. Notice transitional expressions in the following two models.

21   Albert H. Marckwardt in *American English*

In considering the history and development of American English we must remember that the courageous bands who ventured westward into the unknown with Captain John Smith or on board the *Mayflower,* as well as those who followed them later in the seventeenth century, were speaking and writing the English language as it was currently employed in England. <u>Consequently</u>, whatever linguistic processes operated to produce the differences between American and British English which exist today must either have taken place in American English after the colonists settled on this continent or have occurred in British English after the emigrants left their homeland. Or, as a third possibility, there may have been changes in both divisions of the language after the period of settlement. We cannot, however, escape the conclusion of original identity and subsequent change.

22   J. B. Priestley in "Other People's Weaknesses"

What delight we give other people by confessing to absurd weaknesses! For example, I cannot endure being tossed about in small boats, where I sweat with terror. Again, the sight and sound of a bat or a bird fluttering and banging about in a room fill me with disgust that can leap to fear and panic. When I have admitted this, I have seen people light up for the first time in their converse with me. At last I have succeeded in pleasing them. Until then, apparently, I have been insufferable. And I behave in the same fashion. I delight in J's terror of public speaking, in M's horror of spiders, in A's fear of being left alone in any old house, in H's rejection of all flying, in W's shuddering withdrawal from any cat. We like to feel that there is an equitable rationing system for this nonsense, and that we are all at times still children huddling together in the dark. A man or woman whose personality had not a speck of such weakness would be intolerable, not one of us at all, a sneering visitor from some other planet. Now and again they turn up, and we are delighted to see them go.

The Writer's Craft

1. What relationship between ideas is indicated by each underscored expression in Models 21 and 22? Reread Model 21, omitting the words *Consequently, Or,* and *however*. Does the para-

graph seem less clear without those transitional expressions? Why? Does the paragraph read less smoothly without them?

2. Most student writers use too few transitional expressions. If you get in the habit of using them liberally, you will inevitably increase the coherence of what you write, because to write the appropriate transitional expression requires that you be clear in your own mind about the relationship between the sentence you are writing and the one you wrote just before it. In Priestley's paragraph, what is the relationship between the seventh sentence and the eighth one? Accordingly, what transitional expression might the author have inserted in sentence 8?

COHERENCE THROUGH THE USE OF LINKING EXPRESSIONS
The thoughts in a paragraph may be linked by means of pronouns that refer to elements in preceding sentences. Words like *he, it, they, this,* and *those* indicate relationships by reminding the reader of earlier ideas and images. Notice how pronouns contribute to the coherence of the following paragraph.

23   Marya Mannes
in "How Do You Know It's Good?"

For the last fifteen or twenty years the fashion in criticism or appreciation of the arts has been to deny the existence of any valid criteria and to make the words "good" or "bad" irrelevant, immaterial, and inapplicable. There is no such thing, we are told, as a set of standards, first acquired through experience and knowledge and later imposed on the subject under discussion. This has been a popular approach, for it relieves the critic of the responsibility of judgment and the public of the necessity of knowledge. It pleases those resentful of disciplines, it flatters the empty-minded by calling them open-minded, it comforts the confused. Under the banner of democracy and the kind of equality which our forefathers did *not* mean, it says, in effect, "Who are you to tell us what is good or bad?" This is the same cry used so long and so effectively by the producers of mass media who insist that it is the public, not they, who decides what it wants to hear and see, and that for a critic to say that *this* program is bad and *this* program is good is purely a reflection of personal taste.

The Writer's Craft

1. In addition to a few pronouns that add little to coherence, the passage contains six pronouns, here underscored, that do indicate relationships by referring to elements in preceding sentences. Find the element to which each of the underscored pronouns refers.

2. Would the paragraph be as coherent if the pronouns were replaced by the nouns or phrases to which they refer? Would the paragraph read as smoothly as it does?

Now You Try It

Using both transitional expressions and linking expressions, develop one of the following topic sentences into a paragraph. Underline the transitional and linking expressions you use.

   a. Some early American presidents are practically forgotten today.
   b. Swimming is one of the best forms of exercise.
   c. Nowadays men's fashions are changing about as fast as women's.
   d. Emily Dickinson's poetry is quite different from Walt Whitman's.
   e. American cities are faced with staggering problems.
   f. Changing an automobile tire is not difficult.
   g. Something has to be done about air pollution.

COHERENCE THROUGH REPETITION Repeating certain key terms contributes to the coherence of a paragraph. In encountering the same word again and again, the reader is reminded of previous sentences in which it appeared. Notice how effectively the repetition of *New York* and *the city* ties together the paragraph that follows.

24   E. B. White in *Here Is New York*

There are roughly three New Yorks. There is, first, the New York of the man or woman who was born here, who takes the city for granted and accepts its size and its turbulence as natural and inevitable. Second, there is the New York of the commuter — the city that is devoured by locusts each day and spat out each night. Third, there is the New York of the person who was born somewhere else and came to New York in quest of something. Of these three trembling cities the greatest is the last — the city of final destination, the city that is a goal. It is this third city that accounts for New York's high-strung disposition, its poetical deportment, its dedication to the arts, and its incomparable achievements. Commuters give the city its tidal restlessness; natives give it solidity and continuity; but the settlers give it passion. And whether it is a farmer arriving from Italy to set up a small grocery store in a slum, or a young girl arriving from a small town in Mississippi to escape the indignity of being observed by her neighbors, or a boy arriving from the Corn Belt with a manuscript and a pain in his heart, it makes no difference: each embraces New York with the intense excitement of first love, each absorbs New York with the fresh eyes of an adventurer, each generates heat and light to dwarf the Consolidated Edison Company.

The Writer's Craft

1. Two terms are repeated here: *New York* and *the city*. Are there any sentences in which one or the other does not appear?

2. How many times are the terms *New York* and *the city* used in the paragraph? Do you think the repetition is excessive? Would the paragraph have been more effective if the author had occasionally substituted for *New York* and *the city* such expressions as *this metropolis, Manhattan, Gotham, this urban giant?* Why, or why not?

3. What transitional expressions occur in the paragraph? If the author had omitted them, what would the effect have been?

Now You Try It

Write a descriptive paragraph about your own town or city, in which you use repetition as the principal means of achieving coherence. After you have finished, underline each repetition of a key word.

Description

LESSON **6**

Skills of Description

Description conveys attributes of persons, objects, or places. Some descriptive writing, such as a police notice for a criminal-at-large or a naturalist's detailed description of a bird, is intended primarily to convey information. Other descriptive writing is intended not so much to convey information as to suggest to the imagination the impression that something makes on the senses. It is that type of description with which the following lesson is for the most part concerned.

In Model 25 below, Wallace Stegner describes the prairie town of his early childhood, to which he returned for a visit after an absence of many years. Notice that he is more concerned with giving his impression of the change in the appearance of the town than with telling exactly how it looks.

25   Wallace Stegner in *Wolf Willow*

My town used to be as bare as a picked bone, with no tree anywhere around it larger than a ten-foot willow or alder. Now it is a grove. My memory gropes uneasily, trying to establish itself among fifty-foot cottonwoods, lilac and honeysuckle hedges, and flower gardens. Searched for, plenty of familiarities are there: the Pastime Theater, identical with the one that sits across Main Street from the

firehouse in my mind; the lumber yard where we
used to get cloth caps advertising De Laval Cream [10]
Separators; two or three hardware stores (a prairie
wheat town specializes in hardware stores), though
each one now has a lot full of farm machinery next
to it; the hotel, just as it was rebuilt after the fire;
the bank, now remodeled into the post office; the [15]
Presbyterian church, now United, and the *Leader*
office, and the square brick prison of the school,
now with three smaller prisons added to it. These
are old acquaintances that I can check against their
replicas in my head and take satisfaction from. But [20]
among them are the evidences of Progress — hospital, Masonic Lodge, at least one new elevator, a
big quonset-like skating rink — and all tree-shaded,
altered, and distorted, and made vaguely disturbing by greenery. In the old days we all used to try [25]
to grow trees, transplanting them from the Hills or
getting them free with any two-dollar purchase
from one of the stores, but they always dried up
and died. To me, who came expecting a dusty hamlet, the change is charming, but memory has been [30]
fixed by time as photographs fix the faces of the
dead, and this reality is dreamlike. I cannot find
myself or my family or my companions in it.

The Writer's Craft

SELECTING DETAILS

A well-written description is like a skillfully executed drawing; in both cases, the effect is as much the result of what is left
out as of what is put in. Both artist and writer include details
they consider important — those that contribute to the impression they want to convey — and omit details they consider un-
important — those that do not contribute to the dominant impression.

Wallace Stegner begins Model 25 with two contrasting
statements in which he describes his town as it used to be —
"bare as a picked bone" — and as it is now — "a grove" (lines 1
and 3). To help the reader visualize the differences that the years
have made, he then supplies a number of details. Where once

there were only a few scrubby trees, none larger than a "ten-foot willow or alder," now, he tells us, there are "fifty-foot cottonwoods, lilac and honeysuckle hedges, and flower gardens" (lines 2–6). To be sure, some town landmarks, such as "the Pastime Theater," "the lumber yard," and "two or three hardware stores," remain nearly as they were when he was a boy (lines 7–12). But among those "old acquaintances" are "evidences of progress" that he doesn't recognize: a hospital, a Masonic Lodge, a new grain elevator, a skating rink (lines 21–23). Still, the major difference between the town of the present and the town of his boyhood, and the dominant impression that the author wants to convey, is the disturbing presence of trees. Everything, the familiar and the unfamiliar, is "tree-shaded, altered, and distorted, and made vaguely disturbing by greenery" (lines 23–25). In the concluding sentences of the passage, he explains the effect the trees have on him by contrasting his recollection of "the old days" when trees "dried up and died" with the present "dreamlike" reality (lines 25–33).

After he has selected details that contribute to a single dominant impression, Stegner must then make them specific. Notice how he links his boyhood memories to several of the town landmarks. The lumber yard is not just any lumber yard; it is "where we used to get cloth caps advertising De Laval Cream Separators" (lines 9–11). Find one or two additional town landmarks presented with comparable specificity.

USING SENSORY DETAILS

In an effective description many specific details are sensory. Very often a writer describes how something looks but may also describe how it sounds, smells, tastes, or feels, if such details contribute to the sought-after impression.

The author of Model 25 is primarily concerned with the change the trees have made in the appearance of his town and with the effect of that change on his own feelings. Because the change is entirely visual, the appeal is mainly to the reader's sense of sight. What words and phrases help you *see* the following features of the town?

the trees, shrubs, and flowers (lines 1–6)
the familiar landmarks (lines 6–18)
the new buildings (lines 20–23)

Effective description results from careful selection and systematic arrangement. The writer must not only decide which details to include but must also decide on the order in which to present them. One pattern often followed is to begin each paragraph of the description with a general statement and then proceed to support the statement with appropriate details. Notice that Stegner organizes his paragraph in that way essentially, but that instead of beginning it with just one general statement, he starts with two. In the first he recollects that his town "used to be as bare as a picked bone"; in the second, he observes that "Now it is a grove." Similarly, in the rest of the paragraph he alternates between recollection and observation, first noting the familiar landmarks, then the unfamiliar. Finally, he concludes with two sentences that summarize his reaction to the changed appearance of the town.

USING SPECIFIC WORDS AND FIGURATIVE LANGUAGE

A good writer chooses all words carefully, preferring the more specific noun to the general, the exact verb to the imprecise, the fresh adjective to the trite. Figures of speech will help make details even more vivid and effective.

Look back over the passage, noting where Stegner makes especially apt or specific word choices and where he uses figures of speech — similes, metaphors, or personification. (For definitions of those terms see page 79.)

Did you note, in particular, the author's use of specific nouns? Not content with the general term *tree*, he mentions three kinds — willow, alder, and cottonwood. He specifies two kinds of hedge: lilac and honeysuckle. Quite frequently he uses proper nouns, such as *De Laval Cream Separators*. How many other proper nouns can you find? What is their effect? Try replacing them with less specific nouns. Do the sentences that result seem less effective?

If you looked carefully through the passage, you should have been able to locate two similes, two metaphors, and an example of personification. The first simile occurs in the opening line: "My town used to be as bare as a picked bone." Writers often begin descriptive passages with metaphors or similes. Do you think this particular one is effective here? Try substituting a phrase, such as *a treeless place*, for *as bare as a picked bone*. Is anything lost? What is the other simile in this passage? Do you find it as effective as the first one?

Stegner uses figures of speech to convey his feelings. For example, instead of saying simply that the trees bother him by confusing his recollections, he says, "My memory gropes uneasily, trying to establish itself among fifty-foot cottonwoods . . ." (personification). In much the same manner, he speaks of the "square brick prison of the school" (metaphor) instead of saying that he used to hate school. Does figurative language seem more effective than literal language in these instances? Can you find the second metaphor?

Now You Try It

Decide on a person, place, or object to describe. If a person, choose one you once disliked but have now come to like and respect. Or choose a town — or perhaps a house — in which you once lived and to which you recently returned for a visit. Next, decide what general impression you want to convey and what general statement you want to make. Then, in a paragraph of about 250 words, make the statement and support it with specific details.

If the subject has changed with the passage of time, or if your attitude toward it has changed, you may wish to make two contrasting statements, as Stegner does in Model 25. For example, you might make one general statement, such as "Mr. Hallenbeck always seemed formidable to me," and follow it with another, such as "I know now that his brusque manner and stern expression conceal a warm and generous nature." In this case, of course, you would make sure that your paragraph contained details supporting both statements, or you would separate the statements and let each introduce its own paragraph.

LESSON **7**

Selecting Details

Your method of selecting details to include in a description varies according to your purpose. If primarily interested in conveying information about something, you will often proceed systematically to enumerate and distinguish all its parts. But if you are less interested in telling your readers about something than in giving them an impression of it, you will usually include only those details that contribute to the impression and omit all those that do not.

CONVEYING INFORMATION   The following selection, written by a highly-respected sports writer, gives the reader a precise word picture of a baseball. The selection also stresses the critical importance that the weight and size of the ball have on the game.

26   Roger Angell in *Five Seasons*

It weighs just over five ounces and measures between 2.86 and 2.94 inches in diameter. It is made of a composition-cork nucleus encased in two thin layers of rubber, one black and one red, surrounded by 121 yards of tightly wrapped blue-gray wool yarn, 45 yards of white wool yarn, 53 more yards of blue-gray wool yarn, 150 yards of fine cotton yarn, a coat of rubber cement, and a cowhide (formerly horsehide) exterior, which is held together with 216 slightly raised red cotton stitches. Printed certifications, endorsements, and outdoor advertising spherically attest to its authenticity. Like most institutions, it is considered inferior in its present form to its ancient archetypes,* and in this case the complaint is probably justified; on occasion in recent years it has actually been known to come apart under the demands of its brief but rigorous, active career. Baseballs are assembled and handstitched in Taiwan (before this year the work was done in Haiti, and before 1973 in Chicopee, Massachusetts), and contemporary pitchers claim that there is a tangible variation in the size and feel of the balls that now come into play in a single game; a true peewee° is treasured by hurlers, and its departure from the premises, by fair means or foul, is secretly mourned. But never mind: any baseball is beautiful. No other small package comes as close to the ideal in design and utility. It is a perfect object for a man's hand. Pick it up and it instantly suggests its purpose; it is meant to be thrown a considerable distance—thrown hard and with precision. Its feel and heft are the beginning of the sport's critical dimensions; if it were a fraction of an inch larger or smaller, a few centigrams heavier or lighter, the game of baseball would be utterly different.

* **archetypes:** original models or types
° **peewee:** a baseball that is slightly smaller than regulation size.

The Writer's Craft

1. The primary purpose of this selection is to give the reader an accurate physical description of a baseball, and to emphasize how important the weight and size of the ball is to the game. The

first sentence gives the size and weight of the ball. What is described in the long, second sentence? In what order is the description in the long, second sentence arranged?

2. To convey a precise picture the author does more than simply name the parts of the ball. He chooses precise words that help the reader visualize the ball. How does he describe the outer stitching of the ball? What precise words does he use to describe the composition of the layers of the ball? How does the phrase "spherically attest" (line 11) help to convey an accurate physical description of the ball?

3. In some instances the author has selected words that do not help create an accurate physical description of the ball. What, for example, is the effect of words such as *treasured, beautiful, ideal,* and *perfect?* Do these words convey any concrete picture of the ball, or do they suggest the author's attitude toward what is being described?

Now You Try It

Choose one of the following assignments:

1. Describe as clearly and objectively as you can any animal that you know well from observation. Because your purpose will be to inform the reader, avoid including personal opinions or reactions, and be careful not to rely on the reader's knowledge of the animal. If you are writing about a dachshund, for instance, assume that the reader has had some experience with dogs but has never seen a dachshund before.

2. Select any object — a tree, a building, an automobile, a piece of furniture — and enumerate and distinguish its parts. You may want to concentrate on a very specific aspect—as Angell concentrates on the composition of the interior and exterior of the ball—but be sure that you include enough details to let the reader form an accurate and adequate mental picture of what you are describing.

The primary purpose of Model 26 was to *convey information* about the baseball— to describe the ball's physical details precisely and objectively. Joseph Wood Krutch's primary purpose in writing the following selection is to *convey an impression* of the desert landscape. His approach resembles less a photograph than a painting, which seeks not to reproduce a scene by including every detail but rather to show its underlying pattern and suggest its mood by means of a few skillfully executed brushstrokes.

27 Joseph Wood Krutch in *The Desert Year*

If I step through the gate in my patio wall, I am in a moment in a kind of sparse wilderness which shows no sign of man's intrusion, which belongs still to the creatures who have always lived here. Besides the animals there are many green, growing 5 things of many kinds. There are cacti, of course, and among them the great barrels which would be specimens in any botanical garden and which, at first, surprise me as much as, in Africa, I should no doubt be surprised to see lions and elephants not 10 attached to any zoo or circus. There are also the flat green pads of the more familiar "prickly pear" grown to unfamiliar size; there are the coppery purple pads of the somewhat less common Santa Rita prickly pear and also, omnipresent, one or an- 15 other variety of the cholla — that fierce touch-me-not of the desert which often assumes the form of a low tree with bark on its trunk and branches of savagely armed cylindrical pads. The spines are not the minute spicules we first think of when we think 20 of cacti but much like darning needles in length, in strength, and in sharpness.

At first sight, the other large growing things — the mesquite, the paloverde and the creosote bush — seem less abnormal. From a distance, this stretch 25 of desert floor looks green enough and almost like the thickets one finds in many cooler, damper lands. But there is much which distinguishes it. For one thing, the green is a grayer green. For another, one realizes as soon as one steps into it that it is not ³⁰ really a thicket at all but a floor on which everything must have — and everything has managed to get — its standing room.

There is no continuous carpet of grass or herbage, no crowding together of exuberantly growing plant ³⁵ life. One does not push one's way through undergrowth; one strolls almost as in a garden. Where water is scarce, roots spread far and shallowly. Hence the area to which a mesquite, for example, has successfully established claim will support little ⁴⁰ else. For a while it is hard to believe that this untouched country has not been thinned by some human gardener. Because of a spacing which nature has attended to, it has a curious air of being a park rather than a wilderness.   ⁴⁵

The Writer's Craft

1. In the brief space of this description, the author could hardly describe every detail of the desert landscape in the same way that Angell describes each part of the interior and exterior of the ball in Model 26. Instead Krutch must choose a few details from the many available and use them to convey an overall impression of the scene. His first sentence hints at that impression by referring to the desert landscape as "a kind of sparse wilderness." The remainder of the first paragraph then describes some of the "many green, growing things," specifically, four varieties of cacti: the great barrels, the common prickly pear, the Santa Rita prickly pear, and the cholla. Notice that the author does not attempt to describe the cacti in detail; his purpose is not to give the reader an exhaustive word picture but merely to suggest their appearance by precisely describing one or two of their prominent features. What comparison does he make in describing his reaction to the barrel cacti (lines 7–11)? Would such a comparison be appropriate in a description intended solely to convey information? What words and phrases help you visualize the prickly pears and the cholla?

2. The second paragraph shifts attention from individual details of the landscape to its overall pattern. "Other large growing things" are named, but because they "seem less abnormal" than the cacti, they are not described in any detail. Krutch does, however, describe the overall appearance of the desert floor. What does he say it looks like from a distance (lines 25–27)? What does he find it like when he steps into it (lines 30–33)?

3. The third paragraph states Krutch's impression of the desert landscape. Of what do the order and spacing of the various plants remind him? In at least two sentences he clearly describes the overall impression created by the landscape. Which sentences are they?

Now You Try It

In a composition of about 350 words, describe an outdoor scene that has made a strong impression on you. It may be beautiful or ugly; it may be in the city or the country. But begin as Krutch does by describing a few individual details of the scene; then consider its overall appearance and the impression it creates. You might be able to compare an aspect of the scene to something it reminds you of.

The more details you use in a description, the more care you must take to make the result unified and coherent. The following passage contains many more details than the previous one, Model 27. Even so, every detail in it helps create the single, dominant impression Rangoon made on the American dancer Doris Humphrey during a tour of the Orient with the Ruth St. Denis–Ted Shawn dance company in the 1920's.

28 Doris Humphrey in "The Orient"

One steamy day in December, we arrived in Rangoon, the most exotic* of the places we had yet visited, and we had a sense of being deep in the Orient. Most of the men were in sarongs, with small

* **exotic:** foreign; fàscinating, striking, or unusual.

turbans; the women in wrapped skirts and trans- ⁵
parent jackets fastened with jeweled pins. Most of
them were barefoot, too, and the boys in the hotel
moved noiselessly through the halls and in the dining
room. According to the new pattern, my mother and
I took a double room, which was fitted with the ¹⁰
usual curtained beds, big overhead fan, and half-
doors to catch any air there was.

On the very first night we heard of a fair on the
outskirts of Rangoon. This was a chance to see something really Burmese, and we all got into rickshaws ¹⁵
to go after dinner. The fair was a delight, although
it was full of imported European gadgets like Ferris
wheels, fireworks, and shooting galleries. Still, by
following our ears, we came upon a native show,
complete with an orchestra and two dancers—the ²⁰
latter being the most charming little creatures imag-
inable. Arriving before the show began, we were
fascinated to see the dancers kneeling before little
mirrored boxes, finishing their make-up, in full view
on the stage. The make-up was not so elaborate, ²⁵
but the costumes were. These consisted of a tightly
wrapped skirt striped in brilliant colors and reaching to the ankles. Over this went a white, transpar-
ent jacket with up-turned, quite exaggerated points
on the hips, all edged with ball fringe. The front ³⁰
was fastened with three brilliantly jeweled pins. The
arms were heavy with many bracelets; the neck
hung with beads. The black hair was dressed in a
most exotic way. It was cut short to just below the
ears, with bangs; above this was a crown of hair ³⁵
wound smoothly over some solid base—quite high
too, three or four inches. On this were jeweled pins
and artificial flowers dangling on long skewers. To
top it all, the dancers had lighted cheroots, which
they puffed on from time to time. The dancers were ⁴⁰
very small—not more than five feet tall—and as ex-
quisite as flowers. We could hardly wait for the
show to begin.

It opened with a couple of men who sang to the

accompaniment of drums in the grating voices of 45
the East. Then the dancers came on. They moved
with bent knees and gliding steps, very close to the
ground, and with incredible flexibility in the hands
and arms. The fingers turned back almost to the
wrist, a phenomenon we were to see many times 50
later. The movements were quick and bird-like;
without an interpreter to tell me I imagined that the
whole dance and the costumes were derived from
some magical feathered creature. Another dance
used two brightly colored parasols, which the dancer 55
whirled expertly while doing quite acrobatic feats,
including a back bend to the floor. I couldn't know
at the time that Miss Ruth would duplicate this
dance for me exactly—with the cheroot, the parasol,
and all. The little girl from Oak Park, Illinois, was 60
to become extremely exotic in the Burmese manner.

I found someone in the crowd who could speak
a little English and ventured backstage with him to
see one of these bird-like creatures after the show.
She was interested that a dancer from far across 65
the sea had come to see her, and I offered her an
invitation to have lunch with me at my hotel. She
also spoke a little English, so I looked forward to
this visit as a chance to find out more about the life
of a dancer in Burma. Came the day, she showed 70
up in bare feet and native dress, looking as strange
as an orchid in a field of daisies in the all-European
dining room. She sat cross-legged on the chair at
the table, where the native waiters were not too
deferential to this little coquette of their own kind. 75
They brought her Oriental food, which she ate with
her tiny hands that were loaded with rings, and we
had a halting conversation about ways of the dance
in Burma. With her black eyes and hair, and her
exotic, brilliantly colored dress, she made me feel 80
very drab—like a big, faded Westerner. She had
been dancing since she was three, she said. Soon
she would marry, and stop dancing. She must have
been all of fifteen.

The Writer's Craft

1. In Model 27, Joseph Wood Krutch presents specific details first, then concludes with a statement of the dominant impression. Humphrey, on the other hand, here indicates in her first sentence the impression of Rangoon that she intends to convey. What is the key word in the sentence? Imagine how different the entire passage might have been had Humphrey used the word *familiar, depressing,* or *boring* instead.

2. The first sentence, which determines the kind of details that follow, could be called a statement of the controlling idea of the passage. It limits the writer to using *exotic* details—details about Burmese people, clothing, dances, customs. Has Humphrey succeeded in conveying an impression of exoticism?

3. Having decided what details to include, the writer must then make them specific. Find words and phrases that make each of the following details specific:

the double room (lines 10–12)
the dancers' costumes (lines 26–31)
the dancers' hair (lines 33–38)
the young girl's hands (line 77)

Now You Try It

Select one of the following topics to describe in 350 words or more. Begin with a general statement (or statements) and proceed to support it with specific details.

a. Any community activity
b. A memorable party
c. A carnival
d. The worst affair you ever attended
e. A family celebration
f. Any busy place or scene of lively activity

LESSON **8**

Using Sensory Details

In forming impressions, you probably tend to rely heavily on your sense of sight. Yet to a greater or lesser extent, you must rely on your other senses as well. You form an impression of the seashore not only by *seeing* the sun shining on sand and water, but also by *hearing* the roar of the breakers and the cry of gulls, by *feeling* the pounding of the surf and the chilliness of ocean spray, by *smelling* the fresh off-shore breeze, and by *tasting* the saltiness of the sea. The task of the writer describing such a scene is not merely to tell about it but actually to give you as a reader an imaginative impression, or experience, of it by supplying a variety of appropriate sensory details. The task is, in the words of Joseph Conrad, "by the power of the written word to make you hear, to make you feel . . . to make you *see*."

APPEALING TO SEVERAL SENSES   The following selection describes a scene of strenuous activity and high spirits. By appealing simultaneously to the senses of hearing, touch, sight, and smell, the author almost compels you to re-create the scene in your imagination.

29   **Michael O'Malley in *Miners Hill***

The picnic shelter quaked with sound: shouting and laughter, the rollicking wail of the fiddles, the quick staccato pounding of the dancers' feet. In the

clouds of pipe smoke wreathing the air and sliding
out like pale-gray sorrow through the screens, the 5
light was filtered yellow, a dim lively brightness,
somehow magical, the color of the tune of "The
Minstrel Boy." A jig, a four-hand reel, another jig
— the floor trembled with the power of the music.
Heads bobbed up and down and tossed jauntily. 10
Stout housewives and massive laborers hopped
about with a mysterious buoyancy, their feet moving faster than eye could follow. Rumpled hair,
reddening faces, fat puffed cheeks, the good strong
smell of sweat and joy as, one after another, the 15
furious dances were called. The musicians were
dripping wet and swollen with exertion. They had
strange grins, a glassy wildness in their eyes, as
the tunes carried the crowd toward wilder motion,
and the high piping of the flutes goaded any foot 20
that slowed. Fresh couples, loose with laughter and
the music, clamored to replace anyone who tired.
The dancers circled and advanced, clasped and retreated, twisted away with heads tossed back, knees
thrown high, to meet again, the men whooping and 25
clapping their big hands.

The Writer's Craft

1. The passage imaginatively conveys an impression of a
scene in a picnic shelter; by doing so, it arouses in you the sensa-
tions you might experience if you were standing in the shelter
yourself. In reading the passage, you see, hear, smell, and feel
things in your imagination. Find words that help you *see:*

the pipe smoke (lines 3–5)
the dancers (lines 10–15, 23–26)
the musicians (lines 16–18)
the couples (lines 21–22)

Find words that help you *hear:*

the fiddles (line 2)
the dancers' feet (line 2)
the flutes (line 20)
the men (lines 25–26)

What words help you *smell* the air in the picnic shelter? What words help you *feel* the shaking of the shelter? To what sense does the author appeal most often?

2. O'Malley selects his sensory details with care, including only those that help convey an impression of the liveliness of the music and the frenzied activity of the scene. He tells you that "the picnic shelter quaked with sound" (line 1), but he does not even hint at its size, shape, or color. Again, he writes that "Stout housewives and massive laborers hopped about with a mysterious buoyancy" (lines 11–12), and provides glimpses of "Rumpled hair, reddening faces, fat puffed cheeks" (lines 13–14), but he does not say what the dancers wore, and he does not describe any of them individually. He says that "The musicians were dripping wet and swollen with exertion," that "They had strange grins, a glassy wildness in their eyes" (lines 16–18), but he does not say how many there were, how they were dressed, or where they stood. Why would such additional details about the picnic shelter, the dancers, and the musicians detract from, rather than contribute to, the impression conveyed by the passage?

3. The author devotes no more than two consecutive sentences to details appealing to the same sense. He moves quickly from one sight, sound, or other sensation to the next in much the same way that you might shift your attention from one thing to another if you were there watching the dance yourself. He keeps his sentences short, and he uses words that help you visualize specific actions: *quaked, rollicking, sliding, trembled, bobbed, tossed, hopped, goaded, clamored, whooping.* Mention other words in the passage that help you visualize specific actions.

Now You Try It

Select one of the following topics for a description of at least 250 words. Concentrate on trying to convey an impression of frenzied activity. Keep most of your sentences short, use specific verbs and verbals, and include details that appeal to several senses. Avoid describing any one thing at length, but move quickly from one part of the scene to the next, and from one kind of sensory detail to another.

   a. A few minutes of a basketball game, or one play in a football game

b. The hectic activity fifteen minutes before a school play
c. Rush hour downtown
d. A dog fight, with the two owners trying to separate the animals
e. A pep rally

Although Model 29 includes a variety of sensory details, it clearly appeals to the sense of sight more often than to the senses of hearing or smell. In the following selection, the reverse is true: the appeal to the senses of hearing and smell is more frequent than to that of sight.

30 Thomas Wolfe in "Circus at Dawn"

[1] At the sculptural still square where at one corner, just emerging into light, my father's shabby little marble shop stood with a ghostly strangeness and familiarity, my brother and I would "catch" the first streetcar of the day bound for the "depot" 5 where the circus was — or sometimes we would meet someone we knew, who would give us a lift in his automobile.

[2] Then, having reached the dingy, grimy, and rickety depot section, we would get out, and walk 10 rapidly across the tracks of the station yard, where we could see great flares and steamings from the engines, and hear the crash and bump of shifting freight cars, the swift sporadic thunders of a shifting engine, the tolling of bells, the sounds of great 15 trains on the rails.

[3] And to all these familiar sounds, filled with their exultant prophecies of flight, the voyage, morning, and the shining cities — to all the sharp and thrilling odors of the trains — the smell of cin- 20 ders, acrid smoke, of musty, rusty freight cars, the clean pineboard of crated produce, and the smells of fresh stored food — oranges, coffee, tangerines and bacon, ham and flour and beef — there would be added now, with an unforgettable magic and 25

familiarity, all the strange sounds and smells of the coming circus.

[4] The gay yellow sumptuous-looking cars in which the star performers lived and slept, still dark and silent, heavily and powerfully still, would be [30] drawn up in long strings upon the tracks. And all around them the sounds of the unloading circus would go on furiously in the darkness. The receding gulf of lilac and departing night would be filled with the savage roar of the lions, the murderously [35] sudden snarling of great jungle cats, the trumpeting of the elephants, the stamp of the horses, and with the musty, pungent, unfamiliar odor of the jungle animals: the tawny camel smells, and the smells of panthers, zebras, tigers, elephants, and [40] bears.

[5] Then, along the tracks, beside the circus trains, there would be the sharp cries and oaths of the circus men, the magical swinging dance of lanterns in the darkness, the sudden heavy rumble of [45] the loaded vans and wagons as they were pulled along the flats * and gondolas,° and down the runways to the ground. And everywhere, in the thrilling mystery of darkness and awakening light, there would be the tremendous conflict of a confused, [50] hurried, and yet orderly movement.

* **flats:** flatcars.
° **gondolas** (gon′dŏ·láz): open-top railroad cars.

The Writer's Craft

1. Sensory details urge the reader to imagine the appearance, sound, feel, smell, and taste of things. Do Wolfe's sensory details cause you to feel the expectancy and excitement that he and his brother experienced on the morning the circus arrived?

2. The first paragraph briefly describes the town square and the marble shop. The adjectives *sculptural* and *still* modify *square*. To which of the senses do those adjectives appeal? Find in the paragraph two or three other modifiers, either single adjectives or adjective phrases, that appeal to the senses. What sort of mood do those words help create?

3. The second paragraph alludes to the depot section's appearance (lines 9–10), mentions the "great flares and steamings from the engines" (lines 12–13), and then concentrates on the sounds of the station yard (lines 13–16). What are those sounds? Does the time of day have anything to do with the author's choice of detail? Why do you think he includes more sounds than sights?

4. In the third paragraph, Wolfe indicates the associations that the sounds of the station yard have for him (lines 17–19) and then enumerates "all the sharp and thrilling odors of the trains" (lines 19–27). What are those odors?

5. Notice that in one instance (lines 23–24) the author simply lists the sources of several odors. Are you able to recall most of those odors from your own experience? Do they, then, appeal adequately to your sense of smell?

6. The fourth and fifth paragraphs concentrate on the strange sounds and smells of the coming circus. Find words that are used to describe the sounds made by each of the following:

the lions (line 35)
the great jungle cats (lines 35–36)
the elephants (lines 36–37)
the horses (line 37)
the circus men (lines 43–44)
the loaded vans and wagons (lines 45–46)

What adjectives are used to describe the odor produced by all the jungle animals (lines 38–39)? Does the author describe the individual smells of each animal, or does he simply name the different kinds of animals in the circus?

7. Are details in paragraphs 4 and 5 confined solely to sounds and smells? To which of the senses does the author appeal in describing the following?

the circus cars (lines 28–31)
the lanterns (lines 44–45)
the early-morning movement (lines 50–51)

Now You Try It

In two paragraphs of about 150 words each, describe an experience you remember vividly. In the first paragraph, concentrate on one kind of sensory detail, and in the second paragraph, concentrate on another. For example, you might describe a visit to an amusement park on a warm summer evening. In the first paragraph you could concentrate on smells in the air: of hamburgers and hot dogs sizzling on the hot plates of the refreshment stands, and the smell of dust in the penny arcade. Then in the second paragraph you might concentrate on the sounds: the screech of the roller coaster, the excited screams of people on the rides, and the mechanical music of the steam calliope. Revise the composition to make each detail as sharp and vivid as possible.

APPEALING PRIMARILY TO ONE SENSE   In the following passage Henry David Thoreau recalls an evening on a trip that he and his brother took in a small boat down the Concord and Merrimack rivers in New England. On this particular night they were camping on the banks of the Concord near Lowell, Massachusetts. Notice how skillfully the author re-creates the experience by concentrating primarily on one kind of sensory detail.

31   Henry David Thoreau in *A Week on the Concord and Merrimack Rivers*

For the most part there was no recognition of human life in the night, no human breathing was heard, only the breathing of the wind. As we sat up, kept awake by the novelty of our situation, we heard at intervals foxes stepping about over the ⁵ dead leaves, and brushing the dewy grass close to our tent, and once a musquash* fumbling among the potatoes and melons in our boat, but when we hastened to the shore we could detect only a ripple in the water ruffling the disk of a star. At intervals ¹⁰ we were serenaded by the song of a dreaming sparrow or the throttled cry of an owl, but after each sound which near at hand broke the stillness of the night, each crackling of the twigs, or rustling among the leaves, there was a sudden pause, and deeper ¹⁵ and more conscious silence, as if the intruder were aware that no life was rightfully abroad at that

* **musquash:** muskrat.

hour. There was a fire in Lowell, as we judged, this night, and we saw the horizon blazing, and heard the distant alarm bells, as it were a faint tinkling 20 music borne to these woods. But the most constant and memorable sound of a summer's night, which we did not fail to hear every night afterward, though at no time so incessantly and so favorably as now, was the barking of the house dogs, from 25 the loudest and hoarsest bark to the faintest aerial palpitation under the eaves of heaven, from the patient but anxious mastiff to the timid and wakeful terrier, at first loud and rapid, then faint and slow, to be imitated only in a whisper; wow-wow-wow- 30 wow—wo—wo—w—w. Even in a retired and uninhabited district like this, it was a sufficiency of sound for the ear of night, and more impressive than any music.

The Writer's Craft

1. As you read this selection, you become aware that even in the darkness of "a retired and uninhabited district like this" there are a great many things to be described. What do you hear? What do you see? To which sense do most of the details in the selection appeal? Why do you think Thoreau concentrates on that kind of sensory detail?

2. In describing something, a writer must be very careful about word choice. Usually a writer prefers the precise term to the more general, and strives to make sensory details as specific as possible. Without looking back at the selection, examine the pairs of phrases below. Each phrase contains a sensory detail from the selection, but only one phrase in each pair is taken directly from the model; the other phrase has been rewritten so that it is less specific than Thoreau's. First, decide which phrase in each pair is worded more effectively and give reasons for your decision. Then look back at the selection to see if your choice is the one Thoreau made.

> only the blowing of the wind
> only the breathing of the wind
> (line 3)

foxes stepping about over the dead leaves, and brushing
the dewy grass
foxes moving over the leaves and through the wet grass
(lines 5–6)

a musquash in our boat making a disturbance among the
supplies
a musquash fumbling among the potatoes and melons in
our boat
(lines 7–8)

a ripple in the water ruffling the disk of a star
a ripple in the water disturbing the image of a reflected
star
(lines 9–10)

sound of twigs breaking
crackling of the twigs
(line 14)

the horizon blazing
the light of a fire on the horizon
(line 19)

3. Onomatopoetic words — words that imitate sounds, such as
hiss, pop, or *buzz* — are particularly appropriate in descriptive
passages that contain details appealing to the sense of hearing.
Find at least three onomatopoetic words in the selection.

Now You Try It

Imagine that you are trying to describe a memorable scene to
a friend who has been blind from birth; you can use any sensory
details except those that appeal to the sense of sight. For example, you might describe a garden by telling not of the colors
and the shapes of flowers and shrubs but of how soft and
fragile the petals feel, how the bittersweet scent of the mari-
golds mingles with the smell of damp earth, how the birds chat-
ter in the birdbath, and how sweet the summer grass tastes. Set
down your description in a composition of approximately 250
words.

LESSON **9**

Organizing a Description

You should no more list details of a description at random than a portrait painter should place details helter-skelter on a canvas. In other words, to write an effective description, you must know not only how to select appropriate sensory details but also how to organize them.

One way to organize details in a description is by introducing them in the order that they might appear to an observer standing still. Another way is by including them in the order in which they would appear to a moving observer, someone, for example, driving through the country in an automobile. A third method of organization is to arrange details for emphasis by placing the most important either at the beginning or at the end of the passage. This lesson considers models that illustrate these three organizational methods.

LOCATING DETAILS FROM A FIXED VANTAGE POINT   In describing a view, a writer avoids merely listing details at random and leaving it to the readers to visualize them in their proper positions. Instead, a writer relates each detail to the others by presenting them in a logical sequence. In the following selection Joseph Conrad describes the Gulf of Siam as it appears from the deck of an anchored ship. Notice how clearly each detail is located.

On my right hand there were lines of fishing
stakes resembling a mysterious system of half-sub-
merged bamboo fences, incomprehensible in its
division of the domain of tropical fishes, and crazy
of aspect as if abandoned for ever by some nomad   5
tribe of fishermen now gone to the other end of the
ocean; for there was no sign of human habitation
as far as the eye could reach. To the left a group of
barren islets, suggesting ruins of stone walls, towers,
and blockhouses, had its foundation set in a blue   10
sea that itself looked solid, so still and stable did it
lie below my feet; even the track of light from the
westering sun shone smoothly, without that ani-
mated glitter which tells of an imperceptible ripple.
And when I turned my head to take a parting   15
glance at the tug which had just left us anchored
outside the bar, I saw the straight line of the flat
shore joined to the stable sea, edge to edge, with a
perfect and unmarked closeness, in one levelled
floor half brown, half blue under the enormous   20
dome of the sky. Corresponding in their insignificance to the islets of the sea, two small clumps of
trees, one on each side of the only fault in the impeccable joint,* marked the mouth of the river
Meinam ° we had just left on the first preparatory   25
stage of our homeward journey; and, far back on the
inland level, a larger and loftier mass, the grove surrounding the great Paknam pagoda,† was the only
thing on which the eye could rest from the vain
task of exploring the monotonous sweep of the hori-   30
zon. Here and there gleams as of a few scattered
pieces of silver marked the windings of the great
river; and on the nearest of them, just within the bar,
the tug steaming right into the land became lost to

---

* **fault in the impeccable joint:** break in the straight line joining
land and sea.
° **Meinam:** now Chao Phraya; a river running past Bangkok into
the head of the Gulf of Siam.
† **Paknam pagoda:** tall temple tower between Bangkok and the
Gulf of Siam.

my sight, hull and funnel and masts, as though the 35
impassive earth had swallowed her up without an effort, without a tremor. My eye followed the light
cloud of her smoke, now here, now there, above the
plain, according to the devious curves of the stream,
but always fainter and farther away, till I lost it at 40
last behind the mitre-shaped hill of the great pagoda. And then I was left alone with my ship, anchored at the head of the Gulf of Siam.

The Writer's Craft

1. The author describes a scene as it is viewed by an observer
on the deck of an anchored ship. First he describes what is on one
side of him (lines 1–8), then what is on the other side and beneath him (lines 8–14), and finally what is behind him (lines
15–42). What words, phrases, and clauses does Conrad use to locate the following details?

the fishing stakes (lines 1–8)
the islets (lines 8–9)
the blue sea (lines 10–12)
the shore (lines 17–21)
the clumps of trees (lines 22–25)
the grove (lines 26–28)
the moving tug (lines 31–42)

2. Although details are introduced in a logical sequence and
their general location is invariably indicated, notice that the author avoids making his description overly precise and mechanical.
He does not, for example, tell you exactly how far the fishing
stakes and the islands are from the ship. Nor does he tell you
exactly where on the shoreline the mouth of the River Meinam
is, or exactly how far back on the land the great pagoda stands.
Why would such details detract from, rather than add to, the
effectiveness of the description?

Now You Try It

In a composition of about 350 words, describe a panoramic
view as seen from the top of a hill, a tall building, or a tree.
Clearly locate the various details of the view by indicating their

positions in relation to you and in relation to other details. Where appropriate, use phrases such as *to my left, on the right,* and *on the horizon.*

LOCATING DETAILS FROM A MOVING VANTAGE POINT The following selection describes a boy's trip to a bazaar, or fair, on the outskirts of Dublin one evening late in the nineteenth century.

33   James Joyce in "Araby"

I held a florin * tightly in my hand as I strode down Buckingham Street towards the station. The sight of the streets thronged with buyers and glaring with gas recalled to me the purpose of my journey. I took my seat in a third-class carriage of a   5
deserted train. After an intolerable delay the train moved out of the station slowly. It crept onward among ruinous houses and over the twinkling river. At Westland Row Station a crowd of people pressed to the carriage doors; but the porters moved them   10
back, saying that it was a special train for the bazaar. I remained alone in the bare carriage. In a few minutes the train drew up beside an improvised wooden platform. I passed out on to the road and saw by the lighted dial of a clock that it was ten   15
minutes to ten. In front of me was a large building which displayed the magical name.°

I could not find any sixpenny entrance and, fearing that the bazaar would be closed, I passed in quickly through a turnstile, handing a shilling to a   20
weary-looking man. I found myself in a big hall girdled at half its height by a gallery. Nearly all the stalls were closed and the greater part of the hall was in darkness. I recognized a silence like that which pervades a church after a service. I walked   25
into the center of the bazaar timidly. A few people were gathered about the stalls which were still

* **florin:** a coin.
° **magical name:** the exotic name of the bazaar — Araby.

open. Before a curtain, over which the words *Café Chantant* were written in colored lamps, two men were counting money on a salver.* I listened to the fall of the coins. 30

Remembering with difficulty why I had come, I went over to one of the stalls and examined porcelain vases and flowered tea-sets. At the door of the stall a young lady was talking and laughing with two young gentlemen. I remarked their English accents and listened vaguely to their conversation. 35

* salver: tray.

The Writer's Craft

1. The journey to the bazaar is described from a moving vantage point. What words and phrases indicate that the observer is moving?

2. What details make each of the following specific?

the streets on the way to the station (lines 2–4)
the train carriage (lines 5–6)
the view from the train window (lines 7–14)
the hall of the bazaar (lines 21–25)
the stalls (lines 26–37)

Now You Try It

In a composition of about 350 words, describe a brief journey that you can recall vividly. You may have made the journey by any means at all — on foot, on a bicycle, in a car, on a small boat, on a ship, on a ski lift, on water skis, on a Ferris wheel, or whatever. But choose details carefully, describe them specifically, and arrange them in the order in which you encountered them on the journey.

ORGANIZING FOR EMPHASIS The following description of an old man includes many specific details. But notice how the organization of the passage helps emphasize the outstanding feature of the man's appearance.

34   Robert Penn Warren in "The Patented Gate and the Mean Hamburger"

You have seen him a thousand times. You have seen him standing on the street corner on Saturday afternoon, in the little county-seat towns. He wears blue-jean pants, or overalls washed to a pale pastel blue like the color of sky after a shower in spring,   5 but because it is Saturday he has on a wool coat, an old one, perhaps the coat left from the suit he got married in a long time back. His long wristbones hang out from the sleeves of the coat, the tendons showing along the bone like the dry twist of grape-   10 vine still corded on the stove-length of a hickory sapling you would find in his woodbox beside his cookstove among the split chunks of gum and red oak. The big hands, with the knotted, cracked joints and the square, horn-thick nails, hang loose off the   15 wristbone like clumsy, homemade tools hung on the wall of a shed after work. If it is summer, he wears a straw hat with a wide brim, the straw fraying loose around the edge. If it is winter, he wears a felt hat, black once, but now weathered with   20 streaks of dark gray and dull purple in the sunlight. His face is long and bony, the jawbone long under the drawn-in cheeks. The flesh along the jawbone is nicked in a couple of places where the unaccus- tomed razor has been drawn over the leather-coarse   25 skin. A tiny bit of blood crusts brown where the nick is. The color of the face is red, a dull red like the red clay mud or clay dust which clings to the bottom of his pants and to the cast-iron-looking brogans * on his feet, or a red like the color of a   30 piece of hewed cedar which has been left in the weather. The face does not look alive. It seems to be molded from the clay or hewed from the cedar. When the jaw moves once, with its deliberate, mas- sive motion on the quid of tobacco, you are still not   35

* **brogans:** workmen's shoes.

convinced. That motion is but the cunning triumph
of a mechanism concealed within.

But you see the eyes. You see that the eyes are
alive. They are pale blue or gray, set back under
the deep brows and thorny eyebrows. They are not 40
wide, but are squinched up like eyes accustomed to
wind or sun or to measuring the stroke of the ax or
to fixing the object over the rifle sights. When you
pass, you see that the eyes are alive and are warily
and dispassionately estimating you from the am- 45
bush of the thorny brows. Then you pass on, and he
stands there in that stillness which is his gift.

The Writer's Craft

1. In describing a person, place, or object, a writer will often
select one or two particularly interesting or characteristic details
for special emphasis and may single them out with a phrase such
as *the most important parts* or *what you first notice is.* On the
other hand, a writer may place those details in an emphatic position — either at the beginning or end of the passage — and devote more words to them than to the other details. What detail
does Warren emphasize in this selection? How does he emphasize it?

2. Did you notice the order in which the author presents the
details? First he locates the man (lines 1–3), then he describes
his blue jeans and coat (lines 3–8), then his wrist and hands
(lines 8–17), then his hat, jaw, neck, and face (lines 17–37), and
finally, in a separate paragraph, the man's most significant feature — his eyes (lines 38–46). Do you see any reason for arrang-
ing the details in that order rather than, for instance, in the reverse? Does Warren describe the details in the order that an observer would be likely to see them as he approached and finally
passed the man on the street? What is the effect of describing the
eyes in a separate paragraph?

3. In the first paragraph, the author uses several *similes,* or
comparisons of unlike things stated with *like* or *as,* in describing
the man's various features. He speaks, for example, of the tendons of the man's wrists as "showing . . . like the dry twist of
grapevines still corded on the stove-length of a hickory sapling"
(lines 10–12) and of the color of the man's face as "red . . . like

the red clay mud . . . or a red like the color of a piece of hewed cedar which has been left in the weather" (lines 27–32). Find another simile in the first paragraph. What impression of the man do the similes help create?

4. All the details in the first paragraph contribute to conveying a single dominant impression. Does the second paragraph contribute to that impression, or does it alter the impression in some way? What is the effect of the first two sentences in the second paragraph (lines 38–39)?

5. After you have considered the impressions conveyed by both paragraphs, do you think the selection would be as effective as it is if the order of details were reversed — that is, if the eyes were described first?

Now You Try It

Describe an unusual person whom you have had an opportunity to observe over an extended period of time. Locate the person in the place where you generally see him or her. Determine the impression you want to convey, and describe details of dress and physical appearance that will most effectively contribute to that impression. Organize the passage for emphasis, as Warren organized his — either by beginning or concluding it with the detail, or details, that you want to emphasize.

LESSON **10**

Using Specific Words and Figurative Language

SPECIFIC WORDS Efforts to select details that appeal to several senses and to organize those details in an effective way will be wasted unless you choose individual words and phrases of a description with care. Exact verbs, precise adjectives and adverbs, and specific nouns are what give writing vividness. In reading the following description, notice where the author has made especially effective word choices.

35   Alfred Kazin in *A Walker in the City*

Ripeness filled our kitchen even at supper time. The room was so wild with light, it made me tremble; I could not believe my eyes. In the sink a great sandy pile of radishes, lettuces, tomatoes, cucumbers, and scallions broke up on their stark greens   5
and reds the harshness of the world's daily monotony. The window shade by the sewing machine was drawn, its tab baking in the sun. Through the screen came the chant of the score being called up from the last handball game below. Our front door   10
was open, to let in air; you could hear the boys on the roof scuffing their shoes against the gravel. Then, my father home to the smell of paint in the hall, we sat down to chopped cucumbers floating in

the ice-cold borscht, radishes and tomatoes and let- ¹⁵
tuce in sour cream, a mound of corn just out of the
pot steaming on the table, the butter slowly melting
in a cracked blue soup plate — breathing hard
against the heat, we sat down together at last.

Daylight at evening. The whitewashed walls ²⁰
have turned yellow in great golden combs, as if the
butter dribbling down our chins from each new
piece of corn we lovingly prepare with butter and
salt were oozing down the walls. The kitchen is
quiet under the fatigue blown in from the parched ²⁵
streets — so quiet that in this strangely drawn-out
light, the sun hot on our backs, we seem to be eating hand in hand. "How hot it is still! How hot
still!" The silence and calm press on me with a
painful joy. I cannot wait to get out into the streets ³⁰
tonight, I cannot wait. Each unnatural moment of
silence says that something is going on outside.
Something is about to happen. The sound of an impending explosion waits in the summer night.

In the open, now. The sun hanging below the end ³⁵
of each block hits me in the face. They have opened
the fire hydrants and have put up a revolving
shower in the middle of the street, and kids stripped
to their underwear run squealing in and out of the
feebly sputtering drops. "*Mama! Look at me, Ma-* ⁴⁰
ma!" Where the gutter is wet now, it glistens like
rhinestones; where dry, it is blue. Halfway down
the block a horse lies dead in the gutter, a cloud
of flies buzzing at his eyes. A little carousel has
drawn up next to the grocery. The hurdy-gurdy ⁴⁵
skips whole notes at a time as if it were being
pressed and squeezed out of shape each time the
wooden horses with long straw manes come round
again. The pony glumly relieves himself in his
traces, and the sparrows float down from the tele- ⁵⁰
phone wires to peck and peck at each fresh steam-
ing mound of manure, and the smell of the milk
scum from the great open cans outside the grocery
is suddenly joined, on a passing breath of wind,
to the smell of varnish and brine from the barrels ⁵⁵

outside the warehouse on Bristol Street. Westward, on the streets that lead to the park, the dusty trees of heaven droop in the sun. You can smell Brownsville's tiredness in the air like smoke. Slowly, how slowly now, the pigeons rise and fall in their unchanging orbits as they go round and round the roofs, the enigmatic spire of the church, and brush against the aged sycamore with sharp leaves. 60

The Writer's Craft

1. Did you observe the author's use of specific nouns that make you see, hear, smell, and feel things? You should be able to visualize the "great sandy pile" in the sink. What nouns help you see it? How would the substitution of the more general noun *vegetables* for "radishes, lettuces, tomatoes, cucumbers, and scallions" (lines 4–5) affect the passage? What specific nouns help you see the food on the dinner table (lines 14–18)? Why does the author use those nouns instead of simply writing, "We sat down to the *evening meal*"? Find other instances in the selection where general nouns are avoided in favor of more specific ones.

2. Look back over the selection, this time to consider Kazin's use of adjectives and adjective phrases. Do any word choices strike you as unusual? Consider the adjective *wild* in the first paragraph (line 2). Would *bright* be as effective there? Consider *painful* in the second paragraph (line 30). Do you understand what the author means by a "painful joy"? What do those adjectives tell you about his state of mind and the appearance of the room?

3. In looking for adjectives, did you notice how often the author uses participles and participial phrases? He speaks of the tab of the window shade "*baking* in the sun," the corn "*steaming* on the table," the butter "slowly *melting* in a cracked blue soup plate," and the family sitting down together, "*breathing* hard against the heat." Do you find the phrases effective? Why?

4. Find participles and participial phrases that help you see, and perhaps hear, the following:

the boys on the roof (lines 11–12)
the sun (lines 35–36)
the kids (lines 38–39)

the waterdrops (line 40)
the flies (line 44)

Which participles and participial phrases appeal simultaneously to the senses of sight and smell? Which appeal to the sense of hearing? Which participles seem especially well chosen?

5. Now look over the selection once more, this time paying particular attention to Kazin's use of verbs. What verbs strike you as being unusually effective choices? Did you notice *float* (line 50)? Try substituting *fly* in its place. Is anything lost?

The following selection describes the sound a locust makes on a hot summer day. If you are familiar with that sound, write a brief description of it before reading the selection. Be careful to choose modifiers — adjectives and adverbs — that are precise. Then, as you read the selection, compare your choice of modifiers with the author's.

36   Robert Penn Warren in *The Cave*

Then the silence is over. The locusts begin again, for this is the year of the locust. In fact, there has not been silence at all, for the air has been full of a dry, grinding metallic sound, so penetrating that it has seemed, paradoxically, to come from within   5
the blood, or from some little buzz saw working fiendishly away at the medulla oblongata.* It is easy to forget that it is not from inside you, that glittering, jittering, remorseless whir so much part of you that you scarcely notice it, and perhaps love it, un-   10
til the time when you will really notice it, and scream.

The locust sound is like that, rising from the long, wooded ridges and the coves, hollows, gaps, water gaps, and valleys, westward where the land breaks   15
toward the river, eastward toward the higher ridges that heave up, rock snagging above woods-growth. The locust sound unremittingly rises, and you live

* **medulla oblongata:** a part of the brain.

so fully in it that it is no longer sound. It is more like the dizzying heat-dazzle that, too, shimmers 20 up from the woods and ridges to make your vision shake. That distant, pervasive, persuasive sound never stops, and that is why, when the sound in your immediate vicinity does suddenly, and inexplicably, stop, you think you are caught in a breath- 25 less hush.

The Writer's Craft

1. In reading the selection, did you notice the modifiers that describe the locust sound? Are any adjectives and adverbs in the passage included in your own description?

2. Examine the following italicized modifiers in their context:

> In fact, there has not been silence at all, for the air has been full of a *dry, grinding metallic* sound, so *penetrating* that it has seemed, *paradoxically*, to come from within the blood, or from some little buzz saw working *fiendishly* away at the medulla oblongata. (lines 2–7)

> It is easy to forget that it is not from inside you, that *glittering, jittering, remorseless* whir . . . (lines 7–9)

> That *distant, pervasive, persuasive* sound never stops, and that is why, when the sound in your immediate vicinity does *suddenly*, and *inexplicably*, stop, you think you are caught in a *breathless* hush. (lines 22–26)

Find ten adjectives in the sentences that describe the sound of the locust; then consider them one by one. Which ones help you hear the sound, and which merely tell you about it? Which seem most effective and appropriate?

3. Warren describes the whir of the locust as "glittering, jittering, remorseless." What effect is achieved by placing *glittering* next to *jittering*? Does such a repetition of sounds suggest what the author is describing? Can you find other adjectives placed together because of their similar sounds?

4. Pick out the four italicized adverbs in the sentences from the selection printed above. Read the sentences first with those adverbs, then without them. Do the adverbs contribute to the vividness of the description? Which do you consider particularly effective choices?

FIGURATIVE LANGUAGE   Besides using exact verbs, precise adjectives and adverbs, and specific nouns, writers often use figures of speech to create vivid impressions. Model 35 in this lesson contains an example of a figure of speech called *personification:* "Each unnatural moment of silence says that something is going on outside." A moment of silence cannot, of course, say anything; but when it is suggested that an abstraction or an inanimate object can behave as a human being does, the writer is using personification.

Model 36 makes use of a figure of speech called a *simile,* when, for example, we are told that the locust sound "is more like the dizzying heat-dazzle that, too, shimmers up from the woods and ridges to make your vision shake." When a writer directly compares two unlike things by saying that one is *like* the other, or that one behaves *as* the other does, he or she is using a simile. But when a writer compares one thing to another indirectly by presenting an object as though it were something else, he or she is using a *metaphor.* This sentence from Model 35 contains a metaphor: "The whitewashed walls have turned yellow in great golden combs." There a comparison between the walls of the kitchen and honeycombs is being made, but by implication rather than directly.

In reading the following selection, notice how frequently the author uses personification, similes, and metaphors.

37   Donald Culross Peattie in *A Natural History of Trees*

[1] The most magnificent display of color in all the kingdom of plants is the autumnal foliage of the trees of North America. Over them all, over the clear light of the aspens and mountain ash, over the leaping flames of sumac and the hellfire flicker-   5
ings of poison ivy, over the warpaint of the many oaks, rise the colors of one tree — the sugar maple — in the shout of a great army. Clearest yellow, richest crimson, tumultuous scarlet, or brilliant orange — the yellow pigments shining through the over-   10
painting of the red — the foliage of sugar maple at once outdoes and unifies the rest. It is like the mighty, marching melody that rides upon the crest

of some symphonic weltering sea and, with its cry- ing song, gives meaning to all the calculated dis- 15 sonance of the orchestra.

[2] There is no properly planted New England village without its sugar maples. They march up the hill to the old white meetinghouse and down from the high school, where the youngsters troop 20 home laughing in the golden dusk. The falling glory lights upon the shoulders of the postman, swirls after the children on roller skates, drifts through the windows of a passing bus to drop like largesse in the laps of the passengers. On a street where great 25 maples arch, letting down their shining benediction, people seem to walk as if they had already gone to glory.

[3] Outside the town, where the cold pure ponds gaze skyward and the white crooked brooks run 30 whispering their sesquipedalian * Indian names, the maple leaves slant drifting down to the water; there they will sink like galleons with painted sails, or spin away and away on voyages of chance that end on some little reef of feldspar and hornblende 35 and winking mica schist. Up in the hills, the hunter and his russet setter stride unharmed through these falling tongues of maple fire that flicker in the tingling air and leap against the elemental blue of the sky where the wind is tearing crow calls to 40 tatters.

* **sesquipedalian:** measuring a foot and a half; also used humorously to refer to long words.

The Writer's Craft

1. The selection contains an unusually large number of metaphors, similes, and personifications — more, indeed, than you would be likely to encounter in most descriptive passages of similar length. Can you explain why the author includes so many figures of speech? Could he have created as vivid an impression of the autumn foliage with fewer figures?

2. Paragraph 1 refers to "the leaping flames of sumac," "the hellfire flickerings of poison ivy," and "the warpaint of the many

oaks" (lines 5–7). Which figures of speech are these? Can you find any other sentences that indirectly compare foliage to fire? The paragraph speaks of the colors of the maple rising "in the shout of a great army" (line 8). Which figure of speech is this? If the author had written that the colors rise "*like* the shout of a great army," which figure of speech would it have been?

3. The last sentence of paragraph 1 (lines 12–16) compares the foliage of the maple to "the mighty, marching melody that rides upon the crest of some symphonic weltering sea." Do you find the direct comparison effective? What figure of speech is it?

4. When the author describes the maples as they "*march* up the hill" (lines 18–19), the ponds as they "*gaze* skyward" (line 30), and the brooks as they "run *whispering* their sesquipedalian Indian names" (lines 30–31), what figure of speech is he using?

Now You Try It

This lesson has examined three examples of descriptive writing that differ from each other in many respects; but all three have at least one characteristic in common: all are descriptions of things with which many of us are familiar — a kitchen and a city street on a summer evening, the sound of locusts, the autumn foliage. As a rule, writers do their best work when they write from first-hand experience, for then they have something concrete against which to judge what they have set down. They can ask: Does this verb effectively describe the action? Will that adjective really help the reader visualize the object? Does this metaphor, simile, or personification contribute to the impression I am trying to make?

Choose a familiar object, scene, or sound and describe it in a composition of 250 to 400 words. *Show* the subject to the readers; don't merely *tell* them about it. Let them see, hear, touch, and smell it. Pick words carefully and use figures of speech where they seem natural and appropriate. Write a first draft; then read the composition critically — just as you have read the models in this lesson. Replace or eliminate any words or figures of speech that do not seem altogether effective.

Sentence Skills

Writing mature sentences demands a variety of skills. In this section you will examine, and then practice, several skills that are necessary for writing clear, varied, and effective sentences. Skills presented here are those used by writers of models in the Description Section. Similar sentence-skill exercises are given for Narration (pages 129–36), Exposition (pages 189–96), and Opinion and Persuasion (pages 245–50).

ADJECTIVE CLAUSES

27 **Joseph Wood Krutch in** *The Desert Year*
(pages 51–52)

The Krutch selection makes effective use of adjective clauses. Compare the original version of lines 1–4 with a version in which the clauses have been eliminated:

Krutch's version:
. . . I am in a moment in a kind of sparse wilderness which shows no sign of man's intrusion, which belongs still to the creatures who have always lived here.

Rewritten version:
I am in a moment in a kind of sparse wilderness. It shows no sign of man's intrusion. It belongs still to the creatures. These creatures have always lived here.

Which version is more effective? Which one more clearly establishes the relationship between ideas? Which is the more adult version?

What word besides *which, who,* and *whom* is often used to introduce adjective clauses? There is an adjective clause in the sentence *He is the man I met.* What is it?

■ **EXERCISE**   Rewrite the following passage, using adjective clauses to combine ideas, show logical relationships, eliminate short, choppy sentences, and make the paragraph read more smoothly.

> Elizabeth Blackwell was born in England in 1821. She became the first woman in the U.S. to earn an M.D. degree from a medical school. Early in life she was very involved in teaching. She found teaching unfulfilling. People told her a woman couldn't study medicine. These people actually challenged her to apply to medical schools. Geneva Medical College accepted her in 1847. Geneva was the forerunner of Hobart College. In 1857 Blackwell established the New York Infirmary. It was staffed by women. Blackwell also helped found the London School of Medicine for Women. She returned to London to teach in the 1860's.

PARTICIPIAL PHRASES

28 Doris Humphrey in "The Orient" (pages 53–55)

Participial phrases, composed of participles and their complements or modifiers, are used as adjectives to modify nouns or pronouns. In the following sentence from Doris Humphrey's excerpt, participial phrases are italicized:

> *Arriving before the show began,* we were fascinated to see the dancers *kneeling before little mirrored boxes, finishing their make-up,* in full view on the stage.

Often the choice between conveying information in a participial phrase or in a complete sentence depends upon the degree of emphasis desired. A complete sentence generally lends emphasis to the information, whereas a participial phrase subordinates the information to the idea expressed in the independent clause. To appreciate the difference in emphasis, compare Humphrey's sentence above with the following rewritten version of it:

> We arrived before the show began. We were fascinated to see the dancers kneeling before little mirrored boxes. They were finishing their make-up in full view on the stage.

Does the rewritten version give more emphasis to the information that the observers arrived early? What did Humphrey want to focus the reader's attention on?

■ **EXERCISE** Combine each of the following pairs into a single sentence by changing one of the sentences in the pair into a participial phrase. Make sure that the idea you want to emphasize is contained in the main clause.

1. Trudy was smiling sweetly. She asked for an increase in her allowance.
2. The police officer stood on the corner. He was twirling his nightstick.
3. We were blinded by the snowstorm. We lost our way.
4. Wilbur lacked confidence. He did not do well in public speaking.
5. The members of the drama club were in the auditorium. They made plans for their next production.

LOOSE AND PERIODIC SENTENCES

30 Thomas Wolfe in "Circus at Dawn" (pages 60–61)

English sentences can be classified according to form: simple, compound, or complex. They can also be classified according to style. Most sentences in English are *loose* in style, as illustrated by the following example from the Wolfe selection:

> Then, having reached the dingy, grimy, and rickety depot section, we would get out, and walk rapidly across the tracks of the station yard, where we could see great flares and steamings from the engines, and hear the crash and bump of shifting freight cars, the swift sporadic thunders of a shifting engine, the tolling of bells, the sounds of great trains on the rails.

In a loose sentence the subject and predicate often come near the beginning, and subordinate parts follow them. The sentence is grammatically complete before its conclusion, as is the case in the model sentence above. Grammatically and logically that sentence could end after *out* or *yard* or *engines*. Where else could it end?

Another kind of sentence, much less frequently used, is the *periodic* sentence. In a periodic sentence the writer withholds the full meaning until the very end; neither grammatically nor logically could the sentence end earlier than it does. Here is an example:

And to all these familiar sounds, filled with their exultant prophecies of flight, the voyage, morning, and
the shining cities — to all the sharp and thrilling odors
of the trains — the smell of cinders, acrid smoke, of
musty, rusty freight cars, the clean pineboard of crated
produce, and the smells of fresh stored food — oranges,
coffee, tangerines and bacon, ham and flour and beef
— there would be added now, with an unforgettable
magic and familiarity, all the strange sounds and
smells of the coming circus.

Why is it impossible to end this sentence before "all the
strange sounds and smells of the coming circus"? What is
the subject of the sentence? What is the predicate? Because
the full meaning of a periodic sentence is withheld to the
end, the result possesses an air of suspense and climax.

Most of the sentences you write will be loose. But for
the sake of contrast and emphasis, you should occasionally
make use of periodic variations.

■ EXERCISE   Some of the following sentences are loose;
some are periodic. Rewrite the loose sentences to make
them periodic, and the periodic sentences to make them
loose. Decide whether the rewritten sentences are as effective as the originals.

1. If we wish to remain free, if we mean to maintain justice, if we hope to be esteemed throughout the world,
   we must be prepared to defend, whenever it is threat-
   ened, the liberty of each individual citizen.
2. With the trumpets blaring, the drums booming, and the
   children screaming their wild delight, the marchers
   passed in review.
3. We have done our best, although our dreams have now
   faded, our efforts have proved fruitless, and we have
   tasted the bitterness of defeat.
4. Even though the day was bright and sunny, and children, unaware of what had happened there twenty-five
   years ago, were playing near the gates, most of the adult
   visitors at the site could still feel the unutterable terror
   of the place.
5. Everyone was laughing, even though our car had a flat
   tire, and it had started to rain, and some large black
   ants were devouring our picnic lunch.

32   Joseph Conrad in *The Secret Sharer*
(pages 67–68)

In most English sentences the subject comes first, the verb next, and the object or the complement, if there is one, last. But within this normal subject-verb-object pattern almost endless possibilities for sentence variety exist. When we say that the subject comes first, we do not mean that the subject must be the very first word in each sentence. In fact, if it were, your writing would be dull and choppy. There are a great many modifiers — adjectives, adverbs, prepositional phrases, participial phrases, subordinate clauses, and so on — that may precede the subject. One of the most effective ways to lend interest to your writing is to vary the beginnings of sentences.

In the Conrad selection only one sentence in seven begins directly with the subject, though the main sentence patterns are in "normal" word order. Here are the ways in which Conrad's seven sentences begin:

1 On my right hand . . . (prepositional phrase)
2 To the left . . . (prepositional phrase)
3 And when I turned . . . (conjunction with adverb clause)
4 Corresponding in their insignificance . . . (participial phrase)
5 Here and there . . . (adverbs)
6 My eye . . . (subject)
7 And then . . . (conjunction with adverb)

Read the last paragraph of Model 27 (Joseph Wood Krutch's *The Desert Year*) on page 52. There are six sentences in the paragraph. How many of them begin directly with the subject? What are some of the other ways in which they begin? Are there any sentences that do not follow the normal subject-verb-object order?

■ **EXERCISE**   Rewrite the following paragraph adapted from Thoreau's *Walden* for the purpose of this exercise. Vary the sentence beginnings in order to produce a more readable and effective paragraph. You may have to change the wording slightly in some sentences. Do not change the beginning of every sentence.

The mice which haunted my house were not the common ones. They were instead a wild native kind not found in the village. One of them made its nest underneath my house when I was building at Walden. It would come out regularly at lunchtime and pick up the crumbs from my meal. It could readily ascend the sides of the room by short impulses, like a squirrel. It ran up my clothes and along my sleeve one day. It came at last to a piece of cheese I was holding between my thumb and finger. It nibbled the cheese, then cleaned its face and paws, and walked away.

VARIETY IN SENTENCE LENGTHS

34 Robert Penn Warren in "The Patented Gate and the Mean Hamburger" (pages 71–72)

One way to increase the effectiveness of your writing is by varying the lengths of your sentences. An unbroken succession of short sentences is usually monotonous, whereas a succession of long sentences is both monotonous and difficult to read. The last paragraph in Model 34 (page 72) is an example of pleasing variety in sentence length.

Sentence beginning	Number of words in sentence
But you see . . .	5
You see that . . .	7
They are pale . . .	15
They are not wide . . .	32
When you pass . . .	24
Then you pass on . . .	15

Warren might have split some of his longer sentences into two, three, or even four brief ones. The paragraph might then have read:

But you see the eyes. You see that the eyes are alive. They are pale blue or gray. They are set back under the deep brows and thorny eyebrows. They are not wide. They are squinched up like eyes accustomed to wind or sun. They seem accustomed to measuring the stroke of the ax or to fixing the object over the rifle sights. You pass by. As you do, you see that the eyes are alive. They are warily and dispassionately estimating you from the ambush of the thorny brows. Then you pass on. He stands there in that stillness which is his gift.

What effect is produced by these very short sentences? Why is the original paragraph with six sentences of varying lengths more effective than it would have been with a dozen or more brief sentences?

■ EXERCISE Rewrite the following paragraph, breaking the single sentence into at least five sentences. Vary sentence lengths so that you have both short and long sentences in pleasing alternation. The wording may have to be changed slightly.

Years ago there were pronounced regional differences in the United States, with the Northeast, the South, the Middle Atlantic States, the Midwest, the West, and the Northwest each having distinctive food specialities, architectural styles, styles of dress, political views, and dialects; but now America seems to be homogenized, everywhere the same, with Boston baked beans sold in Texas supermarkets, the California rancher at home in New York, Florida sports attire sold in Dubuque, the Solid South a political myth, and a general American dialect spoken from Maine to Florida and from Delaware to Alaska — all signaling the end of diversity.

Narration

LESSON **11**

Skills of Narration

Narration tells a story, presented as a connected series of events usually in chronological order. The events may be true or imaginary. In any case, a narrative always answers the question, "What happened?" Below, Mark Twain tells what happened to one of his friends during an ill-fated night in the 1840's.

38 **Mark Twain**
in *The Autobiography of Mark Twain*

It was back in those far-distant days that Jim Wolf came to us. He was from Shelbyville, a hamlet thirty or forty miles back in the country, and he brought all his native sweetness and gentleness and simplicities with him. He was approaching seven- 5
teen, a grave and slender lad, trustful, honest, honorable, a creature to love and cling to. And he was incredibly bashful. He was with us a good while, but he could never conquer that peculiarity; he could not be at ease in the presence of any woman, 10
not even in my good and gentle mother's; and as to speaking to any girl, it was wholly impossible.

It is to this kind that untoward * things happen. My sister gave a "candy-pull" on a winter's night. I was too young to be of the company and Jim was 15
too diffident. I was sent up to bed early and Jim followed of his own motion. His room was in the new

* **untoward:** unlucky, inconvenient.

part of the house and his window looked out on the roof of the L annex. That roof was six inches deep in snow and the snow had an ice crust upon it which was as slick as glass. Out of the comb of the roof projected a short chimney, a common resort for sentimental cats on moonlight nights — and this was a moonlight night. Down at the eaves, below the chimney, a canopy of dead vines spread away to some posts, making a cozy shelter, and after an hour or two the rollicking crowd of young ladies and gentlemen grouped themselves in its shade, with their saucers of liquid and piping-hot candy disposed about on the frozen ground to cool. There was joyous chaffing and joking and laughter — peal upon peal of it.

About this time a couple of old disreputable tomcats got up on the chimney and started a heated argument about something; also about this time I gave up trying to get to sleep and went visiting to Jim's room. He was awake and fuming about the cats and their intolerable yowling. I asked him, mockingly, why he didn't climb out and drive them away. He was nettled and said overboldly that for two cents he *would*.

It was a rash remark and was probably repented of before it was fairly out of his mouth. But it was too late — he was committed. I knew him; and I knew he would rather break his neck than back down if I egged him on judiciously.

"Oh, of course you would! Who's doubting it?"

It galled him and he burst out, with sharp irritation, "Maybe *you* doubt it!"

"I? Oh no! I shouldn't think of such a thing. You are always doing wonderful things, with your mouth."

He was in a passion now. He snatched on his yarn socks and began to raise the window, saying in a voice quivering with anger:

"*You* think I dasn't — you do! Think what you blame please. I don't care what you think. I'll show you!"

The window made him rage; it wouldn't stay up.
I said, "Never mind, I'll hold it."   60

Indeed, I would have done anything to help. I
was only a boy and was already in a radiant heaven
of anticipation. He climbed carefully out, clung to
the windowsill until his feet were safely placed,
then began to pick his perilous way on all fours   65
along the glassy comb, a foot and a hand on each
side of it. I believe I enjoy it now as much as I did
then; yet it is nearly fifty years ago. The frosty
breeze flapped his short shirt about his lean legs;
the crystal roof shone like polished marble in the in-   70
tense glory of the moon; the unconscious cats sat
erect upon the chimney, alertly watching each
other, lashing their tails, and pouring out their hollow grievances; and slowly and cautiously Jim crept
on, flapping as he went, the gay and frolicsome   75
young creatures under the vine canopy unaware,
and outraging these solemnities with their mis-
placed laughter. Every time Jim slipped I had a
hope; but always on he crept and disappointed it.
At last he was within reaching distance. He paused,   80
raised himself carefully up, measured his distance
deliberately, then made a frantic grab at the nearest cat — and missed it. Of course he lost his balance. His heels flew up, he struck on his back, and
like a rocket he darted down the roof feet first,   85
crashed through the dead vines and landed in a sitting position in fourteen saucers of red-hot candy in
the midst of all that party — and dressed as *he* was
— this lad who could not look a girl in the face with
his clothes on. There was a wild scramble and a   90
storm of shrieks and Jim fled up the stairs, dripping broken crockery all the way.

The Writer's Craft

SELECTING KEY EVENTS

Stories that recount experiences require that the writer select
certain events to include; the events selected are the ones that
help tell the story effectively by making a point. The point of

Mark Twain's narrative is to develop the humor of Jim Wolf's escapade on the night of the candy-pull. From all the events that undoubtedly took place that night, the author has selected and included only the pertinent ones. The following key events occur in the narrative:

Jim Wolf arrives at Mark Twain's house (lines 1–2)
The narrator is sent to bed early, and Jim goes too (lines 16–17)
The young men and women gather under the canopy of vines to wait for the candy to cool (lines 26–30)
Two tomcats begin yowling on the chimney (lines 33–35)
Jim makes his boast and the narrator urges him to act (lines 38–61)
Jim crosses the roof (lines 63–79)
Jim slips, crashes through the vines, and disrupts the party (lines 80–90)
Jim flees up the stairs (lines 90–92)

In lines 26–28 the author says that "after an hour or two" the young people gathered under the canopy of vines, but he does not reveal what happened during that hour or two. Nor does he tell us how the tomcats got on the chimney or what happened to them after Jim fell. How do you account for those omissions?

USING NARRATIVE DETAILS

The key events in the narrative could be presented in a brief summary, which would still be narration, but would lack the rich detail of Mark Twain's story:

> One winter night, when Jim Wolf was staying at our house, my sister gave a "candy-pull." Jim and I went to bed early. After an hour or two, the noise from the party, plus the yowling of a couple of cats on the roof, was too much for me. I went visiting Jim and found him complaining about the cats, so I urged him to crawl out on the roof and drive them away. He boasted that "for two cents" he would, and I goaded him into carrying out the boast. It might have worked out differently had the roof not been so slippery and Jim not been so anxious. But in grabbing for one of the cats, he lost his balance and fell off the roof, right into the middle of my sister's party. Amid a storm of shrieks, he fled back up to his room.

This summary contains all the important facts about Jim Wolf's embarrassing experience, but the interest is gone. *Narrative details* are essential if Jim is to seem alive and the events real and vivid. Here are examples of some of the different kinds of details in Mark Twain's narrative:

Details that reveal character:

> I asked him, mockingly, why he didn't climb out and drive them away. (lines 38–40)
>
> The window made him rage; it wouldn't stay up. (line 59)
>
> I said, "Never mind, I'll hold it." (line 60)
>
> . . . this lad who could not look a girl in the face with his clothes on. (lines 89–90)

Details that make actions specific:

> . . . slowly and cautiously Jim crept on, flapping as he went . . . (lines 74–75)
>
> He paused, raised himself carefully up, measured his distance deliberately, then made a frantic grab at the nearest cat — and missed it. (lines 80–83)
>
> . . . like a rocket he darted down the roof feet first, crashed through the dead vines and landed in a sitting position in fourteen saucers of red-hot candy . . . (lines 85–87)

Details that offer explanations or reasons:

> It is to this kind that untoward things happen. (line 13)
>
> I was too young to be of the company and Jim was too diffident. (lines 15–16)
>
> I knew him; and I knew he would rather break his neck than back down if I egged him on judiciously. (lines 44–46)

Find other details that help make the events in the narrative seem vivid and the experience it relates seem real.

USING DIALOGUE

In a narrative, dialogue — the direct quotation of speakers' words — serves a number of purposes. Dialogue helps convey action, foretell events, or reveal character, either of a speaker or of the person spoken to. What is the function of the dialogue in lines 47–60? Do you think the story would have been as interesting if it had contained no dialogue at all? Why, or why not? Would it have been as interesting if it had been written entirely in dialogue? Explain.

USING DESCRIPTION IN NARRATION

Because narration is concerned with events, the writer concentrates on action rather than on descriptions of persons, places, and objects. At times, though, some description is necessary if the reader is to picture the action and understand the events fully. Below is a list of the people, places, and objects that Mark Twain describes in the model. Look back at the descriptions and explain what they contribute to the narrative.

Jim Wolf (lines 1–12)
the roof outside Jim's window (lines 18–24)
the scene beneath the eaves (lines 24–32)
the view as Jim crawls across the roof (lines 68–78)

POINT OF VIEW

"Who is telling the story?" is a question that must be answered before an author can begin to write; the answer affects the way the material will be selected and arranged. If the story is told from the *personal* point of view, as in Mark Twain's narrative, the narrator functions as a character in the story. That is, Twain participates in the action, which he depicts at close range, and he is able to inject his own opinions, explanations, and judgments. Find at least three places where Mark Twain expresses his own opinions in the model narrative.

Now You Try It

Select one of the following assignments:

1. Write a narrative of from 500 to 750 words depicting a sequence of events that led to a dramatic conclusion. Base the story on a personal experience — one that interested you and is likely to interest readers. Before starting the narrative, outline it by listing the key events in chronological order.

2. Think about an important decision you had to make recently, and recall the sequence of events leading up to it. After listing the key events in chronological order, write a narrative of 500 to 750 words showing how and why you made your decision.

LESSON **12**

Selecting Key Events

Narratives are composed of sequences of events. To be sure, a writer cannot and would not want to include every single event that occurred in the course of an experience. Instead, a writer selects those events that (1) move the action forward, (2) provide turning points or a conclusion for the action, (3) give insight into characters in the story, and (4) help create a desired emotional effect. An event that serves one or more of those functions is called a *key event*. Look for such events in the following narrative.

39 Burl Ives in *Wayfaring Stranger*

[1] When I was in about the sixth grade at school, our two-year high school, which was in another building, decided to put on a play.

[2] The play was put on in the Odd Fellows Hall over the brick mercantile store in the center of our town. We made the scenery, the girls made the costumes, and everybody turned out for the amateur theatricals. People from the other towns came to see them, and before we knew it, we were putting on plays in the neighboring towns, Willow Hill, Yale, St. Marie, Rose Hill, and others.

[3] Between the acts I played the banjo, cracked jokes, and sang minstrel songs and the old ballads. Because of my extensive theatrical commitments I saved

money and bought from Oliver Ditson in Boston a makeup box which had greasepaint, eyebrow pencils, and all kinds of makeup equipment.

[4] One night after our week's theatrical season was over and forgotten, I began to experiment with makeup. I sat before the glass and made myself up as a Chinese with a wig and queue.* Then I made myself up as old men with various kinds of whiskers. One of these I liked very much. I really looked like a very old man with whiskers.

[5] In an old trunk in my father's bedroom, there was a cape and hat, such as gamblers on the Mississippi River used during the turn of the century. This hat and cape had belonged to my father's brother who was the black sheep of the family. He had actually been a Mississippi gambler, and it was said that his body lay unfound at the river's bottom.

[6] I took the cape and hat out of the old trunk and put them on. With my whiskers and gray makeup on, with a cane in my right hand and in a stooped position I walked toward the restaurant. As I came to the corner to turn toward the restaurant, I met Ide Chatman, a neighbor woman. I walked slowly past her and I saw that she was mighty curious, that she did not recognize me. She went on toward home, looking back over her shoulders at one whom she supposed a stranger in town.

[7] I went up past the restaurant but stayed far enough away so that the people in the restaurant saw only the outline of an old man with a cane, a cape, and a tall hat.

[8] When I had moved from the light into the darkness, I ripped off the cape and hat, flew home, and took off the makeup. Then I ran back as fast as I could to the restaurant. The place was buzzing with excitement. Ide Chatman had come in and reported what she had seen on the street. Several of the loafers had seen the old man as he passed in front of the restaurant. I knew in a moment that I was not suspected, so

* queue: a pigtail.

I said, "Why, I saw him not two or three minutes ago as I came up. He was going toward the church."

[9] That night people who had not locked their doors in years locked them. Children waited to walk home with their parents, and there was an air of mystery around the town. During the day drummers * would come to the town taking orders for goods, and occasionally visitors would come to some family, but everyone who came into town was accounted for. The appearance of this stranger was curious and everyone was afraid down in his heart of the mysterious old man.

[10] After a couple of weeks he was forgotten and I thought it time he should make another appearance. It was in the spring of the year, and the roads were muddy, and it was difficult for anybody to get into or out of town. Horseback and carriage were the only practical ways of travel; the roads were impassable to automobiles. Thus the town had fewer visitors than at other times of the year.

[11] It was a beautiful moonlight night when an old man with a cape, tall hat, and cane again moved slowly down the street in Hunt City. Various people passed him, and he walked on, saying nothing. Ten minutes later, after shedding my disguise, I went into the restaurant again, and this time the intensity of the excitement was even greater. People ran into the restaurant to report that they had seen him in various other parts of town where he had not been. Ide Chatman reported that she had seen him walking across the road and that as she went toward him all at once there was a flash and a puff of smoke and he was no more.

[12] Again fear gripped this little town. I fell in with their attitude and soon was not sure but that there was another old man and that actually there was something to be afraid of. For many weeks various people came in to tell of having seen the strange old man at one place or another in the town. One person said he

* **drummers:** traveling salespeople.

had seen him sitting on the steeple of the church, balancing himself and then fading away.

[13] Summer came and the old man had been forgotten except as a legend. Then one night, feeling the need of a little excitement, I put on my costume again and ventured into the streets. Four young men were coming toward me and I thought, should I give ground or should I walk directly past them? I pulled the hat down over my face, bent on the cane, and walked by the four frightened young men. I kept walking and they stopped. One of them said, "Let's catch the old —"

[14] They started walking after me. I started walking a little faster and I realized that they intended to catch me. Also I sensed their fear. I turned, with my cape in the same hand as my cane, and lifted them both high in the air. The young men stopped for a second, then flew in terror down the street. I ran and disrobed, then hurried into the restaurant and reported that I had seen him.

[15] The town was abuzz and again he was reported many times and in many places by various people. One woman said that she had seen him in her back yard and that he had looked up at her and his eyes were afire, that his face was pale, that stringy hair hung down from under his tall hat, and that he had no lips, only a pair of teeth.

[16] During all of this I became very fearful lest I should be caught and I did not appear again in this outfit for a very long time. Then I could not resist and again I appeared on the street as the old man.

[17] The last time I appeared was in the fall of the year. There was a vacant lot down one of the streets where we boys had made beds in the tall Jimson weeds. The weeds had grown eight feet high and through them we had made tunnels.

[18] It happened that on the night when the old man appeared there was a group of men and boys in the street. Somebody said, "Let's get him." All at once they came at me, fifteen or twenty men and boys, running as fast as they could go. I came to the weed patch

which was next to an implement building. I went through a hole in the fence into the Jimson weed patch, threw off my cape and hat, and escaped.

[19] They did not see where I had gone because I had faded into the dark shadow of the implement building. Some of the men said, as they cut back to the restaurant, that as the old man flew down the street his feet had not touched the ground and as he had come to the implement building he had raised in flight and they had seen him soar into the sky.

[20] I was so excited at all of these stories and at all of the wonderful things which were manufactured in the minds of the people that I felt I wanted to tell somebody that I was the old man. But there was no one to tell. I couldn't let this get out. It had to be my secret but I was bursting to tell someone. I thought of telling my father but realized that the consequences might not be pleasant.

[21] So again in two weeks the old man appeared on the street and this time was chased into the weed patch by five or six men, one of them Frank Ives. After I had crawled into the weed patch a little distance, I took off the cape and hat and threw them into the thick weeds some distance. Then I went back by tunnel and joined those who were seeking the old man.

[22] I started down the street ahead of the men who had been seeking the old man and my father said, "Burl, are you going home?"

[23] I said, "Yes, I think I will."

[24] He said, "Wait, I will come with you."

[25] As we neared our house, from underneath his coat he pulled out a cape, a hat, and a cane, and said, "Did you ever see these before?"

[26] And I said, "Yes, they were Uncle John's."

[27] He said, "Yes, they were."

[28] He took the costume and put it back in the trunk which had belonged to my uncle, then came back to me and said, "Let's take a walk."

[29] We walked what seemed to be a very long time down the streets, and finally he said, "You might have been killed, pulling a trick like that."

[30] I said, "Yes."

[31] Then he said, "If the old man never appears again, I will tell no one. It will be our secret."

[32] We stopped and looked directly into each other's eyes and Frank Ives held out his right hand to his son. Until this day it has remained our secret.

The Writer's Craft

1. A key event early in Burl Ives's narrative occurs in paragraphs 6–9, with the first appearance of the strange old man. How do paragraphs 1–5 set the stage for that event?

2. How many excursions into town did Ives make with the cape, hat, and cane? Is each venture a key event in the narrative? Explain. How long a period of time did those events occupy?

3. Every appearance of Ives as the old man is followed by an account of the reactions of the townspeople. Is their behavior important in the narrative? Explain.

4. Transitions indicate that events in the story are presented in chronological order: "One night after our week's theatrical season" (paragraph 4); "After a couple of weeks" (paragraph 10). Find other transitions that indicate chronological order.

5. In a narrative each key event is part of a sequence of events, which should reach a clear-cut conclusion. Does Ives's narrative reach a conclusion? Is Burl Ives's encounter with his father a key event in the narrative? Explain.

Now You Try It

Select one of the following assignments:

1. Write a narrative in which you tell about an adventure or a remarkable experience you had as the result of a decision to act on your own. Before starting the composition, carefully select the key events to include in the narrative.

2. In his *Autobiography* Mark Twain writes: "All my life I have been the easy prey of the cheap adventure." Burl Ives in his narrative demonstrates how he was such "easy prey." Write a narrative about a situation in your own life that reveals how such an insight could be applied to you. Select the key events carefully before starting the composition.

LESSON **13**

Using Narrative Details

An effective narrative includes details that give the reader an interesting and comprehensive view of an experience. To appreciate the difference that narrative details can make, compare the following brief account with Maya Angelou's model that follows it. Both cover the same events, but the latter contains narrative details.

> My friend Paul and I decided to leave London and visit my friend James Baldwin in southern France. We took a ferry to northern France and then drove south. It was a frustrating car trip. When we got to Baldwin's house, we stayed just a short while. Then I went back home to Berkeley.

40   Maya Angelou in "Letter from France"

James Baldwin had invited me many times to come and see his house in the south of France. He has long been my friend, brother, and favorite writer. Since I was so near, since London was reminding me more and more of northern Califor-   5
nia, since Paul was beginning to show just an edge of edginess, I suggested that we tear ourselves loose and bound over to southern France. He agreed readily.

We packed the hardly used gardening tools, put

the borrowed house in order, and telephoned BEA* [10] for reservations to Nice. When we were told the ticket rates (seventy-eight pounds sterling° each, one way, London–Nice) we were nearly shocked into remaining in London. But Paul, the intrepid adventurer, suggested buying a car, an old used car, [15] preferably a retired post-office van ("one driver, whose use of it was mostly in parking along shady streets"). Fortunately, a friend had an Austin Mini Countryman he needed to rid himself of. The car was in "excellent condition," only nine years old, [20] and had spent most of those years "parked along shady streets."

We drove aboard the British Sea Link Ferry in New Haven at 10:00 P.M., and at midnight, as the ship pulled out into the channel, we toasted each [25] other in the well-appointed dining room with a solid French wine that was nearly as good as Gallo's Hearty Burgundy.

Dawn in Dieppe. Three times the morning lifted for two seconds as I picked the car's way through [30] the town's narrow cobbled streets and out onto a gray highway. An arrow promised Rouen and, since Paul was sleeping off our shipboard celebration, I had no choice but to trust the promise. A pale sun rose on the Normandy countryside, and it was a [35] dreary setting for an Ingmar Bergman film. But as the light strengthened, the fertility of the land was more evident. Thatched cottages and prosperous farmhouses sat back from the highway in San Joaquin Valley green. I tried to people the land- [40] scape with conquering Normans from old history books or allied troops from World War II, but the tiny car wrestled along the road like a hooked trout, and before I could let my attention wander, I had driven through Rouen and reached the outskirts of [45] a fairly large town.

Paul awoke, ashamed that he had slept through the hard part of the drive. . . .

* BEA: abbreviation for British European Airways.
° seventy-eight pounds sterling: about $170.

"Are we in Chartres?"

"*Oui.*" 50

We sat at a sidewalk restaurant off a cobbled square and had our first *petit pain* and *café au lait.* The wonders of fresh bread, sweet butter, and hot coffee were partly lost on me since I was still try- 55 ing to unfold my six-foot frame from the pattern the small car was molding me into. Paul popped under the wheel and guided the car back to the highway. Over the rooftops I spied the spires of the cathedral called by Rodin the "Acropolis of France." Once 60 back on the road, I mentally ticked off Chartres. It had been done. . . .

The meadows and pastures unfolded slowly out the Austin's sliding windows in nearly the same rhythm that my legs, shoulders, and arms were atro- phying within the car. By five-thirty we drove into 65 Roanne, and I thought it would be easier to sleep where I was than to demand the improbable of my aching body.

We moved into the fading but elegant Hôtel Cen- trale as if we planned to stay for a month. Paul and 70 a too-thin bellboy carried our six large bags and a box of books into the hotel's strong room, since one of the car doors refused to lock securely. A long steamy bath cajoled my muscles into resuming their work, and by nine o'clock we followed the hotel 75 manager's directions to the Restaurant Alsace-Lor- raine. We ate a well-prepared and abundantly served dinner and walked the quiet dark streets back to the hotel.

Morning found us pleated back into the car and 80 on the highway. Lyons flew by in a haze of pink hill châteaux and modern high-rise buildings.

The car, designed for the wet and misty isle of Britain, began to act stroppy in the warming air. I steered it onto the hot pavement of Autoroute N & 85 7, and it reared on its back wheels and developed a little cough under the hood. . . .

We were coasting along innocently when thick steam bubbled out of the hood accompanied by an

ominous hissing. Before I could pull to the side of 90
the road, more steam issued from the dashboard,
the glove compartment, and, finally, the ashtray.

"The car's overheated." Paul was a school teacher
before he became Britain's one-time highest-paid
comic-strip writer. "Pull over." I did. 95

He lifted the hood and, for a moment, totally
disappeared in a cloud. He materialized at the
side window and asked for the one-quart Thermos
that held my English drinking water.

After shaking the last drop into the rusty radi- 100
ator, Paul got behind the wheel again and eased
us back on the road and to my first French highway
lay-by.* It was a meeting which heralded a long
and affectionate relationship.

For the next week, I was to become familiar with 105
nearly every lay-by from Lyons to Cannes. The car
always needed water, and every 75 kilometers we
filled it from the Thermos and two ex-wine bottles.
As we passed the outskirts of Avignon, Avallon,
Fréjus, we would sally to the nearest charcuterie, 110
buy cheese, bread, butter, wine, and then gently
float out of town to the nearest lay-by. Lunches,
teas, and late afternoon snacks were eaten as we
brooded over the opened hood and tenderly patted
the doll-size tires. Paul would fill each empty wine 115
bottle, and we'd start out again for the next lay-by.

We drove, finally, to Cannes and up the twisting
roads to St. Paul. Near midnight we parked our
pressure cooker at the edge of a tiny square and
saw men in short sleeves playing *boule*° under the 120
lights. The elegant Colombe d'Or restaurant, where
Picasso, Yves Montand, Simone Signoret, and Baldwin were known to "lift a few," faced the square.
We ordered drinks at a lesser known bistro nearby
and telephoned Jimmy. In minutes he strode into 125
the square, jacket flung casually across his shoulders,
a wide grin across his face. He is a celebrity. Tour-
ists and natives alike recognized him, and he re-

* lay-by: British term for roadside area where cars may wait.
° boule: a bowling game.

turned their salute warmly—then gave me a family embrace. He said he'd guide us to his house. 130

The villa suits a great writer and especially James Baldwin. It is glamorous. It is romantic. The romance of Baldwin lies in the fact that his warmth makes us nearly forget that he is a giant. And the house is comfortable to be near. 135

Yet, with the exception of a gay reunion with my friend, the destination was to prove anticlimactic. My soreness resisted the solace of a bed. The smells of old bread, melting butter and stale wine from the car, clung to the lining of my nostrils and made 140 it difficult for me to appreciate the talents of Baldwin's highly praised cook.

We sat under a grapevine-laced arbor that has its counterpart on a ranch in Sonoma owned by a winegrowing friend. The company's conversation 145 dealt with Life, Taxes, Politics, Love, and the Arts. The same subjects we had all discussed in Paris, London, New York, and Berkeley. . . .

"How long do you want to stay?"

I hoped I was reading Paul correctly. "I'm ready 150 to head north," I answered.

He smiled. "We'll leave at dawn."

That suited me.

I said good-by to my friends in St. Paul and spent the next day and the next waving fond adieus to 155 the familiar lay-bys. A day later, I was gathering fresh zucchini, eggplant, and onions from my backyard in Berkeley. I made a *ratatouille provençale*.

The Writer's Craft

1. Narrative details may specify actions, provide reasons for actions, add interest, reveal character, or create atmosphere. Most narrative details serve more than one of those purposes. What purposes do the following details in Model 40 serve?

> I tried to people the landscape with conquering Normans . . . . (lines 40–41)

Paul popped under the wheel . . . . (lines 56–57)

The meadows and pastures unfolded slowly . . . . (line 62)

. . . the fading but elegant Hôtel Centrale . . . (lines 69–70)

He lifted the hood and, for a moment, totally disappeared in a cloud of smoke. (lines 96–97)

2. Narrative details give substance to the key events in a story. Find the details that lend substance and interest to the following events in the narrative.

The author and her friend leave London. (lines 9–22)
The author drives from Dieppe to Chartres. (lines 29–46)
They stop in Roanne. (lines 65–79)
They arrive in St. Paul. (lines 117–30)

EMPHASIS THROUGH IRONY

Irony is a figure of speech that states something quite different from what is actually meant. It is frequently used in writing, both for humor and for emphasis. Maya Angelou writes in lines 103–04 that their first stop at a lay-by was "a meeting which heralded a long and affectionate relationship." Do you see the force of irony in that statement? A more literal mind would have simply written that it was the first of many such interruptions on the trip south. But in so doing emphasis and humor would have been lost.

The term *irony* can also be used to refer to a situation in which the outcome is contrary to what might have been expected. In the last sentence of the model, Maya Angelou tells us that when she got back to Berkeley she cooked a *ratatouille provençale,* which is a French vegetable stew. We might have expected her to have prepared or eaten this dish in southern France. What, then, is ironic about the last sentence?

Now You Try It

Journeys lend themselves to narratives—and, sometimes, to humorous and entertaining narratives. The key events of a trip are usually easy to determine, but narrative details must then be added if the material is to result in something more impressive than a summary. Think of a journey (long or short) that you have taken that would make an interesting narrative. Using Model 40 as an example, write a narrative that takes the reader along with you. You might consider using irony judiciously to add humor and emphasis to the narrative.

LESSON **14**

Using Dialogue

The writer of a narrative wants the reader to see and hear events that are taking place. One way that events may be made vivid is through the use of direct conversation, or *dialogue*, as in the following narrative.

41   John Updike in "Pigeon Feathers"

. . . His parents tried to think of ways to entertain him.

"David, I have a job for you to do," his mother said one evening at the table.

"What?"   5

"If you're going to take that tone, perhaps we'd better not talk."

"What tone? I didn't take any tone."

"Your grandmother thinks there are too many pigeons in the barn."   10

"Why?" David turned to look at his grandmother, but she sat there staring at the burning lamp with her usual expression of bewilderment.

Mother shouted, "Mom, he wants to know why!"

Grandmom made a jerky, irritable motion with   15
her bad hand, as if generating the force for utterance, and said, "They foul the furniture."

"That's right," Mother said. "She's afraid for that old Olinger furniture that we'll never use. David, she's been after me for a month about those poor pigeons. She wants you to shoot them." 20

"I don't want to kill anything especially," David said.

Daddy said, "The kid's like you are, Elsie. He's too good for this world. Kill or be killed, that's my motto." 25

His mother said loudly, "Mother, he doesn't want to do it."

"Not?" The old lady's eyes distended as if in horror, and her claw descended slowly to her lap. 30

"Oh, I'll do it, I'll do it tomorrow," David snapped, and a pleasant crisp taste entered his mouth with the decision.

"And I had thought, when Boyer's men made the hay, it would be better if the barn doesn't look like 35 a rookery," his mother added needlessly.

The Writer's Craft

1. Suppose the author, avoiding dialogue, had written:

> David's mother asked him to shoot the pigeons in the barn, and his father and grandmother agreed that the birds should be killed. At first David said he didn't want to kill them, but then he changed his mind and said he would.

Clearly the summary lacks the interest and force of Updike's narrative. Does the brief version reveal the personalities of the members of David's family? Does it show the conflicts among them?

2. Dialogue can tell the reader a great deal about the person speaking. Do the words that Updike's speakers use help indicate their attitudes and personalities? From the way they speak, how would you characterize David? Father? Mother? Grandmother?

DIALOGUE TAGS

A writer using dialogue must make clear who is speaking. In lines 3–4 of the model, Updike writes:

> "David, I have a job for you to do," *his mother said.* . . .

The italicized words are the dialogue tag. But such tags are not needed every time someone speaks; indeed, of the four speeches in lines 5–10, none uses a dialogue tag. Why are tags unnecessary in those speeches?

When a tag is needed, the verb *said* is usually adequate. At times, though, a writer may wish to show precisely how the speaker's words were uttered. This can be done with specific verbs (*shouted* — line 14), with adverbs modifying the verb *said* (*said loudly* — line 27), or with a combination of specific verbs and adverbs (*added needlessly* — line 36).

Here is another model in which dialogue is used effectively. The speeches in this instance are in dialect; the scene is a village in northern Mississippi, where wild and ornery horses are being auctioned.

42 William Faulkner in "Spotted Horses"

"Now, boys," the Texan said. "Who says that pony ain't worth fifteen dollars? You couldn't buy that much dynamite for just fifteen dollars. There ain't one of them can't do a mile in three minutes; turn them into pasture and they will board themselves; work them like hell all day and every time you think about it, lay them over the head with a single-tree and after a couple of days every jack rabbit one of them will be so tame you will have to put them out of the house at night like a cat." He shook another cake from the carton and ate it. "Come on, Eck," he said. "Start her off. How about ten dollars for that horse, Eck?"

"What need I got for a horse I would need a bear-trap to catch?" Eck said.

"Didn't you just see me catch him?"

"I seen you," Eck said. "And I don't want nothing as big as a horse if I got to wrastle with it every time it finds me on the same side of a fence it's on."

"All right," the Texan said. He was still breathing harshly, but now there was nothing of fatigue or breathlessness in it. He shook another cake into his palm and inserted it beneath his moustache. "All right. I want to get this auction started. I ain't come here to live, no matter how good a country you folks claim you got. I'm going to give you that horse." For a moment there was no sound, not even that of breathing except the Texan's.

"You going to give it to me?" Eck said.

"Yes. Provided you will start the bidding on the next one." Again there was no sound save the Texan's breathing, and then the clash of Mrs. Littlejohn's pail against the rim of the pot.

"I just start the bidding," Eck said. "I don't have to buy it lessen * I ain't over-topped." Another wagon had come up the lane. It was battered and paintless. One wheel had been repaired by crossed planks bound to the spokes with baling wire and the two underfed mules wore a battered harness patched with bits of cotton rope; the reins were ordinary cotton plowlines, not new. It contained a woman in a shapeless gray garment and a faded sunbonnet, and a man in faded and patched though clean overalls. There was not room for the wagon to draw out of the lane so the man left it standing where it was and got down and came forward — a thin man, not large, with something about his eyes, something strained and washed-out, at once vague and intense, who shoved into the crowd at the rear, saying,

"What? What's that? Did he give him that horse?"

"All right," the Texan said. "That wall-eyed horse with the scarred neck belongs to you. Now. That one that looks like he's had his head in a flour barrel. What do you say? Ten dollars?"

"Did he give him that horse?" the newcomer said.

"A dollar," Eck said. The Texan's mouth was still open for speech; for an instant his face died so behind the hard eyes.

"A dollar?" he said. "One dollar? Did I actually hear that?"

"Durn it," Eck said. "Two dollars then. But I ain't — "

"Wait," the newcomer said. "You, up there on the

* **lessen**: unless.

post." The Texan looked at him. When the others turned, they saw that the woman had left the wagon too, though they had not known she was there since they had not seen the wagon drive up. She came among them behind the man, gaunt in the gray shapeless garment and the sunbonnet, wearing stained canvas gymnasium shoes. She overtook the man but she did not touch him, standing just behind him, her hands rolled before her into the gray dress.

"Henry," she said in a flat voice. The man looked over his shoulder.

"Get back to that wagon," he said.

"Here, missus," the Texan said. "Henry's going to get the bargain of his life in about a minute. Here, boys, let the missus come up close where she can see. Henry's going to pick out that saddle-horse the missus has been wanting. Who says ten — "

"Henry," the woman said. She did not raise her voice. She had not once looked at the Texan. She touched the man's arm. He turned and struck her hand down.

"Get back to that wagon like I told you." . . .

The Writer's Craft

1. Few narratives are written entirely as conversation. Rather, dialogue is used only in appropriate places and for a particular purpose, often to dramatize an event or reveal character convincingly. Other sections of the narrative may be presented without dialogue, so that a satisfying balance between dialogue and straight narration can be achieved; too much dialogue (like too much narration) runs the risk of becoming monotonous. Notice how this process of alternation is used in Faulkner's narrative. Do you find it effective?

2. In dialogue, differences in levels of usage can tell the reader much about the education, intelligence, and attitudes of various speakers. Why is dialogue often a more satisfactory way than straight narration to tell readers that a character in a story is, for example, immature, crafty, illiterate, or cruel?

3. Dialogue looks easier to write than it actually is. For one thing, it should never be talk for talk's sake. Nor is it usually a

word-for-word transcript of ordinary conversation, for speech in real life tends to be either rambling or cryptic. By contrast, effective dialogue is carefully selected and edited speech. Why is it important to be selective in choosing dialogue for a narrative? Why may actual conversation have to be edited for use in a narrative? Why may it be desirable to add some dialogue that did not really occur in the events you are narrating?

Now You Try It

Select one of the following assignments:

1. Using Updike's characters in Model 41, write a narrative that contains the next day's conversation at the dinner table. Decide whether or not David has killed the pigeons, and then have the father mention the subject and have the mother willing to forget it. The grandmother may remain the same.

2. Write a narrative using one of the following situations or one of your own choice. Use appropriate dialogue to help develop the situation and characterize the people involved.

   a. A mother and daughter prepare for a weekend guest that one of them doesn't like.
   b. An inquisitive youngster pesters a stranger at a ball game.
   c. A shopper discovers that she has been shortchanged; when she returns to the counter, the clerk remembers neither her nor the merchandise.
   d. A boy tries to explain something about automobiles to a person who has almost no knowledge of cars and little apparent interest in them.
   e. Two girls of quite different appearance and temperament discover they have been dating the same boy.
   f. Two boys very much unlike each other discover they have been dating the same girl.

LESSON **15**

Using Description in a Narrative

In narratives, events are vital, and anything else included should help make the events clear and vivid. Narrative details serve just that purpose. So does dialogue. Still another way to add vividness to a narrative is through the use of descriptive details, examples of which you will have noticed in Model 42. The following narrative also contains description.

43 **Edwin Way Teale in *The Lost Woods***

A back-country road was carrying us south, carrying us through a snow-filled landscape and under the sullen gray of a December sky. Minute by minute, the long chain of the Indiana dunes receded behind us. Ahead, beyond the bobbing ears of the   5
horses, I could catch glimpses of the blue-white, faraway ridges of the Valparaiso moraine.*

Our low bobsled tilted and pitched over the frozen ruts. Beside me, my bearded grandfather clung to the black strips of the taut reins and   10
braced himself with felt-booted feet widespread. At every lurch, my own short, six-year-old legs, dan-

* **moraine:** glacial land formation.

gling below the seat, gyrated wildly like the tail of an off-balance cat.

We had left Lone Oak, my grandfather's dune-country farm, that winter morning, to drive to a distant woods. In the late weeks of autumn, my grandfather had been busy there, felling trees and cutting firewood. He was going after a load of this wood and he was taking me along. At first, we drove through familiar country — past Gunder's big red barn, the weed lot and the school house. Then we swung south and crossed the right-of-way of the Pere Marquette railroad. Beyond, we journeyed into a world that was, for me, new and unexplored. The road ran on and on. We seemed traversing vast distances while the smell of coming snow filled the air.

Eventually, I remember, we swung off the road into a kind of lane. The fences soon disappeared and we rode out into open country, onto a wide, undulating sea of whiteness with here and there the island of a bush-clump. As we progressed, a ribbon of runner-tracks and hoofmarks steadily unrolled, lengthened, and followed us across the snow.

Winter trees, gray and silent, began to rise around us. They were old trees, gnarled and twisted. We came to a frozen stream and turned to follow its bank. The bobsled, from time to time, would rear suddenly and then plunge downward as a front runner rode over a low stump or hidden log. Each time the sled seat soared and dropped away, I clung grimly to my place or clawed wildly at my grandfather's overcoat. He observed with a chuckle:

"Takes a good driver t' hit *all* th' stumps."

Then, while the snow slipped backward beneath the runners and the great trees of that somber woods closed around us, we rode on in silence. As we advanced, the trees grew steadily thicker; the woods more dark and lonely. In a small clearing, my grandfather pulled up beside a series of low, snow-covered walls. Around us were great white mounds that looked like igloos. The walls were the corded stovewood; the igloos were the snow-clad ⁵⁵ piles of discarded branches.

Wisps of steam curled up from the sides of the heated horses and my grandfather threw blankets over their backs before he bent to the work of tossing stovewood into the lumber-wagon bed of ⁶⁰ the bobsled. The hollow thump and crash of the frozen sticks reverberated through the still woods.

I soon tired of helping and wandered about, small as an atom, among the great trees — oak and beech, hickory and ash and sycamore. An air of ⁶⁵ strangeness and mystery enveloped the dark woods. I peered timidly down gloomy aisles between the trees. Branches rubbed together in the breeze with sudden shrieks or mournful wailings and the cawing of a distant crow echoed dismally. ⁷⁰ I was at once enchanted and fearful. Each time I followed one of the corridors away from the clearing, I hurried back to be reassured by the sight of my bundled-up grandfather stooping and rising as he picked up the cordwood and tossed it into ⁷⁵ the sled.

He stopped from time to time to point out special trees. In the hollow of one great beech, he had found two quarts of shelled nuts stored away by a squirrel. In another tree, with a gaping rectangu- ⁸⁰ lar hole chopped in its upper trunk, the owner of the woods had obtained several milk pails full of dark honey made by a wild swarm of bees. Still another hollow tree had a story to tell. It was an immense sycamore by the stream-bank. Its interior, ⁸⁵ smoke-blackened and cavernous, was filled with a damp and acrid odor. One autumn night, there, hunters had treed and smoked out a raccoon.

There were other exciting discoveries: the holes of owls and woodpeckers; the massed brown ⁹⁰ leaves of squirrel-nests high in the bare branches; the tracks of small wild animals that wound about among the trees, that crisscrossed on the ice, that linked together the great mounds of the discarded

branches. In one place, the wing feathers of an ⁹⁵
owl had left their imprint on the snow; and there,
the trail of some small animal had ended and
there, on the white surface, were tiny drops of red.
From the dark mouth of a burrow, under the far
bank of the frozen stream, tracks led away over ¹⁰⁰
the ice. I longed to follow them around a distant
bend in the stream. But the reaches beyond, for-
bidding under the still tenseness of the ominous
sky, slowed my steps to a standstill. However, my
mind and imagination were racing.   ¹⁰⁵

Behind and beyond the silence and inactivity of
the woods, there was a sense of action stilled by
our presence; of standing in a charmed circle
where all life paused, enchanted, until we passed
on. I had the feeling that animals would appear, ¹¹⁰
their interrupted revels and battles would recom-
mence with our departure. My imagination invested the woods with a fearful and delicious atmosphere of secrecy and wildness. It left me with
an endless curiosity about this lonely tract and all ¹¹⁵
of its inhabitants.

After nearly half an hour had gone by, my
grandfather's long sled was full and he called me
back to the seat. As we rode away, I looked back
as long as I could see the trees, watching to the ¹²⁰
last the gloomy woods, under its gloomy sky,
which had made such a profound impression on
me. All the way home, I was silent, busy with my
own speculations.

The Writer's Craft

1. Because the selection tells a story, the events that take
place are of primary importance. What are the key events in the
narrative?

2. Descriptive details help create atmosphere and make the
experience vivid. Find specific details in the model that describe:

grandfather at the reins (lines 9–11)
the narrator beside him (lines 11–14)

the open country (lines 30–33)
the trail left by the sleigh (lines 33–35)
the horses (lines 57–58)

Many other scenes and objects in this passage are made vivid through descriptive details. Point out at least five, and indicate the specific details that describe them.

WORD CHOICE: CONVEYING SENSORY IMPRESSIONS

The selection creates vivid sensory impressions. Which words in the sentences that follow are especially effective in creating such impressions? To which senses do the details appeal?

> A back-country road was carrying us south, carrying us through a snow-filled landscape and under the sullen gray of a December sky.

> At every lurch, my own short, six-year-old legs, dangling below the seat, gyrated wildly like the tail of an off-balance cat.

> . . . we rode out into open country, onto a wide, undulating sea of whiteness with here and there the island of a bush-clump.

> As we progressed, a ribbon of runner-tracks and hoofmarks steadily unrolled, lengthened, and followed us across the snow.

> The hollow thump and crash of the frozen sticks reverberated through the still woods.

Now You Try It

Select one of the following assignments:

1. Think of a tradition, custom, routine, or ritual followed in your home; then write a narrative based on one particular observance of it. Employ all the narrative skills. Select the key events; choose effective narrative details; use dialogue; and include appropriate description.

2. Recall a place, like the lonely woods of Model 43, that impressed you deeply. Write a narrative in which you arrange material much as Teale did, first telling about the journey to the place, next describing what you saw and did there, then concluding with your departure from it.

LESSON **16**
Point of View

Before writing a narrative, you must decide on the most effective point of view from which to tell it. If you want to write as a participant in the action, you will use the *personal* point of view. On the other hand, you may write all-knowingly, observing the action from a position outside the story. In such cases you will be writing from what is called the *omniscient* point of view. This lesson considers both narrative methods.

PERSONAL POINT OF VIEW The following narrative, based on a recollection of a childhood experience, is written from the point of view of a participant in the events.

44 William O. Douglas in *Of Men and Mountains*

[1] The night was pitch-black. A soft, warm southwest wind was blowing over the ridges of the Cascades. Spring was coming to the Yakima Valley. I felt it in the air. It was after midnight. The houses of Yakima were dark. Only the flickering street lights marked the way. We had just arrived by train from California. Father was up ahead with the suitcases, walking with giant strides. Mother came next, with a lad of a few months in her arms. My sister and I brought up the rear.

[2] There were strange noises among the occasional trees and shrubs that we passed. There were creepy sounds coming from the grass and from the

irrigation ditch that ran along the sidewalk. I wondered if they were from snakes or lizards or the dread tarantula that I had been taught to fear in California! Maybe snakes were sticking out their forked tongues as they used to do under the steps of the house in Estrella! Maybe a tarantula would lie in wait and drop off a tree and get me when I passed! Maybe lizards in Yakima were giant lizards! And then there were the dread rattlesnakes that Mother spoke of with fear and trembling. Did they gulp young boys alive, like the snakes in the picture books that could swallow a whole sheep? Was the rustle in the grass the rustle of a rattler? These were alarming thoughts to a boy of five.

[3] I looked anxiously over my shoulder. The trees and bushes with the strange noises in them seemed to take the form of monsters with long arms. I ran to catch up. Then, by the time I had once more looked furtively over my shoulder at the shapeless pursuing forms of the darkness, I discovered that I was far behind again. Why did Father walk so fast? I ran again to catch up. And so, block after block, I alternately lagged behind and ran, fearful of being lost and swallowed up in the night or grabbed by some demon of the dark.

[4] Father walked west from the Northern Pacific railroad station up Yakima Avenue. At Fifth Avenue he turned north, looking in the darkness for the house where our relatives, the Pettits, lived. He apparently did not have their exact address, or having it, was not able to read the house numbers in the dark. He stopped several times to arouse a household, only to find he had picked the wrong place.

[5] At one house he had hardly entered the yard before the two great dogs came racing around opposite sides of the house, barking and snarling. I was frozen with fear. But Father did not hesitate or pause. He continued on his way, speaking to the dogs in a voice that was firm and that to the dogs as well as to me seemed to have the authority of the highest law behind it. The dogs became silent and trotted out to

investigate us. They circled and sniffed me, putting their noses right into my face. I can still feel their hot, stinking breath. To me they seemed to be real demons of the darkness that had come to hold me for ransom. I wanted to scream. But the crisis was quickly passed. Father was soon back. He dismissed the dogs with ease, resumed his search, and presently found the house we wanted. A friendly door soon closed on all the strange noises and on the dangers of the outer darkness.

The Writer's Craft

1. Who are the participants in this narrative? Through whose eyes are the events of the narrative seen and interpreted? Point to specific sentences that show that the point of view is personal — in other words, that all the events are revealed through the consciousness of someone within the story.

2. If the narrative had been written by Douglas's father, would it be substantially different? Explain. Would the story be worth telling from the father's point of view? Why, or why not?

3. A limitation of the personal point of view is that it does not allow the writer to tell what is going on in the minds of other participants. Do you think the disadvantage is a serious one in the Douglas narrative? Explain.

WORD CHOICE: CONVEYING EMOTION

The author's choice of vivid words and phrases throughout the model helps convey the fright of the five-year-old narrator. Consider the italicized words in the following sentences:

> The night was *pitch-black*.
> There were *creepy* sounds coming from the grass and from the irrigation ditch that ran along the sidewalk.
> I was *frozen with fear*.

Compare those sentences with the following:

> The night was *very dark*.
> There were *odd* sounds coming from the grass and from the irrigation ditch that ran along the sidewalk.
> I was *afraid*.

Do the sentences in the second group convey the narrator's emotions as well as those in the first group? Find at least three other instances in the model where vivid words and phrases convey the narrator's emotions forcefully.

Now You Try It

Select one of the following assignments:

1. Start with the opening sentence in Model 44: "The night was pitch-black." Then, using the personal point of view, develop a situation that conveys a sense of impending crisis. Increase the suspense by imagining what could happen — or telling what did happen — in such a place, at such a time. Conclude by showing how the crisis or sense of crisis passed.

2. Write a narrative from the personal point of view in which you show how a decision you made or an action you took led to unexpected results.

Most stories told from the personal point of view are told in the first person. Most, but not all — for the only requirement of such a narrative method is that whatever events and details are included be limited to those a single person within the story would be aware of. In the following portion of a short story, details are limited to those that Vincent notices; accordingly, the point of view is personal, even though revealed in the third person.

45   Truman Capote in "The Headless Hawk"

So Vincent began walking in earnest, and his umbrella tapped codelike block after block. His shirt was soaked through with itchy sweat, and the noises, now so harsh, banged in his head: a trick car horn hooting "My Country, 'Tis of Thee," electric spray of sparks crackling bluely off thundering rails, whiskey laughter hiccuping through gaunt doors of beer-stale bars where orchid juke machines manufactured U.S.A

music — "I got spurs that jingle jangle jingle. . . ."
Occasionally he caught a glimpse of her, once mirrored in the window of Paul's Seafood Palace where
scarlet lobsters basked on a beach of flaked ice. She
followed close with her hands shoved into the pock-
ets of her raincoat. The brassy lights of a movie mar-
quee blinked, and he remembered how she loved
movies: murder films, spy chillers, Wild West shows.
He turned into a side street leading toward the East
River; it was quiet here, hushed like Sunday: a sailor-
stroller munching an Eskimo pie, energetic twins
skipping rope, an old velvety lady with gardenia-
white hair lifting aside lace curtains and peering list-
lessly into rain-dark space — a city landscape in July.
And behind him the soft insistent slap of sandals.
Traffic lights on Second Avenue turned red; at the
corner a bearded midget, Ruby the Popcorn Man,
wailed, "Hot buttered popcorn, big bag, yah?" Vincent shook his head, and the midget looked very put
out, then: "Yuh see?" he jeered, pushing a shovel inside of the candlelit cage where bursting kernels
bounced like crazy moths. "Yuh see, de girlie knows
popcorn's nourishin'." She bought a dime's worth, and
it was in a green sack matching her raincoat, matching her eyes.

This is my neighborhood, my street, the house with
the gateway is where I live. To remind himself of this
was necessary, inasmuch as he'd substituted for a
sense of reality a knowledge of time, and place. He
glanced gratefully at sourfaced, faded ladies, at the
pipe-puffing males squatting on the surrounding steps
of brownstone stoops. Nine pale little girls shrieked
round a corner flower cart begging daisies to pin in
their hair, but the peddler said, "Shoo!" and, fleeing
like beads of a broken bracelet, they circled in the
street, the wild ones leaping with laughter, and the
shy ones, silent and isolated, lifting summer-wilted
faces skyward: the rain, would it never come?

Vincent, who lived in a basement apartment, descended several steps and took out his keycase; then,

pausing behind the hallway door, he looked back through a peephole in the paneling. The girl was waiting on the sidewalk above; she leaned against a brownstone banister, and her arms fell limp — and popcorn spilled snowlike around her feet. A grimy little boy crept slyly up to pick among it like a squirrel.

The Writer's Craft

1. From the many details that make up "a city landscape in July," the author has selected relatively few. Are all the details limited to those that Vincent would notice on his walk? Do we stay with Vincent throughout the passage, or do we sometimes leave him and follow another character? Is the passage told from Vincent's point of view? Is the narrative told in the first person or the third?

2. At the beginning of the second paragraph the personal pronoun changes. To what? Did the change confuse you? How do you account for the author's change of personal pronoun there? In other words, what effect does it achieve?

3. Try reading the passage with *I* substituted throughout for *Vincent* and *he*. Is the alteration possible? In this instance, how does the effect of using the first person differ from that of Capote's version?

Now You Try It

Write a narrative of three or four paragraphs in the third person but from a personal point of view. What you write should include some action, description, and dialogue, but all the details you mention must be those observed by the central character, from whose point of view the narrative is told. If you turn out to be the central character, refer to yourself in the third person throughout the narrative.

OMNISCIENT POINT OF VIEW The narrator of the following events is not a participant in the action, nor does he observe the action with his own eyes. Instead, he stands outside the story, apparently knowing the thoughts and feelings of those within it. Thus, the point of view is omniscient.

46 J. Donald Adams in *Copey of Harvard*

As a small boy, Charles had often been attracted by some bright red berries which grew beside the fence outside the house of an old lady "with corkscrew curls," he remembered, who lived down the street from the Copeland home. One day as the boy came by, the blinds were drawn, and the opportunity to indulge his longing seemed at hand. He plucked a berry and ate it, but its taste was bitter, and he took no more. As he was about to turn away, the blinds of a window flew open, the old lady leaned out and cried, "Now, you naughty boy, you have found your reward. Those berries are deadly poison, which I keep especially for naughty boys. Tomorrow you will be dead!"

Charles's heart leaped in his breast. Reflecting on how sad a fate it was to die when his life had scarcely begun, he hurried, panic-stricken, to his home. There he found his brother Lowell in the hall, and poured out the dreadful story, begging his brother's forgiveness for all the injuries he had done him, exacting a promise that he would attend the funeral, and telling him of certain prized possessions he would leave to him. Charles then kissed his brother, who was by this time in tears, told him he would see him once more, and went out of the house. In the garden he found his father, and told him all that had happened. His father, he remembered, seemed to smile, took him by the hand, and led him back to the scene of his crime. Quivering before the old lady, Charles implored her forgiveness and begged her to give him something which would forestall his imminent end. She exacted his eager promise that never again would he molest her property, whereupon she produced a gumdrop and plopped it in his mouth. Thus comforted, he took his father's hand and left for home.

The Writer's Craft

1. The omniscient narrator of Model 46 seems to know what Charles is thinking as well as doing. Point out places where the writer reports on Charles's thought.

2. The omniscient writer may look at a narrative from the point of view of one or more participants. In this narrative, Adams limits his view pretty much to the mind of Charles, although he could have reported on the thoughts of other participants as well. Why do you think he considered it unnecessary to enter the minds of the father and the old lady?

3. The omniscient point of view gives the writer an opportunity to call attention to any and all details, to make interpretations, and to draw conclusions. Moreover, it permits the writer to know things that one or more of the participants do not know. In this selection, for example, the author knows that the old lady's antidote for the "poison" was a gumdrop. Did Charles know that?

4. Which of the two narrative methods — personal or omniscient — is likely to involve the reader more intimately in the action? Which allows the writer more freedom of movement?

Now You Try It

Select one of the following assignments:

1. Rewrite the J. Donald Adams narrative, telling it from Charles's point of view. Afterwards, compare the two versions and record in note form the different effects achieved by the omniscient point of view on the one hand and the personal point of view on the other.

2. Select a significant episode in the life of a national figure — a political leader or a sports hero, for instance — and describe the episode from the omniscient point of view. You should do research to obtain important facts, but many narrative details you include will be your own.

Sentence Skills

VARIETY IN THE SIMPLE SENTENCE

38 Mark Twain in *The Autobiography of Mark Twain* (pages 91–93)

1. A simple sentence has one independent clause and no subordinate clauses. But though the pattern seems limiting, there are many ways to add variety to it without using subordinate clauses. Notice the variety in these short, simple sentences from Mark Twain's *Autobiography:*

> My sister gave a "candy-pull" on a winter's night.
>
> He was in a passion now.
>
> At last he was within reaching distance.
>
> Indeed, I would have done anything to help.

In the first sentence, a prepositional phrase (*on a winter's night*), modifying the verb *gave,* adds information to the independent clause. In the second and third, prepositional phrases (*in a passion* and *within reaching distance*) are used as predicate adjectives. In the fourth, a conjunctive adverb (*Indeed*) *is* used to begin the sentence, and an infinitive (*to help*) ends it. These are only a few of the many grammatical elements that may be employed in constructing simple sentences.

Short, simple sentences, like those above, serve a number of useful purposes. They state ideas simply and directly. They emphasize important aspects of the subject matter. And when used sparingly with other types of sentences, they provide a change of pace and add pleasing rhythm to a composition.

2. The following simple sentences use two common, effective devices for achieving sentence variety: the appositive and the compound predicate.

Simple sentences with appositives:

> He was approaching seventeen, a grave and slender lad, trustful, honest, honorable, a creature to love and cling to.

> Out of the comb of the roof projected a short chimney, a common resort for sentimental cats on moonlight nights . . .

> There was joyous chaffing and joking and laughter — peal upon peal of it.

Simple sentences with compound predicates:

> He was awake and fuming about the cats and their intolerable yowling.

> I was only a boy and was already in a radiant heaven of anticipation.

> He paused, raised himself carefully up, measured his distance deliberately, then made a frantic grab at the nearest cat — and missed it.

In your own writing you can use appositives and compound predicates to achieve sentence variety effectively.

■ **EXERCISE** The following paragraph contains too many sentences of the same length. Rewrite the paragraph, retaining a few of these short, simple sentences but combining the others by using *appositives* and *compound predicates*. Do not add subordinate clauses. Be sure your revised paragraph reads well.

> Tommy Hobbs was a tall boy from Boonesville. He had a habit of creating disturbances. He was ridiculed by the seniors. He was ignored by the juniors and sophomores. He was feared by the freshmen. He had the reputation of being a bully. One day he stalked into the cafeteria. He pushed into line ahead of a group of timid freshmen. He took a tray from the smallest one. One of the others began to protest mildly. This was a boy named Marvin Ruggles. Tommy turned to argue. His loud voice carried across the cafeteria. It attracted the attention of most of the other students there. For some reason, Tommy suddenly took a step backward. It was a short but fatal step. Not seeing an overturned chair, he stumbled over it. He fell to the floor. All of those watching laughed at Tommy's look of pained surprise.

39 Burl Ives in *Wayfaring Stranger* (pages 97–102)

A compound sentence has two or more independent clauses but no subordinate clauses. Like simple sentences, the compound sentence can be long or short, well constructed or poorly constructed. Examine the following examples from the Burl Ives selection:

> We made the scenery, the girls made the costumes, and everybody turned out for the amateur theatricals.
>
> Children waited to walk home with their parents, and there was an air of mystery around the town.
>
> It was in the spring of the year, and the roads were muddy, and it was difficult for anybody to get into or out of town.
>
> Horseback and carriage were the only practical ways of travel; the roads were impassable to automobiles.
>
> Various people passed him, and he walked on, saying nothing.
>
> Ten minutes later, after shedding my disguise, I went into the restaurant again, and this time the intensity of the excitement was even greater.
>
> I kept walking and they stopped.

All of these examples are compound sentences. Refer to them in answering the following questions:

1. What is the minimum number of independent clauses that a compound sentence must have?
2. Can a compound sentence have more than that minimum number of independent clauses?
3. Do prepositional phrases have any bearing upon whether a sentence is simple, compound, or complex?
4. Do infinitive phrases have any bearing upon whether a sentence is simple, compound, or complex?
5. Do participial phrases have any bearing upon whether a sentence is simple, compound, or complex?
6. The independent clauses in a compound sentence are not always joined by a coordinating conjunction (*and, but, or*). What else may they be joined by?

By using a compound sentence, the writer implies that the ideas in the independent clauses are of equivalent importance and are closely related. An effective compound sentence, therefore, contains two or more closely related ideas of approximately equal importance.

■ **EXERCISE** Decide which of the following pairs of sentences contain related ideas of approximately equal importance. Combine the sentences in those pairs into an effective compound sentence by using a suitable coordinating conjunction (*and, but, or*).

1. The movie received excellent reviews. It was a failure at the box office.
2. George Eliot's real name was Mary Ann Evans. She lived from 1819 to 1880.
3. I drank about a pint of grape juice. My father drank the rest.
4. You must learn the difference between a participle and a gerund. You will lose points on the final exam.
5. Our star basketball player is Toni Galassi. She is five feet ten inches tall.
6. Joel was elected president of the student council last week. He immediately sought to put his program into effect.
7. Nancy Chin would like to take a long vacation. Her business will not permit it.
8. She took her driver's test last Thursday. She is an excellent debater.
9. I must go to bed early tonight. I will oversleep tomorrow morning.
10. Whitman's "When Lilacs Last in the Dooryard Bloom'd" is considered a great elegy. Many people prefer his other tribute to Lincoln, "O Captain! My Captain."

SUBORDINATION IN THE COMPLEX SENTENCE

44 William O. Douglas in *Of Men and Mountains* (pages 121–23)

Complex sentences contain one independent clause and one or more subordinate clauses. A subordinate clause is a group of words containing a subject and a predicate; but even though such a clause has both subject and predicate, it does not function as a sentence. Rather, it serves as an adjective, adverb, or noun within the sentence in which it appears. A clause that modifies a noun or pronoun is an *adjective clause*. If it modifies a verb, an adjective, or an adverb, it is an *adverb clause*. If it serves the same purpose as a one-word noun, it is a *noun clause*. The following passage from the Douglas selection contains four subordinate clauses:

> There were creepy sounds coming from the grass and from the irrigation ditch *that ran along the sidewalk*. I wondered *if they were from snakes or lizards or the dread tarantula that I had been taught to fear in California!* Maybe snakes were sticking out their forked tongues *as they used to do under the steps of the house in Estrella!*

Which two are the adjective clauses in this passage? Which clause is an adverb clause? Which is a noun clause?

By changing the words slightly, each subordinate clause could be made into an independent clause:

> There were creepy sounds coming from the grass and from the irrigation ditch. The ditch ran along the sidewalk. I wondered about the sounds. Were they from snakes or lizards or the dread tarantula? I had been taught to fear these creatures in California! Maybe snakes were sticking out their forked tongues. They used to do this under the steps of the house in Estrella!

Compare the rewritten version with the original. What does your comparison suggest about the value of using subordinate clauses?

▪ **EXERCISE** Rewrite the following paragraph, combining the numbered groups of sentences into single complex sentences. Use both adjective and adverb clauses.

(1) I was in the eighth grade. I had a friend, Willie Gifford. He was an avid stamp collector. (2) Willie received stamps from a small company. This company specialized in unusual items. (3) The company would offer Willie something like "The World's Smallest Hexagonal Stamp with a Portrait of Augustus Caesar." They were asking fifty cents for it. (4) Willie had no use for such a stamp. He would buy it. (5) One day I decided to cure him of buying such trash. This was after I had seen him waste many dollars. (6) I took

an ordinary six-cent stamp. I had bought it at the post office. (7) I cut it into eight pieces. I mounted the pieces on a sheet of paper and mailed them to him. (8) Beside one of the tiny corner pieces of the stamp I wrote, "World's Rarest Triangular Stamp." This in a sense was true. There was no other stamp in the world just like it. (9) Beside another piece I had written, "Here Is an Unusual Stamp. It Contains Nothing But a Picture of Washington's Eye." (10) The price for all eight stamps was $5.25. I set the price. (11) Willie was not amused by my trick. He did stop buying worthless stamps.

VARIETY IN SENTENCE TYPES

46 J. Donald Adams in *Copey of Harvard* (page 127)

A *simple* sentence has one independent clause. A *compound* sentence has two or more independent clauses but no subordinate clauses. A *complex* sentence has one or more subordinate clauses and an independent clause.

A sentence may, of course, be written with two or more independent clauses as well as one or more subordinate clauses:

> Johnny Santo, who coaches Tech's basketball team, has an excellent squad this year, but he will not speculate about his team's chances for the title.

This sentence has two independent clauses: (1) *Johnny Santo has an excellent squad this year;* (2) *he will not speculate about his team's chances for the title.* Moreover, it has one subordinate clause: *who coaches Tech's basketball team.* Because it contains elements of both a compound and a complex sentence, it is called a *compound-complex* sentence, the fourth basic sentence type.

Ordinarily writers use all four types of sentences. The following extract from the Adams selection is illustrative:

> One day as the boy came by, the blinds were drawn, and the opportunity to indulge his longing seemed at hand. (compound-complex sentence) He plucked a berry and ate it, but its taste was bitter, and he took no more. (compound sentence) As he was about to turn away, the blinds of a window flew open, the old

lady leaned out and cried, "Now, you naughty boy, you have found your reward. (compound-complex sentence) Those berries are deadly poison, which I keep especially for naughty boys. (complex sentence with adjective clause) Tomorrow you will be dead!" (simple sentence)

Charles's heart leaped in his breast. (simple sentence) Reflecting on how sad a fate it was to die when his life had scarcely begun, he hurried, panic-stricken, to his home. (complex sentence with noun clause and adverb clause) There he found his brother Lowell in the hall, and poured out the dreadful story, begging his brother's forgiveness for all the injuries he had done him, exacting a promise that he would attend the funeral, and telling him of certain prized possessions he would leave to him. (complex sentence with three adjective clauses)

Consider how the first paragraph would read if simple sentences had been used throughout:

One day the boy came by. The blinds were drawn. The opportunity to indulge his longing seemed at hand. He plucked a berry and ate it. Its taste was bitter. He took no more. He was about to turn away. The blinds of a window flew open. The old lady leaned out and cried, "Now, you naughty boy, you have found your reward. Those berries are deadly poison. I keep them especially for naughty boys. Tomorrow you will be dead!"

The rewritten paragraph sounds choppy and childish. What, then, is gained by combining simple, compound, complex, and compound-complex sentences in a composition?

■ EXERCISE   Rewrite the following paragraph, combining each numbered group of sentences into the kind of sentence indicated in brackets.

(1) On September 6, 1901, the people were in a gala mood. They were attending the Pan-American Exposition in Buffalo. [simple sentence with participial phrase] (2) By nightfall many of them would have seen President McKinley. They would have shaken hands with him. [simple sentence with compound predicate] (3) Exposition officials had designated their Temple of Music as the place. McKinley's

reception would be held in it. [complex sentence with adjective clause] (4) At four o'clock the door of the music hall was opened. People began to file in. [compound sentence] (5) Everyone was intent upon seeing the President. No one noticed a thin, little man with a vacant stare. He was standing in the reception line. [compound-complex sentence with adjective clause] (6) The man was Leon Czolgosz. He was a crazed anarchist, twenty-eight years old. [simple sentence with appositive] (7) Czolgosz advanced in the reception line. He wrapped his hand in a large white handkerchief. [complex sentence with adverb clause] (8) Czolgosz stepped up to the President. He extended his hand. He fired his concealed revolver twice. [simple sentence with compound predicate] (9) McKinley was mortally wounded. His face showed neither pain nor fear, only astonishment. [compound sentence] (10) Some of the guards began striking the assassin. McKinley said weakly, "Don't let them hurt him." [complex sentence with adverb clause]

Exposition

LESSON **17**

Organizing Exposition

Exposition is prose that gives information, develops an idea, or provides an explanation. A history textbook, a how-to-do-it manual, articles in the daily newspaper, entries in an encyclopedia, a travel guide, a governmental report — all are examples of exposition.

No single organizational pattern serves for every kind of expository prose, nor is the most effective pattern usually as obvious as it is in description or narration. The nature of the subject, your purpose in writing, and the audience for which the writing is intended all have a bearing on the type of organization you decide to use. In explaining how to bake a cake, for instance, you would organize the composition as a series of logical steps. A comparison of American football with English Rugby might begin by telling how the games are similar, and follow with a discussion of how they differ. An analysis of the structure of an automobile engine might effectively devote separate paragraphs to each of the major parts. But in every case you would need an organizational plan appropriate to the subject, your purpose, and the audience reading the explanation.

An effective expository composition has the same characteristics as an effective expository paragraph: unity, adequate development, coherence, and appropriate emphasis, all of which are illustrated in the composition below. Notice, incidentally, the effectiveness of the organizational plan.

47   John A. Kouwenhoven
in "What's 'American' About America"

[1] Those engaged in discovering America often begin by discovering the Manhattan skyline, and here as well as elsewhere they discover apparently irreconcilable opposites. They notice at once that it doesn't make any sense, in human or aesthetic terms. It is the product of insane politics, greed, competitive ostentation, megalomania,* the worship of false gods. Its by-products, in turn, are traffic jams, bad ventilation, noise, and all the other ills that metropolitan flesh is heir to. And the net result is, illogically enough, one of the most exaltedly beautiful things man has ever made.

[2] Perhaps this paradoxical result will be less bewildering if we look for a moment at the formal and structural principles involved in the skyline. It may be helpful to consider the skyline as we might consider a lyric poem, or a novel, if we were trying to analyze its aesthetic quality.

[3] Looked at in this way, it is clear that the total effect which we call "the Manhattan skyline" is made up of almost innumerable buildings, each in competition (for height, or glamour, or efficiency, or respectability) with all of the others. Each goes its own way, as it were, in a carnival of rugged architectural individualism. And yet — as witness the universal feeling of exaltation and aspiration which the skyline as a whole evokes — out of this irrational, unplanned, and often infuriating chaos, an unforeseen unity has evolved. No building ever built in New York was placed where it was, or shaped as it was, because it would contribute to the aesthetic effect of the skyline — lifting it here, giving it mass there, or lending a needed emphasis. Each was built, all those under construction are being built, with no thought for subordination to any overall effect.

* **megalomania:** a mania for greatness, especially for big things.

[4] What, then, makes possible the fluid and ever-changing unity which does, in fact, exist? Quite simply, there are two things, both simple in themselves, which do the job. If they were not simple, they would not work; but they are, and they do.

[5] One is the gridiron pattern of the city's streets — the same basic pattern which accounts for Denver, Houston, Little Rock, Birmingham, and almost any American town you can name, and the same pattern which, in the form of square townships, sections, and quarter sections, was imposed by the Ordinance of 1785 on an almost continental scale as what Wolfgang Langewiesche has called "a diagram of the idea of the Social Contract," a blueprint for a future society in which men would live each in his own domain, free and equal, each man's domain clearly divided from his neighbor's.

[6] Whatever its shortcomings when compared with the "discontinuous patterns" of modern planned communities, this artificial geometric grid — imposed upon the land without regard to contours or any pre-conceived pattern of social zoning — has at least the quality of rational simplicity. The section lines, along which roads and fences ran due north-south and due east-west, and which are so clearly visible from a plane over most of the U.S.A., make most of the nation exactly what an airplane pilot wants the country to be: graph paper. As Langewiesche, the pilot, has said: "You can time your plane's shadow with a stop-watch across two lines, and get your exact speed. You can head the airplane down a section line and check your compass. But you hardly need a compass. You simply draw your course on the map and see what angle it makes. Then you cross the sections at the same angle. You can't miss. If you want to go exactly west, you get on a fence and follow it." And this simple gridiron pattern, mimicked in the city's streets, horizontally controls the spacing and arrangement of the isolated rectangular shafts which go to make up the skyline.

[7] The other thing which holds the skyline's diversity together is the structural principle of the skyscraper. When we think of individual buildings, we tend to think of details of texture, color, and form, of surface ornamentation or the lack of it. But as elements in Manhattan's skyline, these things are of little consequence. What matters there is the vertical thrust, the motion upward; and that is the product of cage, or skeleton, construction in steel — a system of construction which is, in effect, merely a three-dimensional variant of the gridiron street plan, extending vertically instead of horizontally.

[8] The aesthetics of cage, or skeleton, construction have never been fully analyzed, nor am I equipped to analyze them. But as a lay observer, I am struck by fundamental differences between the effect created by height in the RCA building at Rockefeller Center, for example, and the effect created by height in Chartres cathedral or in Giotto's campanile.* In both the latter (as in all the great architecture of the past) proportion and symmetry, the relation of height to width, are constituent to ° the effect. One can say of a Gothic cathedral, this tower is too high; of a Romanesque dome, this is top-heavy. But there is nothing inherent in cage construction to invite such judgments. A true skyscraper like the RCA building could be eighteen or twenty stories taller, or ten or a dozen stories shorter, without changing its essential aesthetic effect. Once steel cage construction has passed a certain height, the effect of transactive upward motion has been established; from there on, the point at which you cut it off is arbitrary and makes no difference.

[9] Those who are familiar with the history of the skyscraper will remember how slowly this fact was realized. Even Louis Sullivan — the greatest of the early skyscraper architects — thought in terms of having to close off and climax the upward motion of the tall building with an "attic" or cornice which should

* campanile: bell tower.
° are constituent to: form or constitute.

be, in its outward expression, "specific and conclusive." His lesser contemporaries worked for years on the blind assumption that the proportion and symmetry of masonry architecture must be preserved in the new technique. If with the steel cage one could go higher than with load-bearing masonry walls, the old aesthetic effects could be counterfeited by dressing the façade as if one or more buildings had been piled on top of another — each retaining the illusion of being complete in itself. You can still see such buildings in New York: the first five stories perhaps a Greco-Roman temple, the next ten a neuter warehouse, and the final five or six an Aztec pyramid. That Aztec pyramid is simply a cheap and thoughtless equivalent of the more subtle Sullivan cornice. Both structures attempt to close and climax the upward thrust, to provide an effect similar to that of the *Katharsis* * of Greek tragedy.

[10] But the logic of cage construction requires no such climax. It has less to do with the inner logic of masonry forms than with that of the old Globe-Wernicke sectional bookcases, whose interchangeable units (with glass-flap fronts) anticipated by fifty years the modular unit systems of so-called modern furniture. Those bookcases were advertised in the nineties as "always complete but never finished" — a phrase which could with equal propriety have been applied to the Model-T Ford. Many of us remember with affection that admirably simple mechanism, forever susceptible to added gadgets or improved parts, each of which was interchangeable with what you already had.

[11] Here, then, are the two things which serve to tie together the otherwise irrelevant components of the Manhattan skyline: the gridiron ground plan and the three-dimensional vertical grid of steel cage construction. And both of these are closely related to one another. Both are composed of simple and infinitely repeatable units.

* *Katharsis:* purification or release of emotions.

1. The primary purpose of the model is to explain why the New York skyline is beautiful. Here, in simple outline, is the organizational plan used:

> *Controlling Idea:* Manhattan Skyline Is Beautiful
> I. Skyline irrational and unplanned, but unified
> II. Unity in skyline derives from two factors
>   A. Gridiron pattern of streets
>   B. Vertical patterns of skyscrapers built on principle of steel cage construction

2. The *introductory paragraph* begins with a rather broad generalization: that the Manhattan skyline is characterized by "apparently irreconcilable opposites." The author then presents the negative aspects of the skyline and concludes with a sentence that states the controlling idea of the composition. Would the paragraph have been as effective if he had stated the controlling idea in the first sentence? Explain.

3. After the introductory paragraph, topic I is treated. Could the position of topics I and II have been reversed without impairing coherence? Why, or why not?

4. The *developmental paragraphs,* those that support the controlling idea of the composition, are arranged in logical order; that is, each has an unalterable position in the composition. Why would the passage be weakened if paragraph 6 preceded paragraph 5?

5. Paragraph 3 concludes the discussion of topic I. Paragraph 4 then leads into a discussion of topic II. Such a device, called a *transitional paragraph,* functions as a means of connecting main sections of the composition. Why are most transitional paragraphs relatively brief? Can you find another transitional paragraph in the selection?

6. The model includes one other type of paragraph, a *concluding paragraph.* Notice in the concluding paragraph (11) that the phrase "otherwise irrelevant components" echoes the thought stated in the introductory paragraph. What is the effect of the restatement? The concluding paragraph summarizes what is said about the unity of the Manhattan skyline. What is the effect of presenting a brief summary in a concluding paragraph? Can you think of other ways that a composition might be concluded effectively?

In addition to transitional paragraphs, the composition frequently uses transitional and linking words and phrases. Paragraph 2, for instance, is linked to the first paragraph by repetition of the word "result." Point out at least five other transitional or linking words and phrases.

Now You Try It

Write an expository composition on some aspect of the community in which you live. You may write about the buildings, the people, the politics, the social life, the recreational facilities, the job opportunities, or any other appropriate aspect. Begin with an introductory paragraph that states the controlling idea; then use three or more developmental paragraphs that explain, clarify, and support that idea. End with a concluding paragraph that summarizes your main points. Be sure to use transitional expressions and, if necessary, transitional paragraphs so that readers can readily follow the steps in your explanation.

LESSON **18**

Organizing an Analysis

Almost any subject can be analyzed: an organization, a person, the causes of a historical event, a problem, a mechanism, a structure, a work of literature. Because analysis, by its nature, divides a subject into parts, writers often *classify* as a means of organizing essays based on an analysis. In the following model, notice how the task of analyzing the English language affects the organization.

48   C. L. Wrenn in *The English Language*

[1] The English language is spoken or read by the largest number of people in the world, for historical, political, and economic reasons; but it may also be true that it owes something of its wide appeal to qualities and characteristics inherent in itself. What are these characteristic features which outstand in making the English language what it is, which give it its individuality and make it of this worldwide significance?
[2] First and most important is its extraordinary receptive and adaptable heterogeneousness — the varied ease and readiness with which it has taken to itself material from almost everywhere in the world and has made the new elements of language

its own. English, which when the Anglo-Saxons ⁱ⁵
first conquered England in the fifth and sixth centuries was almost a "pure" or unmixed language —
which could make new words for new ideas from
its own compounded elements and had hardly any
foreign words — has become the most "mixed" of ²⁰
languages, having received throughout its history
all kinds of foreign elements with ease and assimi-
lated them all to its own character. Though its
copiousness * of vocabulary is outstanding, it is its
amazing variety and heterogeneousness which is ²⁵
even more striking; and this general receptiveness
of new elements has contributed to making it a
suitable and attractive vehicle in so many parts of
the world.

[3] A second outstanding characteristic of Eng- ³⁰
lish is its simplicity of inflection — the ease with
which it indicates the relationship of words in a
sentence with only the minimum of change in their
shapes or variation of endings. There are languages, such as Chinese, that have surpassed Eng- ³⁵
lish in the reduction of the language in the matter of inflections to what looks like just a series of
fixed monosyllabic roots; but among European
languages, taken as a whole, English has gone as
far as any in reducing the inflections it once had ⁴⁰
to a minimum. A natural consequence of this
simplifying of inflection by reduction, however, is
that since the relationship of words to each other
is no longer made clear by their endings, this must
be done in other ways. ⁴⁵

[4] A third quality of English, therefore, is its
relatively fixed word order. An inflected language
like Latin or Russian can afford to be fairly free
in the arrangement of its words, since the inflections show clearly the proper relationship in the ⁵⁰
sentence, and ambiguity is unlikely. But in a language which does not change the forms of its
words according to their relationship in the sen-

* **copiousness:** abundance.

tence-significance, the order of the words is likely to be relatively fixed; and a fixed word order in 55 relation to meaning in the sentence takes the place of the freedom made possible by the system of inflections.

[5] Another consequence, fourthly, of the loss or reduction to the minimum of the inflections which 60 English once had, is the growth of the use of periphrases or roundabout ways of saying things, and of the use of prepositions to take the place of the lost inflections. The English simplified verb uses periphrases and compound tenses made with 65 auxiliary verbs to replace the more elaborate system of tenses that once existed (though tenses had already become fairly simple before the Anglo-Saxons came to England). Similarly, English, which once had nearly as many case endings as 70 Latin, has come to use prepositions instead of these, as can easily be seen if one translates any piece of Latin into English.

[6] A fifth quality of English — though this, like the loss of inflections and its consequences, is 75 shared with some other languages — is the development of new varieties of intonation to express shades of meaning which were formerly indicated by varying the shapes of words. This is perhaps somewhat comparable (though only in a small 80 way) to the vast use of intonation in Chinese as a method of expressing meaning in sentences which would otherwise seem like series of unvarying monosyllabic roots. Consider, for instance, the wonderful variety of shades of meaning we may 85 put into the use of the word *do*, merely by varying the intonation — that is, the pitch and intensity, the tone of the voice.

[7] Not all the above qualities are in themselves necessarily good, nor have they all contributed to 90 the general success of English. But it seems probable that of them all it is the adaptable receptiveness and the simplicity of inflection that have done most in this regard. On the other hand, the very

copiousness and heterogeneousness of English ⁹⁵
leads to vagueness or lack of clarity. Its resources
are too vast for all but the well educated to use to
full advantage; and such phenomena as "pidgin
English," "journalese," jargon, woolliness of expression and slatternly speech and writing, are every- ¹⁰⁰
where likely to be met with. It may fairly be said
that English is among the easiest languages to
speak badly, but the most difficult to use well.

The Writer's Craft

1 An introductory paragraph should arouse the reader's interest and state the topic of the composition. Does Wrenn's opening paragraph accomplish both objectives? The topic of the selection is presented in the form of a question. Do you find that
device effective? Explain.

2. The first characteristic the author discusses is the heterogeneousness of the language, and he stresses the importance of
that characteristic. How? Second, he mentions the simplicity of
inflection in the English language. Are the third, fourth, and fifth
characteristics related to that simplicity of inflection? Would you
understand the third, fourth, and fifth characteristics as well if
you did not know what was meant by "simplicity of inflection"?

3. There are good reasons for the order in which the first
two characteristics are treated. Are there equally good reasons
for the order of the last three? Would it really matter if the
sixth paragraph had been placed fourth, or if the fifth paragraph
had been placed sixth? In other words, is the author's order for
paragraphs 4, 5, and 6 *arbitrary?* When is an arbitrary arrangement of paragraphs justified?

4. Whatever method of organization is used, a writer should
make the organizational plan clear to the reader. How is the organizational plan of this model made clear?

5. In each of the five developmental paragraphs, the topic
sentence appears in the same position. What is that position?
Why is it an especially appropriate position for the topic sentence in an essay of analysis?

6. One function of a concluding paragraph may be to summarize, as Wrenn's last paragraph summarizes, the content of
what has gone before. What else does the paragraph do?

The nature of Wrenn's subject makes it necessary for him to include some words that he knows may be unfamiliar to his readers: *heterogeneousness* (line 11), *inflection* (line 31), *periphrases* (line 62), and *intonation* (line 77). But he does try to make the meanings of those words clear by giving a brief definition in context. The technique is one you will find useful when you write about subjects that have special vocabularies. What, incidentally, do each of the four italicized words mean?

Now You Try It

Select a topic that can be carefully and logically analyzed; then write an essay of analysis that begins with an introductory paragraph, contains three or more developmental paragraphs, and ends with a summary paragraph. The following questions may suggest an appropriate topic:

a. What is an atom?
b. What are the three branches of our national government?
c. What are the essential characteristics of slang?
d. What features characterize all popular dances?
e. What are the reasons for the popularity of folk songs?
f. What is a "good" college?
g. What are the essential parts of a short story?
h. What are the characteristics of a successful student leader?
i. What makes a student newspaper outstanding?

LESSON **19**

Explaining a Process

A process may be explained in one of two ways. Instructions may be given on how to *do* something: to build a bookcase, to tune an engine, to hem a skirt. Alternatively, the explanation may reveal how something operates or how it occurred or was done: how the stock market operates, how glass is made, how gold was discovered in California, how the frontier gradually disappeared. But in both kinds of explanation, details are usually presented in chronological order.

The following selection includes a brief explanation of how dictionaries are made.

49 S. I. Hayakawa
in "How Dictionaries Are Made"

[1] It is an almost universal belief that every word has a correct meaning, that we learn these meanings principally from teachers and grammarians (except that most of the time we don't bother to, so that we ordinarily speak "sloppy English"), 5 and that dictionaries and grammars are the supreme authority in matters of meaning and usage. Few people ask by what authority the writers of dictionaries and grammars say what they say. The docility with which most people bow down to the 10 dictionary is amazing, and the person who says, "Well, the dictionary is wrong!" is looked upon as out of his mind.

[2] Let us see how dictionaries are made and how the editors arrive at definitions. What follows, [15] applies, incidentally, only to those dictionary offices where first-hand, original research goes on — not those in which editors simply copy existing dictionaries. The task of writing a dictionary begins with the reading of vast amounts of the literature [20] of the period or subject that it is intended to cover. As the editors read, they copy on cards every interesting or rare word, every unusual or peculiar occurrence of a common word, a large number of common words in their ordinary uses, and also the [25] sentences in which each of these words appears, thus:

pail

The dairy *pails* bring home increase of milk

Keats, *Endymion*   [30]

I, 44–45

[3] That is to say, the context of each word is collected, along with the word itself. For a really big job of dictionary writing, such as the *Oxford English Dictionary* (usually bound in about twenty- [35] five volumes), millions of such cards are collected, and the task of editing occupies decades. As the cards are collected, they are alphabetized and sorted. When the sorting is completed, there will be for each word anywhere from two to three to [40] several hundred illustrative quotations, each on its card.

[4] To define a word, then, the dictionary editor places before him the stack of cards illustrating that word; each of the cards represents an actual [45] use of the word by a writer of some literary or historical importance. He reads the cards carefully, discards some, rereads the rest, and divides up the stack according to what he thinks are the several senses of the word. Finally, he writes his defini- [50] tions, following the hard-and-fast rule that each definition *must* be based on what the quotations in front of him reveal about the meaning of the word.

The editor cannot be influenced by what *he* thinks a given word *ought* to mean. He must work according to the cards, or not at all.

[5] The writing of a dictionary, therefore, is not a task of setting up authoritative statements about the "true meanings" of words, but a task of *recording*, to the best of one's ability, what various words *have meant* to authors in the distant or immediate past. *The writer of a dictionary is a historian, not a lawgiver.* If, for example, we had been writing a dictionary in 1890, or even as late as 1919, we could have said that the word "broadcast" means "to scatter" (seed and so on) but we could not have decreed that from 1921 on, the commonest meaning of the word should become "to disseminate audible messages, etc., by wireless telephony." To regard the dictionary as an "authority," therefore, is to credit the dictionary writer with gifts of prophecy which neither he nor anyone else possesses. In choosing our words when we speak or write, we can be *guided* by the historical record afforded us by the dictionary, but we cannot be *bound* by it, because new situations, new experiences, new inventions, new feelings, are always compelling us to give new uses to old words. Looking under a "hood," we should ordinarily have found, five hundred years ago, a monk; today, we find a motorcar engine.

The Writer's Craft

1. Paragraph 1 begins with the author's statement of a widely held belief — a belief that he proceeds to attack. The tone of the paragraph suggests that Hayakawa does not share the "almost universal belief that every word has a correct meaning." Point to specific words and phrases that reveal the tone.

2. The first sentence of paragraph 2 indicates that the writer is about to explain a process. Why is that sentence at the beginning of the second paragraph rather than at the end of the first? Does the sentence state, or merely imply, that the explanation to follow will refute the idea that dictionaries and grammars are the "supreme authority"?

3. In explaining a simple process (such as how to build a campfire), the writer will often include a list of the equipment, tools, or materials needed. Would such a list be helpful here; that is, should the author have said, "In making a dictionary, be sure you have a supply of index cards, a list of the words you want to define, and a generous number of books, magazines, and newspapers"? If Hayakawa's topic had been "How to Make a Dictionary" instead of "How Dictionaries Are Made," would such a list have been appropriate? What is the essential difference between the two topics?

4. Paragraphs 2, 3, and 4 deal with the process of making a dictionary. In what kind of order are the details in those paragraphs arranged? Why is that order effective for explaining a process?

5. Paragraph 5 is a summary paragraph intended to refute the popular belief that the dictionary is a supreme authority. Do you find it convincing? On what evidence has the author based his case? Would you say that his explanation of a process is subordinate to his purpose of proving that dictionary makers are not lawgivers?

PARAGRAPH SKILLS

1. Paragraphs 2, 3, and 4, all of which deal with the process of making a dictionary, contain no topic sentences. In paragraphs developed chronologically, why are explicit topic sentences frequently unnecessary? Would such sentences be of any real help to the reader?

2. What is the topic sentence of paragraph 5? Why does that paragraph have a topic sentence whereas the preceding three paragraphs do not?

3. Notice the transitional expressions in paragraphs 2, 3, and 4:

> *As* the editors read (line 22)
> *As* the cards are collected (lines 37–38)
> *When* the sorting is completed (line 39)

Find two other transitional words or phrases that indicate chronological sequence. Why are transitional expressions vital in paragraphs that explain a process?

4. The sentence beginning on line 47 presents a series of chronological details. Why are transitional expressions unnecessary in that sentence?

Now You Try It

Write a composition of three or four paragraphs explaining a process. In choosing the process, avoid one that is too simple (the result will be little more than a cookbook recipe) or one that is too complex (the intricacies of the subject will detract from the task of writing effectively). In addition, choose one with which you are thoroughly familiar. While writing the composition, use chronological order and transitional words and phrases. You may want to write about one of the following topics:

a. How to write a criticism of a short story
b. How to get the most benefit from a college visit
c. How to dance the _____
d. How a dog can be taught to obey
e. How parliamentary rules function in a committee meeting
f. How cryptographers break codes
g. How to make photographic enlargements

Comparing and Contrasting

Sometimes an expository composition, like an expository paragraph (page 32), may be developed effectively by showing how two subjects are alike (comparison) or how they differ (contrast). An essay developed with comparisons and contrasts presents special problems of organization. The problems and Bruce Catton's solutions to them are illustrated in the selection that follows.

50   Bruce Catton in *This Hallowed Ground*

[1] Until this Palm Sunday of 1865 the word Appomattox had no meaning. It was a harsh name left over from Indian days, it belonged to a river and to a country town, and it had no overtones. But after this day it would be one of the haunted possessions of the American people, a great and unique word that would echo in the national memory with infinite tragedy and infinite promise, recalling a moment in which sunset and sunrise came together in a streaked glow that was half twilight and half dawn.

[2] The business might almost have been stage-managed for effect. No detail had been overlooked. There was even the case of Wilmer McLean, the Virginian who once owned a place by a stream named Bull Run and who found his farm overrun by soldiers

in the first battle of the war. He sold out and moved to southern Virginia to get away from the war, and he bought a modest house in Appomattox Court House; and the war caught up with him finally, so that Lee and Grant chose his front parlor — of all the rooms in America — as the place where they would sit down together and bring the fighting to an end.

[3] Lee had one staff officer with him, and in Mr. McLean's front yard a Confederate orderly stood by while the war horse Traveler nibbled at the spring grass. Grant came with half a dozen officers of his own, including the famous Sheridan, and after he and Lee had shaken hands and taken their seats, these trooped into the room to look and to listen. Grant and Lee sat at two separate tables, the central figures in one of the greatest tableaus of American history.

[4] It was a great tableau not merely because of what these two men did but also because of what they were. No two Americans could have been in greater contrast. (Again the staging was perfect.) Lee was legend incarnate — tall, gray, one of the handsomest and most imposing men who ever lived, dressed today in his best uniform, with a sword belted at his waist. Grant was — well, he was U. S. Grant, rather scrubby and undersized, wearing his working clothes, with mud-spattered boots and trousers and a private's rumpled blue coat with his lieutenant general's stars tacked to the shoulders. He wore no sword. The men who were with them noticed the contrast and remembered it. Grant himself seems to have felt it; years afterward, when he wrote his memoirs, he mentioned it and went to some lengths to explain why he did not go to this meeting togged out in dress uniform. (In effect, his explanation was that he was just too busy.)

[5] Yet the contrast went far beyond the matter of personal appearance. Two separate versions of America met in this room, each perfectly embodied by its chosen representative.

[6] There was an American aristocracy, and it had had a great day. It came from the past and it looked to the past; it seemed almost deliberately archaic,

with an air of knee breeches and buckled shoes and powdered wigs, with a leisured dignity and a rigid code in which privilege and duty were closely joined. It had brought the country to its birth and it had provided many of its beliefs; it had given courage and leadership, a sense of order and learning, and if there had been any way by which the eighteenth century could possibly have been carried forward into the future, this class would have provided the perfect vehicle. But from the day of its beginning, America had been fated to be a land of unending change. The country in which this leisured class had its place was in powerful ferment, and the class itself had changed. It had been diluted. In the struggle for survival it had laid hands on the curious combination of modern machinery and slave labor, the old standards had been altered, dignity had begun to look like arrogance, and pride of purse had begun to elbow out pride of breeding. The single lifetime of Robert E. Lee had seen the change, although Lee himself had not been touched by it.

[7] Yet the old values were real, and the effort to preserve them had nobility. Of all the things that went to make up the war, none had more poignance than the desperate fight to preserve these disappearing values, eroded by change from within as much as by change from without. The fight had been made and it had been lost, and everything that had been dreamed and tried and fought for was personified in the gray man who sat at the little table in the parlor at Appomattox and waited for the other man to start writing out the terms of surrender.

[8] The other man was wholly representative too. Behind him there was a new society, not dreamed of by the founding fathers: a society with the lid taken off, western man standing up to assert that what lay back of a person mattered nothing in comparison to what lay ahead of him. It was the land of the mudsills,* the temporarily dispossessed, the people who had noth-

---

* **mudsills:** foundation beams placed directly on the ground.

ing to lose but the future; behind it were hard times, humiliation, and failure, and ahead of it was all the world and a chance to lift oneself by one's bootstraps. It had few standards beyond a basic unformulated belief in the irresponsibility and ultimate value of the human spirit, and it could tramp with heavy boots down a ravaged Shenandoah Valley or through the embers of a burned Columbia without giving more than a casual thought to the things that were being destroyed. Yet it had its own nobility and its own standards; it had, in fact, the future of the race in its keeping, with all the immeasurable potential that might reside in a people who had decided that they would no longer be bound by the limitations of the past. It was rough and uncultivated, and it came to important meetings wearing muddy boots and no sword, and it had to be listened to.

[9] It could speak with a soft voice, and it could even be abashed by its own moment of triumph, as if that moment were not a thing to be savored and enjoyed. Grant seems to have been almost embarrassed when he and Lee came together in this parlor, yet it was definitely not the embarrassment of an underling ill at ease in a superior's presence. Rather it was the diffidence of a sensitive man who had another man in his power and wished to hurt him as little as possible. So Grant made small talk and recalled the old days in the Mexican War, when Lee had been the polished staff officer in the commanding general's tent and Grant had been an acting regimental quartermaster, slouching about like the hired man who looked after the teams. Perhaps the oddest thing about this meeting at Appomattox was that it was Grant, the nobody from nowhere, who played the gracious host, trying to put the aristocrat at his ease and, as far as might be, to soften the weight of the blow that was about to come down. In the end it was Lee who, so to speak, had to call the meeting to order, remarking (and the remark must have wrenched him almost beyond endurance) that they both knew what they were there for and that perhaps they had better get down to

business. So Grant opened his orderly book and got out his pencil. He confessed afterward that when he did so he had no idea what he was going to write.

The Writer's Craft

1. The selection depicts the scene of Lee's surrender to Grant — the meeting at Appomattox that concluded the American Civil War. Paragraphs 1–3 set the stage for the meeting. Paragraph 1 gives the time and place of the encounter and also suggests what the meeting has come to mean to the American people. How do paragraphs 2 and 3 help set the stage for the meeting?

2. Paragraph 3 concludes with the assertion that the meeting was "one of the greatest tableaus of American history." Then, the beginning of paragraph 4 states that it was "a great tableau" not only because of what Lee and Grant did there but also because of the contrasts between the two men. The rest of the paragraph deals with their contrasting appearance. From the many possible details that might have been mentioned, the author selects the following four:

LEE	GRANT
gray, handsome, imposing	scrubby
tall	undersized
best uniform	working clothes
sword belted at waist	no sword

Why do you suppose he chose those particular details and not others? We know, for example, that both men wore beards. Why is that detail not mentioned?

3. Having selected the four sets of contrasting details in paragraph 4, Catton had to decide how to arrange them. He could have considered them item by item, setting them off against each other:

> Lee was tall; Grant was undersized. Lee was one of the most imposing men who ever lived; Grant was rather scrubby. Lee was dressed in his best uniform; Grant wore his working clothes. Lee had his sword belted at the waist; Grant had no sword.

Do you think the author's arrangement of details is more effective than the one above? Explain.

4. Paragraph 5 is a transitional paragraph, linking two main sections of a longer composition. Each of the two sentences in the paragraph serves a distinct purpose. What does the first sentence do? What does the second one do?

5. The second part of the selection, paragraphs 6–8, contrasts the two versions of America that Grant and Lee represented. Here the pattern of organization is the same as that in paragraph 4: a detailed depiction of the old aristocracy is presented first, followed by a contrasting picture of the new society. Why do you think the author once more chose to follow that pattern, rather than the pattern of contrasting individual items of the two societies one at a time?

6. In contrasting the appearance and background of Lee and Grant, the author describes Lee first. Why do you think he put Lee before Grant in both instances?

7. The last paragraph of the selection shows Grant and Lee together in the parlor, preparing to negotiate the formal terms of surrender. Do you find the paragraph effective? Would the selection have been as effective if the two men had not been shown together at the end? Discuss.

Now You Try It

Select one of the following assignments:

1. Write a composition in which you depict a significant encounter between two people. It may be a meeting between yourself and someone else, between two historical figures, between two fictional characters, or between two people you know. Include a comparison or contrast of the two as part of the account, limiting the comparison or contrast to aspects that will add interest to your composition. Possible details of interest and significance are their appearances, their personalities, their backgrounds, and their feelings during the meeting. Incidentally, if differences between your subjects are more interesting than their similarities, put the similarities first and treat the differences at greater length; likewise, if the similarities are more interesting than the differences, put the differences first. That way, your composition will gain in interest as it proceeds.

2. Write a composition that you develop by comparing two subjects. Begin by making a general statement about the two sub-

jects in the introductory paragraph and conclude by summarizing the points in the comparison. Use an organizational pattern that enables you to achieve the emphasis you desire. If, for example, you want the reader to receive a total impression of each of the subjects separately, devote the first part of the composition to a treatment of all the aspects and characteristics of Subject A; after you have covered Subject A completely, treat parallel aspects of Subject B. On the other hand, if your primary purpose is to compare and contrast individual features of the two subjects, set corresponding features in Subject A and B off against each other, as was done with Catton's details in item 3 of The Writer's Craft. In either case, select the points of comparison carefully and be sure to cover the same points with both subjects.

You may compare one of the pairs of subjects listed below or choose a pair of your own.

a. Two contemporary public figures
b. Classical music and popular music
c. Two characters from literature who face and resolve a similar problem
d. Two stories by the same author
e. A movie version of a book and the book itself

LESSON **21**

Narration and Description in Exposition

To clarify techniques appropriate to different types of writing, this book is divided into separate sections on description, narration, and exposition. But the division should not mislead you into thinking that the three types exist apart from each other. Narration frequently involves both description and exposition, and a descriptive essay may well include narrative and expository elements. This lesson shows the way appropriate narration and description can make expository writing more effective.

NARRATION IN EXPOSITION   The following selection discusses the devotion of the Japanese to the art of appreciation. In doing so, it uses two brief narratives effectively.

51   Santha Rama Rau in "Aspects of Beauty"

[1] There is a very famous story in Japan about a man who was renowned throughout the country for the magnificent chrysanthemums he cultivated in his garden. Soon his fame reached even to the imperial palace, and the emperor announced that he wished to see these remarkable chrysanthemums. Greatly honored, the man went out into his garden before the em-

peror arrived and cut down all except one of his treasured flowers, leaving only the most beautiful of all to delight the eyes of the emperor. It was the highest compliment he could offer.

[2] To foreigners this story needs, perhaps, a little explanation. But to the Japanese the point is immediately clear — the appreciation of something beautiful is so important a human activity that there is nothing surprising (only admirable) in the action of a man who can destroy hundreds of wonderful plants so that the emperor may enjoy the one flawless flower undistracted by lesser blooms, so that he can offer perfection the concentration it deserves. A friend of mine once explained the matter to me fairly succinctly. "Almost anyone," he said, "has at least some appreciation of art, but the Japanese have gone a little further. They have made an art of appreciation. Other people don't always realize that this is a genuinely creative function."

[3] In more vigorously externalized societies one is apt to feel that one must express oneself, be "creative," be active and contributing in some way. There is a subtle but constant pressure on one to meet the demands of an aggressive society in outward expressions even if the medium is only conversation. Many people mean by this that you must have something to *show* for your effort — to be creative you must write or paint or even be a good cook. You must express yourself in conversation, in music, or perhaps in dancing. The aspect of living that is so often forgotten — or at best relegated to an inferior position — is the sense of appreciation. What of the people who read the books, see the pictures, hear the music, or even eat the cooking? What about their "creative" offering, their sensitive and developed art of appreciation? It is just as hard to come by, and to the Japanese, at least, just about as valuable.

[4] Whether this sense of appreciation is a cause or an effect in Japanese society I suppose only anthropologists can decide, but certainly to the traveler or the foreigner in Japan, it lends a surprising and new per-

spective to a life that has often been interpreted as too rigidly mannered for spontaneity. It adds, besides, a richness and an unsuspected depth to a society in which women (on the surface at least) appear to lead dull and restricted lives.

[5] An American friend of mine, a girl who had lived in Japan for the two years that her husband was stationed there, told me the story of one of her most unexpectedly pleasant experiences in Tokyo. In Japan, with servants to do her housework, an amah to help with the children, she suddenly and disconcertingly found herself with a good deal of time on her hands. She had rather despairingly decided that she was "uncreative" and had no particular inclination to take up amateur painting or attend classes in flower arrangement. At a fairly pedestrian party one day, she expressed something of the sort to a Japanese woman there, the wife of one of her husband's business associates.

[6] "I see," the Japanese woman replied seriously, "but what do you *like* to do?"

[7] "Well, in America," my friend said, feeling rather frivolous, "I keep house for my husband, and the children take up a lot of time, and I like pretty clothes and good perfumes — "

[8] "Perfumes?" the Japanese woman interrupted with interest. "Perfumes are very difficult to appreciate."

[9] And eventually my American friend found herself attending the meetings of an "incense-smelling society," where a number of Japanese women spent the afternoon enjoying the fragrances of scented wood smoke — cedar, lime, verbena, camphor, pine, plum, and many more — learning their special characteristics, appreciating the subtle changes of quality in a piece of wood a hundred years old as contrasted with a new fragment cut the day before. It was an activity that the members of the society considered important enough to employ an expert to instruct them, and my American friend discovered not only a new and fascinating pastime but began to understand a whole new

approach to the pleasure and appreciation of daily living, to the smells, sounds, textures, or sights that previously had not seemed worth her notice. It all contributed to a fresh and sharper awareness of the world about her.

The Writer's Craft

1. The expository purpose of the selection is to explain the importance the Japanese place on the art of appreciation. In developing her topic, the author has included two narratives: a brief one in paragraph 1 and a longer one in paragraphs 5–9. These narrative sections are subordinate to her overall purpose, which is expository; nonetheless, they are important in developing the selection fully. If you were to read only the expository sections in the passage, paragraphs 2–4, what would be lost? One obvious answer is that the selection would lose interest if the narration were omitted. But what, besides interest, do the narrative paragraphs contribute?

2. The unit on narration stressed the importance of narrative details (pages 94–95 and 103–09). Yet the first paragraph in this selection is greatly compressed, with almost no detail; the entire story is told in four sentences without dialogue. Why do you think the narrative is written in the barest outline?

3. On the other hand, the second narrative section utilizes a substantial amount of detail; it includes a setting, some characterization, three paragraphs of dialogue, and a number of specific details about the "incense-smelling society." How do you account for the difference in the amount of detail in the two narratives? Does part of your answer involve their respective positions in the selection?

Now You Try It

Write an expository composition based on one of the topics listed below, or an appropriate topic of your own choice. Include at least one narrative incident in developing the topic.

    a. Characteristics of a New Englander (or Texan, or some other inhabitant of an area of the United States)
    b. America's greatest leader

c. The outstanding team sport of them all
d. How to avoid work
e. The techniques of bird-watching
f. How to win an election
g. How to stay in good physical condition

DESCRIPTION IN EXPOSITION   In explaining how to grow roses, you might describe the characteristics of two or three particular species. If you were explaining the attractions of small colleges, you might describe a typical campus. The selection that follows discusses pool and surf swimming and, in doing so, employs descriptions of both indoor pools and the surf.

52   John Knowles in "Everybody's Sport"

[1] In many ways a pool is the best place to do real swimming. Free water tends to be too tempestuous, while in a pool it is tamed and imprisoned; the challenge has been filtered out of it along with the bacteria.   5

[2] I did my first swimming in a pool, and have tried pools in many places since then. The most glittering was the Eden Roc pool of the Hotel du Cap d'Antibes, and the most enjoyable was at a kind of oasis in Texas where I was stationed with the Air   10 Force. Here, a swimming pool was a real blessing, for this part of Texas lacked water to drink, let alone to swim in. Many days a cloud of dust — "Oklahoma!" the Texans called it — blew over and settled down upon us, our cots, and everything else.   15 Finally we learned that water had been struck nearby and that two crude swimming pools had been built.

[3] One of the pools was very cold, and the other was colder. To us in Texas in July, they had the   20 power to exhilarate, to free us from the sunlight which fell like metal from the blank sky. They offered all you could ask of water, all you could wish for in swimming. No indoor pool could rival them.

[4] Nevertheless, indoor pools excel in one way ²⁵ — in the use of artifice to enhance the pleasure of swimming. The best artificial effects I have seen are in the Exhibition Pool at Yale University.

[5] It is surrounded by a large, dark green amphitheater which slopes steeply upward. Shining in ³⁰ the center of this somber oval is the pool, its white tile deck and pastel blue water glittering frivolously away. If you stand beside it alone, with no one in the water or the seats, you become aware of an august silence, as though you were in a mecha- ³⁵ nized cathedral.

[6] I was there alone one day when someone began throwing control switches. Banks of lights overhead and along the sides went out and only the pool remained lighted, from below the surface, glow- ⁴⁰ ing like a luminous, smoky, green-blue cloud suspended in a black cavern. I dived in. The light seemed amazingly to increase my buoyancy; the water bore me up as though I were made of cork and could float forever. ⁴⁵

[7] In fierce contrast to such peace and glamour is the surf, which is charged with challenge. Surf swimming is much better managed now, of course; in the old days people who had come near drowning were revived by being hanged from the heels, ⁵⁰ or bled, or rolled over a barrel, or, as sometimes happened, pushed back into the water lest God consider it impious for men to bring back someone so close to eternity. We know better now, but even so, the surf's disturbing undercurrent is there for ⁵⁵ every swimmer to feel, and on rough days the warnings go up and the swimmers are restricted to a particular area or kept out of the water altogether.

[8] The surf at such moments is not to be trifled ⁶⁰ with. In fact you never trifle with the surf; when it is in a playful mood, the surf trifles with you. That's the joy of swimming in it. Along comes a large playful wave. It rises up and smacks you, shoves you along, knocks you off your feet like a big clumsy ⁶⁵

dog trying to ingratiate itself with a child. You are the child. It doesn't matter if you hold an Olympic gold medal; in the surf you wallow and are knocked around like any dog-paddler.

[9] Another wave swells up, growing more intimidating by the moment. As it nears you, the great crest breaks, an immense amount of rushing water is about to crash over your head. You are just a morsel of flotsam, but you happen to be human and you have the ingenuity which raised your ancestors out of the water in the first place. You put your arms in front of you, your head between them, and dive through the wave. Despite its tremendous force, it hurtles harmlessly over you and smashes its energy ineffectually against the shore.

[10] A new swell approaches, and you decide to ride it in. This is a much trickier feat. You turn your body toward shore and glance coolly over your shoulder to note how big the wave is, how fast it is coming and, most crucially of all, when it will break. Your judgment, let's say, is just right. You are already planing toward the beach when the wave reaches you. It bears you surgingly up and forward, and just then the threatening tracery along its crest breaks, not over you but under you. You can feel its chaotic turbulence beating all along your body. It goes on and on, like some rolling hydraulic engine beneath you, shooting you wildly toward shore. At last it beaches you, with a certain grudging gentleness. Victory.

[11] More usually, you are too far from shore and begin to plane too soon, so that the wave lifts you up briefly like King Kong balancing a matchbox, then contemptuously lets you fall and sweeps on. Or worse, you are too close to shore, and as you watch the approach of the wave with that cool glance over your shoulder, you notice that the foam is thickening too soon along its crest. The wave suddenly transforms itself into a top-heavy, rushing wall; it's too late to turn and dive into it, too late to run, too late to duck. The wave breaks on top of

you. Now you're helpless; the breaker embroils you, grinds you in its vortex, somersaults you six or eight times and then tosses you up on the shore like a piece of spent seaweed. Surf swimming is perhaps 110 the most elemental of all athletic experiences; you give over your being to the action of waves, currents, tides — things titanic and even cosmic.

[12] These are some of the joys of swimming. In all its forms, even in competitive swimming, the 115 source of our pleasure is facing and conquering the challenge of water. Watch any child, after he has been alarmed by a ducking or two, gingerly find his way to a delighted confidence when he learns that water will actually support him. As he learns to 120 deal with it, the water will become the best playground he ever had, with just enough echo of the challenge left in it to keep him always stimulated.

[13] Swimming is essentially a simple and even a humble sport. It inspires none of the mass adula- 125 tion of baseball, or the protocol of tennis or the folklore of fishing or the *esprit de corps* of skiing. Most sports require equipment ranging from a ball to a bull, but swimming is independent even of the fins and goggles and other innovations that have 130 brought so much new fun in the water. This is the sport of commoners. All you need to enjoy it is a certain amount of water — the most abundant substance on earth.

The Writer's Craft

1. In a sense, all exposition contains some description. Even a medical report stating that "the incision is two inches long" has, by the use of adjectives, described the incision. However, this kind of description requires no special attention; it is used unconsciously by all writers, experienced or inexperienced. What you should notice in the model is the use of extended description, as in paragraphs 5–6, which describe the Exhibition Pool at Yale. Why would the selection have been less effective if the author had simply said that the Yale pool is "glamorous," and had not described it in any detail?

2. What is gained by describing in detail the experience of swimming in the surf?

3. What is gained by the extended comparison between swimming and other sports in paragraph 13?

The paragraphs of the selection are coherent. Which word is repeated to link the second paragraph to the first? How does the first sentence of paragraph 3 link that paragraph with the one preceding it? What two devices are used to connect paragraphs 3 and 4? How are the remaining paragraphs in the selection joined together? Are there any places where transitions between paragraphs do not seem adequate?

As you know, writers of description often use figures of speech to convey vivid images of whatever they are describing. The extracts below contain some of the metaphors, similes, and personifications that appear in this selection. Explain why the italicized figures of speech are effective. As you examine the sentences, notice the writer's choice of verbs. Which verbs do you find especially effective?

> To us in Texas in July they [the pools] had the power to exhilarate, to free us from *the sunlight* which *fell like metal from the blank sky.* (lines 20–22)
>
> The surf at such moments is not to be trifled with. In fact you never trifle with the surf; *when it is in a playful mood, the surf trifles with you.* That's the joy of swimming in it. Along comes a large *playful wave. It rises up and smacks you, shoves you along, knocks you off your feet like a big clumsy dog trying to ingratiate itself with a child.* (lines 60–66)
>
> As it nears you, the great crest breaks, an immense amount of rushing water is about to crash over your head. *You are just a morsel of flotsam* . . . (lines 71–74)
>
> It [*the wave*] goes on and on, like some rolling hydraulic engine beneath you . . . (lines 89–93)
>
> . . . *the breaker* embroils you, grinds you in its vortex, somersaults you six or eight times and then *tosses you up on the shore like a piece of spent seaweed.* (lines 107–10)

Now You Try It

In an expository essay on one of the topics below, or a topic of your own choice, use description wherever appropriate to add interest and clarity.

a. Baseball as the typical American sport
b. Apple pie as the typical American food
c. Why I want to go to _____ College
d. How to mow a lawn and like it
e. The superiority of wood as a craft material
f. A rare stamp or coin
g. Examples of local architecture
h. Television personalities this season

LESSON

Combining Expository Techniques

The models in this section illustrate how various techniques can be used in the developmental paragraphs of an expository composition. These expository techniques — development with examples, analysis, the explanation of a process, comparison and contrast, narration, description — can be used singly or in whatever combination best suits the writer's purpose.

The following selection makes use of several expository techniques. Do you find the combination effective?

53   Alexander Petrunkevitch in "The Spider and the Wasp"

[1] In the feeding and safeguarding of their progeny the insects and spiders exhibit some interesting analogies to reasoning and some crass examples of blind instinct. The case I propose to describe here is that of the tarantula spiders and their archenemy, the digger wasps of the genus Pepsis. It is a classic example of what looks like intelligence pitted against instinct — a strange situation in which the victim, though fully able to defend itself, submits unwittingly to its destruction.

[2] Most tarantulas live in the tropics, but several

species occur in the temperate zone and a few are common in the southern U.S. Some varieties are large and have powerful fangs with which they can inflict a deep wound. These formidable looking spiders do not, however, attack man; you can hold one in your hand, if you are gentle, without being bitten. Their bite is dangerous only to insects and small mammals such as mice; for a man it is no worse than a hornet's sting.

[3] Tarantulas customarily live in deep cylindrical burrows, from which they emerge at dusk and into which they retire at dawn. Mature males wander about after dark in search of females and occasionally stray into houses. After mating, the male dies in a few weeks, but a female lives much longer and can mate several years in succession. In a Paris museum is a tropical specimen which is said to have been living in captivity for 25 years.

[4] A fertilized female tarantula lays from 200 to 400 eggs at a time; thus it is possible for a single tarantula to produce several thousand young. She takes no care of them beyond weaving a cocoon of silk to enclose the eggs. After they hatch, the young walk away, find convenient places in which to dig their burrows, and spend the rest of their lives in solitude. Tarantulas feed mostly on insects and millepedes. Once their appetite is appeased, they digest the food for several days before eating again. Their sight is poor, being limited to sensing a change in the intensity of light and to the perception of moving objects. They apparently have little or no sense of hearing, for a hungry tarantula will pay no attention to a loudly chirping cricket placed in its cage unless the insect happens to touch one of its legs.

[5] But all spiders, and especially hairy ones, have an extremely delicate sense of touch. Laboratory experiments prove that tarantulas can distinguish three types of touch: pressure against the body wall, stroking of the body hair, and riffling of certain very fine hairs on the legs called trichobothria. Pressure against the body, by a finger or the end of a pencil, causes the

tarantula to move off slowly for a short distance. The touch excites no defensive response unless the approach is from above where the spider can see the motion, in which case it rises on its hind legs, lifts its front legs, opens its fangs, and holds this threatening posture as long as the object continues to move. When the motion stops, the spider drops back to the ground, remains quiet for a few seconds, and then moves slowly away.

[6] The entire body of a tarantula, especially its legs, is thickly clothed with hair. Some of it is short and woolly, some long and stiff. Touching this body hair produces one of two distinct reactions. When the spider is hungry, it responds with an immediate and swift attack. At the touch of a cricket's antennae, the tarantula seizes the insect so swiftly that a motion picture taken at the rate of 64 frames per second shows only the result and not the process of capture. But when the spider is not hungry, the stimulation of its hairs merely causes it to shake the touched limb. An insect can walk under its hairy belly unharmed.

[7] The trichobothria, very fine hairs growing from disklike membranes on the legs, were once thought to be the spider's hearing organs, but we now know that they have nothing to do with sound. They are sensitive only to air movement. A light breeze makes them vibrate slowly without disturbing the common hair. When one blows gently on the trichobothria, the tarantula reacts with a quick jerk of its four front legs. If the front and hind legs are stimulated at the same time, the spider makes a sudden jump. This reaction is quite independent of the state of its appetite.

[8] These three tactile responses — to pressure on the body wall, to moving of the common hair, and to flexing of the trichobothria — are so different from one another that there is no possibility of confusing them. They serve the tarantula adequately for most of its needs and enable it to avoid most annoyances and dangers. But they fail the spider completely when it meets its deadly enemy, the digger wasp Pepsis.

[9] These solitary wasps are beautiful and formidable creatures. Most species are either a deep shiny blue all over, or deep blue with rusty wings. The largest have a wingspan of about four inches. They live on nectar. When excited, they give off a pungent odor — a warning that they are ready to attack. The sting is much worse than that of a bee or common wasp, and the pain and swelling last longer. In the adult stage the wasp lives only a few months. The female produces but a few eggs, one at a time at intervals of two or three days. For each egg the mother must provide one adult tarantula, alive but paralyzed. The tarantula must be of the correct species to nourish the larva. The mother wasp attaches the egg to the paralyzed spider's abdomen. Upon hatching from the egg, the larva is many hundreds of times smaller than its living but helpless victim. It eats no other food and drinks no water. By the time it has finished its single Gargantuan meal and become ready for wasphood, nothing remains of the tarantula but its indigestible chitinous skeleton.

[10] The mother wasp goes tarantula-hunting when the egg in her ovary is almost ready to be laid. Flying low over the ground late on a sunny afternoon, the wasp looks for its victim or for the mouth of a tarantula burrow, a round hole edged by a bit of silk. The sex of the spider makes no difference, but the mother is highly discriminating as to species. Each species of Pepsis requires a certain species of tarantula, and the wasp will not attack the wrong species. In a cage with a tarantula which is not its normal prey the wasp avoids the spider, and is usually killed by it in the night.

[11] Yet when a wasp finds the correct species, it is the other way about. To identify the species, the wasp apparently must explore the spider with her antennae. The tarantula shows an amazing tolerance to this exploration. The wasp crawls under it and walks over it without evoking any hostile response. The molestation is so great and so persistent that the tarantula often rises on all eight legs, as if it were on stilts. It may

stand this way for several minutes. Meanwhile the wasp, having satisfied itself that the victim is of the right species, moves off a few inches to dig the spider's grave. Working vigorously with legs and jaws, it excavates a hole 8 to 10 inches deep with a diameter slightly larger than the spider's girth. Now and again the wasp pops out of the hole to make sure that the spider is still there.

[12] When the grave is finished, the wasp returns to the tarantula to complete her ghastly enterprise. First she feels it all over once more with her antennae. Then her behavior becomes more aggressive. She bends her abdomen, protruding her sting, and searches for the soft membrane at the point where the spider's leg joins its body — the only spot where she can penetrate the horny skeleton. From time to time, as the exasperated spider slowly shifts ground, the wasp turns on her back and slides along with the aid of her wings, trying to get under the tarantula for a shot at the vital spot. During all this maneuvering, which can last for several minutes, the tarantula makes no move to save itself. Finally the wasp corners it against some obstruction and grasps one of its legs in her powerful jaws. Now at last the harassed spider tries a desperate but vain defense. The two contestants roll over and over on the ground. It is a terrifying sight and the outcome is always the same. The wasp finally manages to thrust her sting into the soft spot and holds it there for a few seconds while she pumps in the poison. Almost immediately the tarantula falls paralyzed on its back. Its legs stop twitching; its heart stops beating. Yet it is not dead, as is shown by the fact that if taken from the wasp, it can be restored to some sensitivity by being kept in a moist chamber for several months.

[13] After paralyzing the tarantula, the wasp cleans herself by dragging her body along the ground and rubbing her feet, sucks the drop of blood oozing from the wound in the spider's abdomen, then grabs a leg of the flabby, helpless animal in her jaws and drags it down to the bottom of the grave. She stays there for many minutes, sometimes for several hours, and what

she does all that time in the dark we do not know. Eventually she lays her egg and attaches it to the side of the spider's abdomen with a sticky secretion. Then she emerges, fills the grave with soil carried bit by bit in her jaws, and finally tramples the ground all around to hide any trace of the grave from prowlers. Then she flies away, leaving her descendant safely started in life.

[14] In all this the behavior of the wasp evidently is qualitatively different from that of the spider. The wasp acts like an intelligent animal. This is not to say that instinct plays no part or that she reasons as man does. But her actions are to the point; they are not automatic and can be modified to fit the situation. We do not know for certain how she identifies the tarantula — probably it is by some olfactory or chemo-tactile sense — but she does it purposefully and does not blindly tackle a wrong species.

[15] On the other hand, the tarantula's behavior shows only confusion. Evidently the wasp's pawing gives it no pleasure, for it tries to move away. That the wasp is not simulating sexual stimulation is certain, because male and female tarantulas react in the same way to its advances. That the spider is not anesthetized by some odorless secretion is easily shown by blowing lightly at the tarantula and making it jump suddenly. What, then, makes the tarantula behave as stupidly as it does?

[16] No clear, simple answer is available. Possibly the stimulation by the wasp's antennae is masked by a heavier pressure on the spider's body, so that it reacts as when prodded by a pencil. But the explanation may be much more complex. Initiative in attack is not in the nature of tarantulas; most species fight only when cornered so that escape is impossible. Their inherited patterns of behavior apparently prompt them to avoid problems rather than attack them. For example, spiders always weave their webs in three dimensions, and when a spider finds that there is insufficient space to attach certain threads in the third dimension, it leaves the place and seeks another, instead of finishing the web in a single plane. This urge to escape seems to

arise under all circumstances, in all phases of life, and to take the place of reasoning. For a spider to change the pattern of its web is as impossible as for an inexperienced man to build a bridge across a chasm obstructing his way.

[17] In a way the instinctive urge to escape is not only easier but often more efficient than reasoning. The tarantula does exactly what is most efficient in all cases except in an encounter with a ruthless and determined attacker dependent for the existence of her own species on killing as many tarantulas as she can lay eggs. Perhaps in this case the spider follows its usual pattern of trying to escape, instead of seizing and killing the wasp, because it is not aware of its danger. In any case, the survival of the tarantula species as a whole is protected by the fact that the spider is much more fertile than the wasp.

The Writer's Craft

1. In the first paragraph of the selection, the author indicates that his purpose is expository: to show that the conflict between the Pepsis wasp and the tarantula is an example of the conflict between reason and blind instinct in the animal world. Is the first paragraph an effective introductory paragraph? Do you think the writer should have specified which of the insects exemplifies reason and which, blind instinct? Or does the omission help arouse interest in the selection?

2. Developmental paragraphs 2–4 give information about the tarantula: its habitat, its habits, and its abilities. Paragraphs 5–8 continue to furnish information, but in them the writer analyzes the tarantula's sense of touch. He classifies each of the three distinct types of touch to which the tarantula responds. Why do you suppose this *analysis* is included? How does it contribute to the development of the topic?

3. Paragraph 9 gives background information about the wasp. What purpose does the information serve? How is it related to the topic?

4. Paragraphs 10–13 *explain a process*. What reasons can you give for the writer's including this detailed account of how the wasp finds and subdues the spider? As you know, the explanation

of a process requires a careful presentation of details in chronological order. Are the details in paragraphs 10–13 presented chronologically? What transitional expressions make the time sequence clear?

5. *Description* occurs throughout the selection. The author describes:

the tarantula's burrow
the tarantula's response to a touch from above
the tarantula's body
the tarantula's trichobothria
the Pepsis wasp
the larva that emerges from the wasp's egg
the tarantula's skeleton
the tarantula's response to the wasp's initial investigation
the grave dug by the wasp
the tarantula after it has been paralyzed

Are these descriptions important to the overall development of the topic? Explain.

6. Paragraphs 14 and 15 *compare and contrast* the wasp's and the spider's behavior during the conflict. Why is it natural for the writer to compare their behavior at this point in the development of the topic?

7. Paragraphs 16 and 17 attempt to answer the question posed in the last sentence of paragraph 15: "What, then, makes the tarantula behave as stupidly as it does?" The author offers some theories but gives no conclusive answer to the question. Inasmuch as no such answer is possible, why do you think the last two paragraphs of theorizing are included? How are paragraphs 14–17 related to the first paragraph in the selection?

8. Expository techniques are not, of course, combined arbitrarily. When several techniques are combined in a long expository composition, they must contribute to the clarity and unity of the selection as a whole. Do you think the author, in this instance, has succeeded in combining expository techniques to produce a clear and unified composition? Explain your answer.

COHERENCE

Transitional expressions and linking expressions help achieve coherence within paragraphs. Moreover, when placed at the beginning of paragraphs, these same devices can help achieve coherence between paragraphs in a composition. Transitional words and phrases (*however, therefore, then, on the other hand,* etc.) show the relationship between ideas in succeeding paragraphs. Linking expressions (*this, these, they, it, that,* etc.) may be used separately or with a noun to show that the writer is continuing to discuss an element mentioned in the preceding paragraph.

The following examples illustrate these devices in some of the paragraph beginnings of Model 53:

> *These three tactile responses* . . . (linking expression, connecting paragraphs 7 and 8)
>
> *These solitary wasps* . . . (linking expression, connecting paragraphs 8 and 9)
>
> *Yet when a wasp finds the correct species* . . . (transitional expression, connecting paragraphs 10 and 11)

The passage uses other transitional and linking expressions. Find two more and explain how they serve to connect succeeding paragraphs.

The following selection also combines several expository techniques.

54 Marchette Chute in *Shakespeare of London*

[1] Acting was not an easy profession on the Elizabethan stage or one to be taken up lightly. An actor went through a strenuous period of training before he could be entrusted with an important part by one of the great city companies. He worked on a raised stage in the glare of the afternoon sun, with none of the softening illusions that can be achieved in the modern theatre, and in plays that made strenuous demands upon his skill as a fencer, a dancer, and an acrobat.

[2] Many of the men in the London companies had been "trained up from their childhood" in the art, and an actor like Shakespeare, who entered the profession in his twenties, had an initial handicap that could only be overcome by intelligence and rigorous discipline. Since he was a well-known actor by 1592, and Chettle

says he was an excellent one, he must have had the initial advantages of a strong body and a good voice and have taught himself in the hard school of the Elizabethan theatre how to use them to advantage.

[3] One of the most famous of the London companies, that of Lord Strange, began its career as a company of tumblers, and a standard production like "The Forces of Hercules" was at least half acrobatics. Training of this kind was extremely useful to the actors, for the normal London stage consisted of several different levels. Battles and sieges were very popular with the audiences, with the upper levels of the stage used as the town walls and turrets, and an actor had to know how to take violent falls without damaging either himself or his expensive costume.

[4] Nearly all plays involved some kind of fighting, and in staging hand-to-hand combats the actor's training had to be excellent. The average Londoner was an expert on the subject of fencing, and he did not pay his penny to see two professional actors make ineffectual jabs at each other with rapiers when the script claimed they were fighting to the death. A young actor like Shakespeare must have gone through long gruelling hours of practice to learn the ruthless technique of Elizabethan fencing. He had to learn how to handle a long, heavy rapier in one hand, with a dagger for parrying in the other, and to make a series of savage, calculated thrusts at close quarters from the wrist and forearm, aiming at either his opponent's eyes or below the ribs. The actor had to achieve the brutal reality of an actual Elizabethan duel without injuring himself or his opponent, a problem that required a high degree of training and of physical coordination. The theatres and inn-yards were frequently rented by the fencing societies to put on exhibition matches, and on one such occasion at the Swan a fencer was run through the eye and died, an indication of the risks this sort of work involved even with trained, experienced fencers. The actors had to be extremely skilled, since they faced precisely the same audience. Richard Talleton, a comic actor of the 80's who was the first great popular star of

the Elizabethan theatre, was made Master of Fence the year before he died and this was the highest degree the fencing schools could award.

[5] Not being content with savage, realistic fights in its theatre productions, the London audience also expected to see bloody deaths and mutilations; and it was necessary to find some way to run a sword through an actor's head or tear out his entrails without impairing his usefulness for the next afternoon's performance. This involved not only agility but a thorough knowledge of sleight of hand, since the players were working close to the audience and in broad daylight. Elizabethan stage management was not slavishly interested in realism, but it was always concerned with good stage effects, and when bloodshed was involved, it gave the audience real blood. It had been found by experience that ox blood was too thick to run well, and sheep's blood was generally used. To stage a realistic stabbing, one actor would use a knife with a hollow handle into which the blade would slip back when it was pressed home, and his fellow actor would be equipped with a bladder of blood inside his white leather jerkin, which could be painted to look like skin. When the bladder was pricked and the actor arched himself at the moment of contact, the blood spurted out in a most satisfactory manner. Sometimes real knives were used and a protective plate, and a juggler once staggered into St. Paul's Churchyard and died there because he had done the trick when he was drunk and forgotten his plate. In *The Battle of Alcazar* there was a disemboweling scene for which the property man supplied three vials of blood and liver, heart and lungs of a sheep. Then it was up to Edward Alleyn and his fellow actors to use skillful substitution in such a way as to create the illusion, before a critical London audience in broad daylight, that their organs were being torn out.

[6] Another test of an actor's physical control was in dancing. Apart from the dances that were written into the actual texts of the plays, it was usual to end the performance with a dance performed by some of

the members of the company. A traveller from abroad who saw Shakespeare's company act *Julius Caesar* said that "when the play was over they danced very marvelously and gracefully together," and when the English actors travelled abroad, special mention was always made of their ability as dancers. The fashion of the time was for violent, spectacular dances and the schools in London taught intricate steps like those of the galliard, the exaggerated leap called the "capriole" and the violent lifting of one's partner high into the air that was the "volte." A visitor to one of these dancing schools of London watched a performer do a galliard and noted how "wonderfully he leaped, flung, and took on"; and if amateurs were talented at this kind of work, professionals on the stage were expected to be very much better.

[7] In addition to all this, subordinate or beginning actors were expected to handle several roles in an afternoon instead of only one. A major company seldom had more than twelve actors in it and could not afford to hire an indefinite number of extra ones for a single production. This meant that the men who had short speaking parts or none were constantly racing about and leaping into different costumes to get onstage with a different characterization as soon as they heard their cues. In one of Alleyn's productions a single actor played a Tartar nobleman, a spirit, an attendant, a hostage, a ghost, a child, a captain, and a Persian; and while none of the parts made any special demands on his acting ability, he must have had very little time to catch his breath. The London theatre was no place for physical weaklings; and, in the same way it is safe to assume that John Shakespeare must have had a strong, well-made body or he would not have been appointed a constable in Stratford; it is safe to assume that he must have passed the inheritance on to his eldest son.

[8] There was one more physical qualification an Elizabethan actor had to possess, and this was perhaps more important than any of the others. He had to have a good voice. An Elizabethan play was full of action,

but in the final analysis it was not the physical activity that caught and held the emotions of the audience; it was the words. An audience was an assembly of listeners and it was through the ear, not the eye, that the audience learned the location of each of the scenes, the emotions of each of the characters, and the poetry and excitement of the play as a whole. More especially, since the actors were men and boys and close physical contact could not carry the illusion of love-making, words had to be depended upon in the parts that were written for women.

[9] An Elizabethan audience had become highly susceptible to the use of words, trained and alert to catch their exact meaning and full of joy if they were used well. But this meant, as the basis of any successful stage production, that all the words had to be heard clearly. The actors used a fairly rapid delivery of their lines and this meant that breath control, emphasis, and enunciation had to be perfect if the link that was being forged between the emotions of the audience and the action on the stage was not to be broken. When Shakespeare first came to London, the problem of effective stage delivery was made somewhat easier by the use of a heavily end-stopped line, where the actor could draw his breath at regular intervals and proceed at a kind of jog-trot. But during the following decade this kind of writing became increasingly old-fashioned, giving way to an intricate and supple blank verse that was much more difficult to handle intelligently; and no one was more instrumental in bringing the new way of writing into general use than Shakespeare himself.

[10] Even with all the assistance given him by the old way of writing, with mechanical accenting and heavy use of rhyme, an Elizabethan actor had no easy time remembering his part. A repertory system was used and no play was given two days in succession. The actor played a different part every night, and he had no opportunity to settle into a comfortable routine while the lines of the part became second nature to him. He could expect very little help from the prompter, for that overworked individual was chiefly

occupied in seeing that the actors came on in proper order, that they had their properties available, and that the intricate stage arrangements that controlled the pulleys from the "heavens" and the springs to the trapdoors were worked with quick, accurate timing. These stage effects, which naturally had to be changed each afternoon for each new play, were extremely complicated. A single play in which Greene and Lodge collaborated required the descent of a prophet and an angel let down on a throne, a woman blackened by a thunderstroke, sailors coming in wet from the sea, a serpent devouring a vine, a hand with a burning sword emerging from a cloud, and "Jonah the prophet cast out of the whale's belly upon the stage." Any production that had to wrestle with as many complications as this had no room for an actor who could not remember his lines.

[11] Moreover, an actor who forgot his lines would not have lasted long in what was a highly competitive profession. There were more actors than there were parts for them, judging by the number of people who were listed as players in the parish registers. Even the actor who had achieved the position of a sharer in one of the large London companies was not secure. Richard Jones, for instance, was the owner of costumes and properties and playbooks worth nearly forty pounds, which was an enormous sum in those days, and yet three years later he was working in the theatre at whatever stray acting jobs he could get. "Sometimes I have a shilling a day and sometimes nothing," he told Edward Alleyn, asking for help in getting his suit and cloak out of pawn.

[12] The usual solution for an actor who could not keep his place in the competitive London theatre was to join one of the country companies, where the standards were less exacting, or to go abroad. English actors were extravagantly admired abroad and even a second-string company with poor equipment became the hit of the Frankfort Fair, so that "both men and women flocked wonderfully" to see them. An actor like Shakespeare who maintained his position on the Lon-

don stage for two decades could legitimately be praised, as Chettle praised him, for being "excellent in the quality he professes." If it had been otherwise, he would not have remained for long on the London stage.

The Writer's Craft

1. Paragraphs 3–11 develop the topic of the selection — the difficulty of being an actor in Elizabethan times, particularly on the London stage — by discussing six qualities required of the Elizabethan actor: acrobatic ability, fencing ability, dancing ability, a strong body, a good voice, and a good memory. At least eight *examples* are given in the developmental paragraphs, each example specifically illustrating a general point the writer wants to make. Paragraph 3, for instance, begins with two examples demonstrating the importance of acrobatic skill to the Elizabethan actor: (1) Lord Strange's acting company actually began as a company of tumblers, and (2) a typical Elizabethan production like " 'The Forces of Hercules' was at least half acrobatics." Look back at the other developmental paragraphs and find six more examples that illustrate and support the writer's generalizations.

2. Paragraph 5 contains a brief *explanation of a process*. What process is explained there? Is an explanation an effective means of developing the paragraph?

3. Notice the *description* of the knife and the jerkin in this extract from paragraph 5:

> To stage a realistic stabbing, one actor would use a knife with a hollow handle into which the blade would slip back when it was pressed home, and his fellow actor would be equipped with a bladder of blood inside his white leather jerkin, which could be painted to look like skin.

Find several other places where descriptive details are included. In the first paragraph, for example, how is the Elizabethan theater described? How, in paragraph 3, is the usual London stage described? How are the rapier and the thrusts the actor had to make in hand-to-hand combat described in paragraph 4?

4. Does the combination of expository techniques in this selection result in an informative, unified, and coherent composition? Explain your answer.

Now You Try It

Write an expository composition in which you combine several expository techniques discussed in this section. Your task is not to combine arbitrarily as many techniques as possible, but to develop a clear, informative, carefully organized composition. Use techniques appropriate to the topic and of value to its development. You may select one of the following topics or choose one of your own.

a. Recent trends in art or music
b. How automation has affected the automobile industry
c. Why the T-formation replaced the single-wing in high school football
d. The work of the Peace Corps
e. How statistics can lie
f. Why the dinosaur became extinct
g. How a television set works
h. What a Presidential campaign manager does
i. The principles of Braille
j. How scientists explore the depths of the ocean
k. Locust plagues
l. Principles of stereo sound
m. The contribution to literature of an American poet or prose writer
n. The significance of a specific current event

Sentence Skills

THE PASSIVE VOICE

47 John A. Kouwenhoven in
"What's 'American' About America" (pages 140–43)

The writer's decision to use either the active or the passive voice within a sentence is in part a matter of taste or style. Generally the active voice is stronger and less apt to lead to stylistic difficulties. But at times the passive voice is useful when, for example, the receiver of an action instead of the doer should be stressed. In the following sentence from Model 47, the verb is in the passive voice:

> Those bookcases *were advertised* in the nineties as "always complete but never finished."

Had the active voice been used, the sentence might have read:

> The manufacturer advertised those bookcases in the nineties as "always complete but never finished."

Compare the original sentence with the rewritten version. Does the passive construction help emphasize the receiver of the action? What is emphasized in the sentence using the active voice?

The sentence Kouwenhoven wrote does not mention the doer, but had he wished to include that information, he could have written:

> These bookcases were advertised *by the manufacturers* in the nineties as "always complete but never finished."

He would then have mentioned the doer, but the passive construction would still have made bookcases the more emphatic element.

A second occasion for using the passive voice is when the writer chooses not to mention the doer of the action in a given sentence. It may be that it is unnecessary to mention the doer at all, or that the doer is unknown. The following sentences from Model 47 do not mention the person or persons who performed the action:

> No building ever built in New York *was placed* where it was, or *shaped* as it was, because it would contribute to the aesthetic effect of the skyline — lifting it here, giving it mass there, or lending a needed emphasis. Each *was built,* all those under construction *are being built,* with no thought for subordination to any overall effect.

The author's concern in these sentences is with *what* has been done, not with *who* has done it; he wants simply to dismiss *all* buildings as not having been designed with an eye to their being a part of a pattern. The passive voice enables him to make the point without naming individual architects responsible for the various buildings. He could, of course, have used "architects" as his subject in sentences using the active voice. Rewrite the sentences, using "architects" as the subject and making the verbs active. Why is the result much less effective than Kouwenhoven's way of expressing the same ideas?

While the passive voice is often useful, it should not be overused. Why is the use of the passive voice *not* desirable in each of the following sentences?

> A thrilling last-minute field goal *was kicked* by Ernie Newlin.
>
> In my last semester a composition *was written* by me for the essay contest, and it *was judged* by three teachers to be the best in our school.
>
> My old scarf *was worn* on the trip to Cleveland.

■ **EXERCISE** Rewrite the following sentences, changing the verbs from active to passive. Eliminate any of the present subjects, the doers of the action, that need not be mentioned.

1. The mayor, three council members, and two newspapers have severely criticized the construction of these new apartment buildings.
2. The newspaper carrier often delivers our newspaper as late as seven o'clock in the evening.
3. They guarantee this vacuum cleaner for one year.
4. For the third time, the officials charged our team with an error.

5. No one has ever openly discussed the reasons for the tariff on snuff.
6. Most of the members of the cast performed *My Sister Eileen* rather ineptly.
7. Someone had placed the street sign on the wrong corner.
8. They had lowered the flag on City Hall to half-mast.
9. A neighbor found our missing beagle and returned him to our house.
10. The House of Representatives impeached Andrew Johnson in February, 1868, but the Senate did not convict him.

ELIMINATION OF UNNECESSARY WORDS

49 **S. I. Hayakawa in "How Dictionaries Are Made"** (pages 151–53)

Eliminating useless words is an important step in revising a composition. Indeed, it is one of the surest ways to improve the quality of your writing. Consider how much better the following paragraph reads, leaving out the canceled words — words that Hayakawa did not include:

> Let us see how dictionaries are made and ~~let us see~~ how the editors arrive at definitions. What follows ~~in this paragraph and in succeeding paragraphs~~ applies, incidentally, only to those dictionary offices where first-hand, original research goes on — ~~it does~~ not ~~apply~~ to those ~~dictionary offices~~ in which editors simply copy existing dictionaries. The task of writing a dictionary ~~commences and~~ begins with the reading of vast amounts of the ~~written~~ literature of the period or subject that it is intended ~~and planned~~ to cover. As the ~~dictionary~~ editors read ~~the literature of the period or subject,~~ they copy on cards every interesting or rare word, ~~they copy~~ every unusual or peculiar occurrence of a common word, ~~they copy~~ a large number of common words in their ~~everyday,~~ ordinary uses, and ~~they~~ also ~~copy~~ the sentences in which each of these words ~~occurs and~~ appears.

The canceled words are either repetitive or superfluous.

Unnecessary repetition. In the first sentence there is no reason to repeat the words *let us see,* which merely slow down the readers without giving any additional information. Nor is there any point in using the verb *commences* in the third sentence; *begins* means precisely the same thing. Find six other crossed-out examples of unnecessary repetition.

Superfluous words. The phrase *in this paragraph and in succeeding paragraphs* is superfluous. The readers do not need to be given that information; they already know it or will soon discover it. The word *written* is superfluous before *literature.* Literature is assumed to be written unless specifically defined otherwise. Find two other examples of crossed-out superfluous words.

▪ **EXERCISE** Rewrite the following paragraph, eliminating at least thirty-five words that are unnecessarily repetitive or superfluous. Do not eliminate facts or change the meaning of the sentences.

It is surprising how many notable events and happenings in American history have occurred between the dates of April 6 and April 21. Four of our important, major wars began in these few days from April 6 to April 21. The American Revolution began on April 19, 1775, with the engagements at Lexington and Concord. The War Between the States started and got underway on April 12, 1865, with the firing on Fort Sumter. According to the Congressional declaration made by Congress, the Spanish-American War began on April 21, 1898. And the United States entered the First World War, World War I, on April 6, 1917. Two famous and renowned presidents died in office during these days. Abraham Lincoln was shot at the place called Ford's Theatre on April 14, 1865; and Franklin D. Roosevelt died at Warm Springs, in the state of Georgia, on April 12, eighty years later. These days have also included two major, serious disasters. The San Francisco earthquake and fire occurred at San Francisco on April 18 and 19, 1906. On the night of April 14, six years later, the White Star liner *Titanic* struck an iceberg and sank in the North Atlantic after striking it, with the loss of many human American lives.

50 Bruce Catton in *This Hallowed Ground*
(pages 156–60)

These extracts from Model 50 contain parallelism:

It came from the past and
it looked to the past . . .
It had brought the country to its birth and
it had provided many of its beliefs . . .
The fight had been made and
it had been lost . . .
. . . behind it were hard times, humiliation, and failure, and ahead of it was all the world and a chance
to lift oneself by one's bootstraps.

The two independent clauses in each sentence are similar
in construction, and in the first three sentences, certain
words are repeated. Notice that the two parallel clauses
in each sentence express parallel or contrasting ideas. Stating parallel or contrasting ideas in similar grammatical
constructions is one effective way of achieving emphasis.
Compare the following two sentences:

Weak:

It is through success that we achieve fame; but when
we fail, we get to know ourselves.

Emphatic:

It is through success that we achieve fame; it is
through failure that we get to know ourselves.

Used too frequently, parallel constructions can seem
contrived and mannered; used appropriately, they add emphasis, rhythm, and variety to your writing.

■ **EXERCISE** Rewrite the following sentences so that the
statements within each sentence are parallel in structure.

1. Behind us lie hard work, frustration, and defeat; but
rest, satisfaction, and success lie ahead of us.
2. We have made our decision, and it will be defended by
us.
3. General Pope promised an easy victory, but a disastrous
defeat was what he led his army to.

4. A pessimist would call the barrel half empty; it would be called half full by an optimist.
5. Let the council continue to work for the success of the honor system, but it should not be forgotten by us that ultimate success lies with every student in the school.

POSITION OF ADVERBS AND ADJECTIVES

51 **Santha Rama Rau in "Aspects of Beauty"**
(pages 163–66)

1. Position of adverbs. Usually adverbs can be moved from one position to another without changing the meaning of a sentence. Consider the following example from Model 51:

> *Soon* his fame reached even to the imperial palace, and the emperor announced that he wished to see these remarkable chrysanthemums.

The adverb *soon* can be moved to other positions in the sentence:

> His fame *soon* reached even to the imperial palace . . .
> His fame reached *soon* even to the imperial palace . . .

Though somewhat more awkward than the original, these sentences have the same meaning and are grammatically correct. Placement of an adverb is often a matter of style. It depends on what the writer wants to emphasize and on where the adverb sounds best in the sentence. In deciding where to place an adverb, consider the sentence that precedes and the sentence that follows the one you are writing. Reading the composition aloud as you revise will help you decide where to place adverbs most effectively.

In the following four sentences from Model 51, the italicized adverbs *cannot be moved:*

> a. Greatly honored, the man went *out* into his garden . . .

Here, *out* is practically a part of the verb. To move it from its position would make the sentence nonsensical.

> b. Other people don't always realize that this is a *genuinely* creative function.

Here, *genuinely,* which modifies the adjective *creative,* must remain in the normal position of an adverb before the adjective it modifies.

   c. A friend of mine once explained the matter to me *fairly* succinctly.

Here, *fairly* modifies the adverb *succinctly.* The two adverbs can be moved together to different positions in the sentence, but *fairly* must remain in its position immediately preceding the adverb it modifies.

   d. Whether this sense of appreciation is a cause or an effect in Japanese society I suppose *only* anthropologists can decide . . .

Here, *only* can be moved without making the sentence grammatically incorrect, but to do so changes the meaning of the sentence. Try putting *only* before *I.* What effect does this move have on the meaning of the sentence? What if *only* precedes *suppose?* In that case, it denotes that the speaker only supposes instead of knows for sure.

2. Position of adjectives. Unless it is a predicate adjective, an adjective almost always comes directly before the word it modifies:

. . . the emperor may enjoy the *one flawless* flower . . .

". . . I like *pretty* clothes and *good* perfumes — "

It all contributed to a *fresh* and *sharper* awareness of the world about her.

In none of these sentences can the adjectives be moved to any other position. Sometimes, though rarely, an adjective or a pair of adjectives may be moved to a position *after* the word modified:

Original sentence:

There is a *subtle but constant* pressure on one to meet the demands of an aggressive society . . .

Rewritten sentence:

There is a pressure on one, *subtle but constant,* to meet the demands of an aggressive society . . .

Although you may prefer the original sentence to the rewritten one, there is nothing grammatically wrong with putting the adjectives after the noun that is modified. Nor is there any possibility of misinterpreting the second sentence, even though the prepositional phrase *on one* splits the adjectives from the noun *pressure*. Notice that in reversing the normal adjective-noun word order, you deemphasize the noun and give special emphasis to the adjectives.

■ **EXERCISE** Some of the italicized adverbs and adjectives in the following paragraph are movable; some are not. Rewrite the paragraph, repositioning each movable modifier within the sentence in which it appears.

> Horatio Alger, Jr., *unquestionably* was one of the most *prolific* and *popular* authors who ever lived. He wrote about 130 books for teen-agers, influencing *directly* the lives of many Americans in *late* nineteenth century. The Alger novel has been called, *caustically*, "one book with 130 *different* titles." The plot does not vary: A young, *penniless but honest* boy rises in the world through pluck and luck. The young hero is *usually* befriended by a rich patron and becomes rich himself *eventually*. Though Alger's heroes succeed *inevitably*, Alger himself led a *rather* unsuccessful life. He lacked shrewdness in business and never made a *substantial* fortune. He wanted to write a *great* novel, but the scores of books he did write are unread and unhonored *today*.

Opinion and
Persuasion

LESSON **23**

Opinion

Essays of opinion are those in which the writer uses an opinion as a topic and develops it with several paragraphs of convincing evidence. Such essays, to be effective, adhere to all the principles of expository writing; they are unified, coherent, carefully organized, and written in a clear and interesting style. The chief difference between an expository essay and an essay of opinion is purpose. Whereas the purpose of an expository essay is to *explain* something, the purpose of an essay of opinion is to *convince* the reader of the validity of the writer's belief. In some essays of opinion, the writer tries to change the reader's mind; in others, the writer simply wants the reader to understand the reasons for holding a particular conviction.

Opinions offer an almost limitless supply of topics for composition, ranging from statements of personal belief to views on national and international affairs. The following essay of opinion is an expression of personal belief. Having defined his "code of living," the writer develops the essay by explaining what he means by it and why he believes in it.

55 Ben Lucien Burman in "Antidote for War"

[1] I became a philosopher early. I *had* to become a philosopher. I was rather badly wounded in the First World War at Soissons, France, when I was twenty-two and as a result I was flat on my back for a long time. It was either get a philosophy or crack up.

[2] My code of living is simple. It consists of three parts. One, never be cruel; two, always be artistic; three, never lose your sense of humor.

[3] Number One I don't believe requires much explanation. Never be cruel means, of course, always be kind. I believe that kindness is the natural human instinct, not cruelty. I have no illusions about humanity. I know its faults, its frequent blindness, its capacity for making terrible mistakes. But my work as a writer takes me among all kinds of men and women, often the very rough and the very poor. Everywhere I have found generosity and nobility; men who would have gladly given their lives for me because I had done them some slight kindness. The vast majority of human beings will do the basically good thing if they are given half a chance.

[4] By the second point in my code, always be artistic, I mean that whatever I do, I try to do with as much grace as possible. If I write a book, I want to make it as beautiful as I can. If I were a shoemaker, I would want to make shoes the same way, as perfect as possible. In our madly commercialized and mechanized world we have lost our sense of the beautiful. I believe we need beauty in our lives as much as we need food on our dining room tables. A world where beauty flourishes is a happy world — a world at peace.

[5] The third part of my code, as I said earlier, is never lose your sense of humor. I don't like pomposity. I don't like stuffed shirts. I'm glad I was born in a small town. It's a wonderful antidote for smugness. I remember years ago when I had a little success in New York with one of my first novels. There was the usual round of autograph parties and literary lunches and I was feeling rather pleased with myself. About this time I happened to go back to my home town in Kentucky and I saw an old fellow I had known as a boy standing on a street corner. He looked me up and down a long time and remarked lazily, "How are you, Benny? You been away a while, ain't you? You still teaching school?" That reduced life to its proper proportions.

[6] I was over in Germany not long ago, in the ru-

ins of Berlin, and a reporter asked me to give his paper a thought for the day. That was a bit of an order for me, who had been in two wars against the Germans and had very definite physical souvenirs from both. I reflected on what I could tell the Germans under these circumstances. And then I wrote: "When all the peoples of the world remember to laugh, particularly at themselves, there will be no more dictators and no more wars."

The Writer's Craft

1. The topic of the essay is one writer's personal beliefs — a code of living that consists of three parts. In which paragraph is the code stated?

2. What is the purpose of the first paragraph? Would the essay be less effective if the first paragraph were omitted? Explain.

3. How do the three parts of the writer's code of living influence the organization of the essay? In other words, what is the function of paragraphs 3–6?

4. Opinions, or personal beliefs, may be supported in various ways. The writer may cite facts, include illustrative examples, relate personal experiences, or give further supporting beliefs. Does Burman support his belief in the first part of his code of living by stating further personal beliefs about the value of being kind? Does he use his own experiences as support? How does he support his belief in parts two and three of his code?

5. Consider these aspects of the essay: (a) the clarity with which opinion is expressed, (b) the support given to the statement of opinion, (c) the organization of the essay, and (d) the unity and coherence of the essay. How would you evaluate the passage in each of those four cases?

Now You Try It

Select one of the following assignments:

1. Write a composition of at least five paragraphs in which you explain your personal philosophy. Follow Burman's organizational pattern: (a) Write an introductory paragraph showing how you came to hold the philosophy or belief; (b) state your code of

living concisely in a separate paragraph; (c) substantiate your belief in the various aspects of the code in at least three paragraphs, using a variety of methods: examples, incidents, and so on. Revise the composition as appropriate.

2. Take Burman's concluding "thought for the day" — "When all the peoples of the world remember to laugh, particularly at themselves, there will be no more dictators and no more wars." In a composition of at least five unified and coherent paragraphs, explain why *you* think a sense of humor is vital.

LESSON **24**

Using Examples
to Support an Opinion

If an expression of opinion is to be convincing, it must be supported with evidence; otherwise a reader may well raise the question, "Why should I believe this?" On the other hand, when substantial evidence is given, a reader is more likely to accept, or at least consider, the validity of the opinion. An excellent way to support an opinion is through the use of examples, as in the following essay, where the writer uses examples to support an opinion he holds about historical inaccuracies in motion pictures.

56   Gilbert Highet in "History on the Silver Screen"

[1] Suppose we go to the movies.

[2] We might see a new epic about the War of Independence, starring Audrey Hepburn as Martha Washington, Charlton Heston as George Washington, and William Holden as all the other Founding Fathers. (He is a very versatile actor, William Holden.) Among the most stirring scenes are the battles. There is a splendid reenactment of the Battle of Trenton. On one side the Hessians, with their red coats and their long muskets and bayonets; on the other side the small forces of General Washington, in motley uniforms and ill armed; but they have the advantage of surprise, and

they are fighting for their own country: they charge gallantly. The Hessians, with the power of long-established discipline, resist. For a moment the issue hangs undecided. Then Charlton Heston jumps forward carrying a heavy machine gun: *trrr, trrrrrr,* he mows down the Hessians, the first rank, the second, and the third; the American forces move onward in triumph, shouting "Victory!"; Washington waves his machine gun, and the camera pans from it to the Stars and Stripes.

[3] Or else we might see an epic about the Civil War. The hero is the Southern general, George Edward Pickett (played by William Holden). The big scene is the Battle of Gettysburg. The forces of North and South struggle, locked in deadly conflict, swaying this way and that. The ground is dark with blood, the sky, with the smoke of guns. Pickett's division is held in reserve, until at last, on the fateful July 3rd, the attack on Cemetery Hill is launched, with Pickett and his men in the forefront. Up the deadly slope they charge, with rebel yells almost drowned by the thunder of Federal cannon. Just at the summit, as the lines are about to meet, up spring the defending Federal troops. They are led by a Sioux Indian in full warpaint, who is followed by eight hundred whooping Indian tribesmen brandishing stone tomahawks. This decides the battle.

[4] Exciting, isn't it? No? Incredible? Almost disgusting? Yes, it is. But neither of these fantastic scenes is any more incredible, any more disgusting to a man with a sense of history than the distortions of historical fact which are repeatedly perpetrated by the makers of motion pictures. The Civil War is usually quite well represented — because we have photographs of it and reminiscences of it; the very weapons and uniforms used by the combatants still exist; and somehow we understand their manners, their attitude toward life. By the time we go as far back as the War of Independence, a certain vagueness sets in — about manners if not about material objects (I still have in my mind's eye a delicious scene in which Meriwether Lewis, played by Fred MacMurray, said to President Jefferson with a genial grin, like a basketball coach talking to a

difficult school principal, "Oh, congratulations on the Louisiana Purchase!"); and any period beyond that seems to be dim and fabulous. By the time we reach the Greeks and the Romans everything is lost in a world of fantasy.

[5] I must say that I am fascinated, in a horrible way, by motion pictures about ancient Greece and Rome. However silly they may be, they are usually photographed quite beautifully; the costumes are very becoming, particularly to the women; there is a certain thrill in seeing all the famous buildings, like the Acropolis at Athens, looking brand-new and so clean; and then the mistakes and the distortions are uproariously funny. They are just as funny as George Washington waving a machine gun, or Meade's troops headed by a detachment of Sioux Indians. And sometimes they are far funnier. The unconscious humor of the movies is one of their strongest assets.

[6] In movies about ancient Greece and Rome, the static parts often look quite real and convincing — no doubt because they have been modeled on pictures and statues. It is the active parts which are usually so funny. Almost every motion picture about ancient Rome I have ever seen showed somebody driving through the streets of the city in a chariot, while the citizens cringed away from his mad career.* This is as absurd as showing a cowboy on horseback galloping along the sidewalk of Fifth Avenue, New York. Chariots and such things were absolutely prohibited in the streets of Rome; they were kept for war, or else for hot-pole driving ° on the highways outside the cities. Everybody walked. The average Roman never rode in a chariot from the day of his birth to the day of his death.

[7] The Greek and Roman armies are usually wrong too. Most Hollywood producers know very little about military tactics, and still less about the more difficult science of strategy. Even in modern movies, they con-

---

* **mad career:** reckless dash or course.
° **hot-pole driving:** a made-up expression analogous to "hot-rod driving."

stantly make both the Good Ones and the Bad Ones commit elementary blunders in the art of war.

[8] In *The Robe* we see a group of Roman legionaries rushing into a town and shooting at everyone visible with bows and arrows. In other pictures about Rome we see the legionaries throwing spears with great care and accuracy, as though those were their essential weapons. The reason for these mistakes is quite obvious. The people in Hollywood think that everyone fights by shooting; if not *bang bang*, then *fft fft;* if not smoking guns, then whizzing arrows and hissing spears. But this is nonsense. The Romans conquered the world with swords — short, strong, efficient swords which were used both for cutting and for thrusting. Spears were thrown at the opening of a battle, much as grenades are thrown now, without very careful aim, merely as a device to disrupt the enemy's line; what mattered was the body-to-body conflict. As for bows and arrows, these were left to Arabs and the like, who stayed out in the wings together with slingers. It is as ridiculous to show the Roman soldiers using bows and arrows as it would be to show the U. S. Marines using blowpipes and poisoned darts. The Romans, like the Marines, were realists; they knew that if you want to kill an enemy and defend yourself, the surest way is to face him, eye to eye, and put a sword into him.

[9] In the same way, and probably for the same reason, Hollywood often gets the strategy of Roman warfare quite wrong. (I believe the people out on the Gold Coast think the Romans were stupid, primitive fellows with no power of long-term planning, no maps and no experience in warfare — early medieval minds; whereas in fact they were shrewd statesmen and hard pragmatic thinkers, with a long, long experience of both war and politics reaching over many countries and many centuries.) There was a good motion picture version of Shakespeare's *Julius Caesar,* in which most of the acting and the characterizations struck me as truly splendid; the conspirators might have been the actual men whose faces one sees on sculptured portraits of the old Roman tombs. But when we came to

one of the great crises of the play — a crisis which Shakespeare himself well understood, and did his best to explain within the limits of his small theater — the battle at which the forces of the Republic were beaten by the forces of dictatorship, then we saw that it was misunderstood, or vulgarized, or both. In actual fact, the battle was touch and go; it was one of those supremely difficult contests in which the two sides are approximately equal and each has a chance of winning. One side was victorious on one wing, the other side on the other wing, the center remaining undecided. It was one of the Republican commanders, Cassius, who misinterpreted the situation, gave up too soon, committed suicide, and wrecked the chances of his army. This is a powerful and highly dramatic situation; Shakespeare grasped it. But as Hollywood presented it to us, the army of the Republic marched blindly into a long canyon, without sending out any reconnaissance units to guard their advance and their flanks. The hills above the canyon were occupied by the enemy; and, at a given moment, Mark Antony (played by Marlon Brando) raised his hand in the old gesture so familiar from Western movies, and the stupid Republican forces were destroyed like walking ducks, mowed down by Sitting Bull.

[10] This kind of oversimplification is supposed to make history clearer, bolder, more dramatic. In fact, it destroys many of the best values in history, and therefore destroys many of the possibilities of drama which lie in history. For example, take the screen treatment of the Polish romance about the emperor Nero and the first persecution of the Christians, *Quo Vadis?* If I remember correctly, the screen play began with a Roman general (well played by Robert Taylor) leading a triumphal procession into the city of Rome — and, as he rode at the head of his victorious troops, saluting the indolent and selfish young emperor Nero. I wrote a piece for *Harper's Magazine* about this absurd scene, pointing out that, under the Roman empire, no Roman general except a member of the imperial family could ever lead a triumphal procession — for a very good

reason: namely, that the triumphant general was, for the time being, supreme in the state, almost God, and could have seized power in fifteen minutes. I got a letter back from Hollywood saying that this was all very well for pedants and specialists, but that people who wrote motion picture scripts had to give the public big spectacular crowd scenes, and what could be better than a triumphal procession? Well, the answer is that truth is always better than falsehood, and that it nearly always makes better drama. The end of the movie version of *Quo Vadis?* was equally false to history; it had the emperor Nero overthrown by a mutiny of some of his troops mixed with a popular revolt stimulated by horror at the persecution of the Christians. The man who was supposed to lead the mutiny was Robert Taylor. Now, the writers could have made this final piece of nonsense more credible, or "motivated" it in depth, by sticking to historical truth in the first scene. They could and should have made the Roman general lead his victorious troops up to the very gate of Rome, and then have them taken over by the young emperor, too weak to command but too vain to omit the opportunity of a triumphal procession; wearing a suit of specially made gold armor, Nero would lead the army through cheering crowds, while the war-hardened officers rode grimly in the rear, smouldering with rancor and beginning to plan his final overthrow.

[11] Sometimes, again, entirely imaginary or palpably false scenes are placed on the screen, for no reason whatever that any sane being can conceive, except sheer carelessness or ignorance. Quite early in the film version of *The Robe* we saw the aging emperor Tiberius — looking fairly convincing (although much less sinister than he was in reality), but complaining bitterly about his troubles with his wife, the empress Julia, who appeared for a moment with a magnificent costume and a proud manner. An amusing domestic scene. But at the time when the drama was supposed to take place, Julia had been dead for about twenty years, and Tiberius' inclinations had turned in far different directions. Think of the trouble, the expense,

and the needless ingenuity expended on writing in a scene, working out dialogue, providing dress and makeup and hairdo, for a character who was not only unnecessary but impossible.

[12] I wonder why they do this sort of thing. Partly it is because they know little or nothing about historical research. They do not believe it is possible to find out the truth about how the Roman army fought, or how a Roman emperor treated his wife. They do not know, apparently, that there are dozens and dozens of reference books filled with details. Often they seem to use cheap and more or less fictional accounts of the life which they are going to put on the screen. Usually, their banquets are as unlike a real Roman banquet as a party given by Al Capone * would be unlike a normal American dinner party. This is because the most detailed description which we have of a Roman banquet is a bitterly satirical account of a vulgar millionaire's party in which everything is either exaggerated or in outrageously bad taste — and yet the simpleminded "researcher" who cannot distinguish satire from truth is apt to accept it as normal. In the same way, I suppose, the Asian nations will accept the portrayal of American life given in such films as *Guys and Dolls* as being truly representative of our culture at its most characteristic.

[13] But partly, also, the people who make such films about history are cynics. They live for the moment. They think that history does not matter; or in the immortal phrase attributed to Henry Ford, "History is bunk." And, what is worse, they think that everyone else believes the same. They believe that no one cares about the truth of anything that happened beyond fifty or a hundred years ago. Perhaps that is the worst thing that could be said about them with any pretense to truth: that they despise us, their fellow citizens and the customers. They imagine that we cannot tell the difference between truth and lies, between sense and stupidity, provided the screen is made extra wide, and

---

* **Al Capone:** American gangster and racketeer.

covered with beautiful colors, lovely women, expensive costumes, and competent actors (Robert Taylor, Charlton Heston, and William Holden). We are all supposed to be seventeen-year-olds. The French had a phrase for this attitude: they said their theater managers sometimes spoke of "les cochons de payants," "those swine who pay for admission," or more bluntly, "the stinking customers." But that is too bitter for Hollywood. The people who make these epics do not think we are swine. They merely think we are children.

The Writer's Craft

1. The essay expresses an opinion: historical films are filled with inaccuracies that insult the viewer's intelligence. Where does the author make a clear statement of his opinion? Would you have preferred the statement at the beginning of the essay? Why, or why not?

2. Examples support an opinion effectively if they are relevant and if there are enough of them to be convincing. Highet's examples have to do with historical inaccuracies in movies. Are enough given to convince you that his opinion is justified? How many examples does he give? Are they presented in sufficient detail?

3. Paragraphs 2 and 3 furnish two hypothetical examples of historically inaccurate films: a movie about the War of Independence and one about the Civil War. Point out at least two obvious misrepresentations of fact in those examples. Why do you think those first examples are of hypothetical or imaginary films rather than real ones?

Now You Try It

Select one of the following assignments:

1. Certain topics, like the one on which Model 56 is based, all but demand support by specific examples. If you believe that baseball is a more complex game than basketball, you can hardly support that opinion without giving a few well-chosen examples of the complexities in the rules and plays in both games. Choose one of the following topics, or one of your own, and support your opinion with examples.

a. Canada is a wonderful vacation area.
b. Chemistry deserves great credit for America's high standard of living.
c. Most American presidents have gained in public esteem after their death or retirement.
d. Crises seem to bring out the best in people.
e. Competition is the basis of progress.

2. Write an essay of opinion, illustrating with examples the *appropriateness* or *ridiculousness* of one of the following aspects of modern society:

a. Architectural design: houses, motels, office buildings, shopping centers, churches, or gas stations
b. Television: commercials, situation comedies, panel shows, documentaries, or children's programs
c. Transportation: car-clogged cities, the Interstate Highway System, commuter railroads, suburban buses, highway speed limits, or driver training

LESSON

Narration and Description in an Essay of Opinion

You are not born with opinions; you acquire them. How? Two common ways of forming opinions are through experiencing events and through observing conditions in the world around you. When you express and support an opinion in writing, narrative may be needed to tell about events you have experienced; the conditions you have observed may call for description. In the following selection, notice how the author has developed and supported his opinion by using both narration and description.

57   H. L. Mencken in "The Libido for the Ugly"

On a winter day some years ago, coming out of Pittsburgh on one of the expresses of the Pennsylvania Railroad, I rolled eastward for an hour through the coal and steel towns of Westmoreland County. It was familiar ground; boy and man, I had been   5 through it often before. But somehow I had never quite sensed its appalling desolation. Here was the very heart of industrial America, the center of its most lucrative and characteristic activity, the boast and pride of the richest and grandest nation ever   10 seen on earth — and here was a scene so dreadfully

hideous, so intolerably bleak and forlorn that it reduced the whole aspiration of man to a macabre
and depressing joke. Here was wealth beyond com-
putation, almost beyond imagination — and here 15
were human habitations so abominable that they
would have disgraced a race of alley cats.

I am not speaking of mere filth. One expects steel
towns to be dirty. What I allude to is the unbroken
and agonizing ugliness, the sheer revolting mon- 20
strousness, of every house in sight. From East Liberty to Greensburg, a distance of twenty-five miles,
there was not one in sight from the train that did
not insult and lacerate the eye. Some were so bad,
and they were among the most pretentious — 25
churches, stores, warehouses, and the like — that
they were downright startling; one blinked before
them as one blinks before a man with his face shot
away. A few linger in memory, horrible even there:
a crazy little church just west of Jeannette, set like 30
a dormer-window on the side of a bare, leprous hill;
the headquarters of the Veterans of Foreign Wars
at another forlorn town, a steel stadium like a huge
rattrap somewhere further down the line. But most
of all I recall the general effect — of hideousness 35
without a break. There was not a single decent
house within eye range from the Pittsburgh sub-
urbs to the Greensburg yards. There was not one
that was not misshapen, and there was not one that
was not shabby. 40

The country itself is not uncomely, despite the
grime of the endless mills. It is, in form, a narrow
river valley, with deep gullies running up into the
hills. It is thickly settled, but not noticeably over-
crowded. There is still plenty of room for building, 45
even in the larger towns, and there are very few
solid blocks. Nearly every house, big and little, has
space on all four sides. Obviously, if there were architects of any professional sense or dignity in the
region, they would have perfected a chalet to hug 50
the hillsides — a chalet with a high-pitched roof, to
throw off the heavy winter snows, but still essen-

tially a low and clinging building, wider than it was tall. But what have they done? They have taken as their model a brick set on end. This they have con- 55 verted into a thing of dingy clapboards, with a narrow, low-pitched roof. And the whole they have set upon thin, preposterous brick piers. By the hundreds and thousands these abominable houses cover the bare hillsides, like gravestones in some gigantic 60 and decaying cemetery. On their deep sides they are three, four, and even five stories high; on their low sides they bury themselves swinishly in the mud. Not a fifth of them are perpendicular. They lean this way and that, hanging on to their bases pre- 65 cariously. And one and all they are streaked in grime, with dead and eczematous * patches of paint peeping through the streaks.

Now and then there is a house of brick. But what brick! When it is new it is the color of a fried egg. 70 When it has taken on the patina of the mills it is the color of an egg long past all hope or caring. Was it necessary to adopt that shocking color? No more than it was necessary to set all the houses on end. Red brick, even in a steel town, ages with some dig- 75 nity. Let it become downright black, and it is still sightly, especially if its trimmings are of white stone, with soot in the depths and the high spots washed by the rain. But in Westmoreland they prefer that uremic yellow, and so they have the most 80 loathsome towns and villages ever seen by mortal eye.

I award this championship only after laborious research and incessant prayer. I have seen, I believe, all of the most unlovely towns of the world; 85 they are all to be found in the United States. I have seen the mill towns of decomposing New England and the desert towns of Utah, Arizona, and Texas. I am familiar with the back streets of Newark, Brooklyn, and Chicago, and have made scientific 90 explorations to Camden, N. J., and Newport News,

* eczematous: as if afflicted with eczema, a skin disease.

Va. Safe in a Pullman, I have whirled through the gloomy, God-forsaken villages of Iowa and Kansas, and the malarious tidewater hamlets of Georgia. I have been to Bridgeport, Conn., and to Los Ange- [95] les. But nowhere on this earth, at home or abroad, have I seen anything to compare to the villages that huddle along the line of the Pennsylvania from the Pittsburgh yards to Greensburg. They are incomparable in color, and they are incomparable in de- [100] sign. It is as if some titanic and aberrant genius, uncompromisingly inimical to man, had devoted all the ingenuity of Hell to the making of them. They show grotesqueries of ugliness that, in retrospect, become almost diabolical. One cannot imagine [105] mere human beings concocting such dreadful things, and one can scarcely imagine human beings bearing life in them.

The Writer's Craft

1. Mencken's essay begins as a narrative: "On a winter day some years ago . . . I rolled eastward. . . ." What sentences and phrases maintain the narrative framework throughout the essay?

2. The narrative does not tell a story simply for its own sake. Instead, narration is used here as a framework for an essay of opinion. Mencken has witnessed a condition about which he has a strong opinion. What is that condition, and what is his opinion of it?

3. Because the author's opinion concerns the *appearance* of coal and steel towns in Westmoreland County, the essay naturally includes many descriptive details. What words and phrases are used to describe the following elements seen and thought about on the train trip from Pittsburgh to Greensburg? Explain how the words and phrases used in the descriptions make the author's opinion clear.

the overall scene (lines 11–17)
every house in sight (lines 19–29 and lines 34–40)
the church just west of Jeannette (lines 30–31)
the steel stadium (lines 33–34)
the country itself (lines 41–47)

the kind of architecture that he would like to see used for
   houses (lines 48–54)
the architecture that actually exists (lines 54–68)
the color of the brick houses (lines 70–72)
the villages (lines 96–108)

4. Sometimes an opinion is made emphatic by demonstrating
the irony of the situation that provokes it. In the first paragraph,
positive and negative facts about a geographical area are juxta-
posed to make the irony apparent:

> Here was the very heart of industrial America, the center
> of its most lucrative and characteristic activity, the boast
> and pride of the richest and grandest nation ever seen on
> earth — and here was a scene so dreadfully hideous, so in-
> tolerably bleak and forlorn that it reduced the whole aspira-
> tion of man to a macabre and depressing joke.

Where else in the first paragraph does the author juxtapose positive and negative facts to make his point? Can you find any other
places later in the essay where he does the same thing? Explain
why the technique is effective.

WORD CHOICE: SPECIFIC VERBS

The opinion in this essay is developed largely through a caus-
tic description of buildings the author saw between Pittsburgh
and Greensburg. Throughout the essay the language is vivid. Although most of the vividness comes from Mencken's use of descriptive adjectives and adverbs, part of it does come from his occasional use of very specific verbs:

> . . . there was not one in sight from the train that did not
> *insult* and *lacerate* the eye. (lines 23–24)
> . . . one *blinked* before them as one *blinks* before a man
> with his face shot away. (lines 27–29)
> . . . on their low sides they *bury* themselves swinishly in
> the mud. (lines 62–63)
> . . . I have *whirled* through the gloomy, God-forsaken
> villages of Iowa and Kansas . . . (lines 92–93)
> . . . villages that *huddle* along the line of the Pennsylva-
> nia from the Pittsburgh yards to Greensburg. (lines 97–99)

When you do the writing assignment that follows, try to add
vividness to it by using specific verbs.

Now You Try It

Write an essay of opinion about the appearance of a village, a city, or a state through which you have traveled. Using a slight narrative framework, in the manner of Model 57, include descriptive details to support your opinion. Remember that an opinion may be favorable as well as unfavorable. Mencken happened to select a subject that to him had many depressing aspects. Your opinion — perhaps even about some of the places Mencken mentions — may be quite different.

LESSON

Persuasion

A persuasive essay and an essay of opinion are similar in that both state an opinion and then attempt to convince the reader by offering evidence to support it. But persuasion differs from opinion in that it generally tries to convince the reader not only to accept an attitude or proposal, but also to take some action as a consequence — an action specified in the essay.

The following persuasive essay urges the reader to make notations in books. Consider the techniques used to persuade you to "write between the lines."

58   Mortimer J. Adler in "How to Mark a Book"

[1] You know you have to read "between the lines" to get the most out of anything. I want to persuade you to do something equally important in the course of your reading. I want to persuade you to "write between the lines." Unless you do, you are not likely to do the most efficient kind of reading.

[2] I contend, quite bluntly, that marking up a book is not an act of mutilation but of love.

[3] You shouldn't mark up a book which isn't yours. Librarians (or your friends) who lend you books expect you to keep them clean, and you should. If you

decide that I am right about the usefulness of marking books, you will have to buy them. Most of the world's great books are available today, in reprint editions, at less than a dollar.

[4] There are two ways in which one can own a book. The first is the property right you establish by paying for it, just as you pay for clothes and furniture. But this act of purchase is only the prelude to possession. Full ownership comes only when you have made it a part of yourself, and the best way to make yourself a part of it is by writing in it. An illustration may make the point clear. You buy a beefsteak and transfer it from the butcher's icebox to your own. But you do not own the beefsteak in the most important sense until you consume it and get it into your bloodstream. I am arguing that books, too, must be absorbed in your bloodstream to do you any good.

[5] Confusion about what it means to *own* a book leads people to a false reverence for paper, binding, and type — a respect for the physical thing — the craft of the printer rather than the genius of the author. They forget that it is possible for a man to acquire the idea, to possess the beauty, which a great book contains, without staking his claim by pasting his bookplate inside the cover. Having a fine library doesn't prove that its owner has a mind enriched by books; it proves nothing more than that he, his father, or his wife, was rich enough to buy them.

[6] There are three kinds of book owners. The first has all the standard sets and best sellers — unread, untouched. (This deluded individual owns woodpulp and ink, not books.) The second has a great many books — a few of them read through, most of them dipped into, but all of them as clean and shiny as the day they were bought. (This person would probably like to make books his own, but is restrained by a false respect for their physical appearance.) The third has a few books or many — every one of them dog-eared and dilapidated, shaken and loosened by continual use, marked and scribbled in from front to back. (This man owns books.)

[7] Is it false respect, you may ask, to preserve intact and unblemished a beautifully printed book, an elegantly bound edition? Of course not. I'd no more scribble all over a first edition of *Paradise Lost* than I'd give my baby a set of crayons and an original Rembrandt! I wouldn't mark up a painting or a statue. Its soul, so to speak, is inseparable from its body. And the beauty of a rare edition or of a richly manufactured volume is like that of a painting or a statue.

[8] But the soul of a book *can* be separated from its body. A book is more like the score of a piece of music than it is like a painting. No great musician confuses a symphony with the printed sheets of music. Arturo Toscanini reveres Brahms, but Toscanini's score of the C-minor Symphony is so thoroughly marked up that no one but the maestro himself can read it. The reason why a great conductor makes notations on his musical scores — marks them up again and again each time he returns to study them — is the reason why you should mark your books. If your respect for magnificent binding or typography gets in the way, buy yourself a cheap edition and pay your respects to the author.

[9] Why is marking up a book indispensable to reading? First, it keeps you awake. (And I don't mean merely conscious; I mean wide awake.) In the second place, reading, if it is active, is thinking, and thinking tends to express itself in words, spoken or written. The marked book is usually the thought-through book. Finally, writing helps you remember the thoughts you had, or the thoughts the author expressed. Let me develop these three points.

[10] If reading is to accomplish anything more than passing time, it must be active. You can't let your eyes glide across the lines of a book and come up with an understanding of what you have read. Now an ordinary piece of light fiction, like, say, *Gone with the Wind,* doesn't require the most active kind of reading. The books you read for pleasure can be read in a state of relaxation, and nothing is lost. But a great

book, rich in ideas and beauty, a book that raises and tries to answer great fundamental questions, demands the most active reading of which you are capable. You don't absorb the ideas of John Dewey * the way you absorb the crooning of Mr. Vallee.° You have to reach for them. That you cannot do while you're asleep.

[11] If, when you've finished reading a book, the pages are filled with your notes, you know that you read actively. The most famous *active* reader of great books I know is President Hutchins, of the University of Chicago. He also has the hardest schedule of business activities of any man I know. He invariably reads with a pencil, and sometimes, when he picks up a book and pencil in the evening, he finds himself, instead of making intelligent notes, drawing what he calls "caviar factories" on the margins. When that happens, he puts the book down. He knows he's too tired to read, and he's just wasting time.

[12] But, you may ask, why is writing necessary? Well, the physical act of writing, with your own hand, brings words and sentences more sharply before your mind and preserves them better in your memory. To set down your reaction to important words and sentences you have read, and the questions they have raised in your mind, is to preserve those reactions and sharpen those questions.

[13] Even if you wrote on a scratch pad, and threw the paper away when you had finished writing, your grasp of the book would be surer. But you don't have to throw the paper away. The margins (top and bottom, as well as side), the endpapers, the very space between the lines, are all available. They aren't sacred. And, best of all, your marks and notes become an integral part of the book and stay there forever. You can pick up the book the following week or year, and there are all your points of agreement, disagreement, doubt, and inquiry. It's like resuming an interrupted

* **John Dewey:** a philosopher.
° **Mr. Vallee:** Rudy Vallee, a popular singer.

conversation with the advantage of being able to pick up where you left off.

[14] And that is exactly what reading a book should be: a conversation between you and the author. Presumably he knows more about the subject than you do; naturally, you'll have the proper humility as you approach him. But don't let anybody tell you that a reader is supposed to be solely on the receiving end. Understanding is a two-way operation; learning doesn't consist in being an empty receptacle. The learner has to question himself and question the teacher. He even has to argue with the teacher, once he understands what the teacher is saying. And marking a book is literally an expression of your differences, or agreements of opinion, with the author.

[15] There are all kinds of devices for marking a book intelligently and fruitfully. Here's the way I do it:

1. *Underlining:* of major points, of important or forceful statements.
2. *Vertical lines at the margin:* to emphasize a statement already underlined.
3. *Star, asterisk, or other doodad at the margin:* to be used sparingly, to emphasize the ten or twenty most important statements in the book. (You may want to fold the bottom corner of each page on which you use such marks. It won't hurt the sturdy paper on which most modern books are printed, and you will be able to take the book off the shelf at any time and, by opening it at the folded-corner page, refresh your recollection of the book.)
4. *Numbers in the margin:* to indicate the sequence of points the author makes in developing a single argument.
5. *Numbers of other pages in the margin:* to indicate where else in the book the author made points relevant to the point marked; to tie up the ideas in a book, which, though they may be separated by many pages, belong together.
6. *Circling of key words or phrases.*

7. *Writing in the margin, or at the top or bottom of the page, for the sake of:* recording questions (and perhaps answers) which a passage raised in your mind; reducing a complicated discussion to a simple statement; recording the sequence of major points right through the book. I use the endpapers at the back of the book to make a personal index of the author's points in the order of their appearance.

[16] The front endpapers are, to me, the most important. Some people reserve them for a fancy bookplate. I reserve them for fancy thinking. After I have finished reading the book and making my personal index on the back endpapers, I turn to the front and try to outline the book, not page by page, or point by point (I've already done that at the back), but as an integrated structure, with a basic unity and an order of parts. This outline is, to me, the measure of my understanding of the work.

[17] If you're a diehard anti-bookmarker, you may object that the margins, the space between the lines, and the endpapers don't give you room enough. All right. How about using a scratch pad slightly smaller than the page size of the book — so that the edges of the sheets won't protrude? Make your index, outlines, and even your notes on the pad, and then insert these sheets permanently inside the front and back covers of the book.

[18] Or, you may say that this business of marking books is going to slow up your reading. It probably will. That's one of the reasons for doing it. Most of us have been taken in by the notion that speed of reading is a measure of our intelligence. There is no such thing as the right speed for intelligent reading. Some things should be read quickly and effortlessly, and some should be read slowly and even laboriously. The sign of intelligence in reading is the ability to read different things differently according to their worth. In the case of good books, the point is not to see how many of them you can get through, but rather how

many can get through you — how many you can make your own. A few friends are better than a thousand acquaintances. If this be your aim, as it should be, you will not be impatient if it takes more time and effort to read a great book than it does a newspaper.

[19] You may have one final objection to marking books. You can't lend them to your friends because nobody else can read them without being distracted by your notes. Furthermore, you won't want to lend them because a marked copy is a kind of intellectual diary, and lending it is almost like giving your mind away.

[20] If your friend wishes to read your "Plutarch's Lives," "Shakespeare," or "The Federalist Papers," tell him, gently but firmly, to buy a copy. You will lend him your car or your coat — but your books are as much a part of you as your head or your heart.

The Writer's Craft

1. Where does the author clearly state both his opinion and his persuasive purpose? Explain why that is a good place for him to make his opinion and purpose clear.

2. Why do you think paragraph 3, the first developmental paragraph, is devoted to explaining that the only books to be marked are those that the reader owns?

3. Paragraphs 4–6 discuss two ways of owning books and three types of book owners. The discussion in these three paragraphs includes reasons why you should write in books; additional reasons appear in paragraphs 8–14. Reasons given in a persuasive essay should serve a double purpose: they should explain why the writer has a particular opinion, and at the same time they should motivate the reader to take the action the writer desires. Do the reasons Adler gives in this essay help convince you that writing in the books you own is a good idea? If you do not already take notes while reading, has Adler succeeded in persuading you to try it? Explain.

4. A good persuasive essay makes clear what the reader is to do. Does the list of devices in paragraph 15 fulfill that requirement? Do you find the list helpful?

5. Several comparisons occur in the development of the essay. How do the comparisons noted below help persuade the reader to mark books? If you find any ineffective comparisons, explain why.

buying books and buying clothes and furniture (paragraph 4)
owning a book and consuming a beefsteak (paragraph 4)
reading a book and conversing with a teacher (paragraphs 13 and 14)
reading books and acquiring friends (paragraph 18)
lending a book and giving your mind away (paragraph 19)

6. The writer of a persuasive essay recognizes that some readers will oppose the opinion or proposal being stated; otherwise, there would be no need to write the essay. Here Adler disposes of several objections to marking books. Paragraphs 7 and 8, for example, deal with opposition from readers who may own rare or expensive editions of books; such books have a right to be respected, the author concedes, but cheaper editions may be purchased for the purpose of marking. How does he dispose of objections mentioned in paragraphs 17, 18, and 19–20? Why is it important for the writer of a persuasive essay to deal with as many of the serious objections as possible?

7. Throughout the essay Adler's style is informal and direct. He addresses the reader as *you* and uses short sentences composed of words and phrases that he would probably employ if he were speaking. Is the style effective as a persuasive technique? Explain.

Now You Try It

Select one of the following assignments:

1. Write a composition persuading your readers to try one of the following activities, or an activity of your choosing.

a. Playing chess or bridge
b. Working early in the morning
c. Traveling by back roads rather than turnpikes
d. Spending at least one week a year away from civilization
e. Working at a part-time job

f. Listening to classical music

g. Painting

2. Some people in other countries still do not fully understand the process of government in the United States. With a definite person in mind — a student your age in Russia, perhaps — write an essay in which you explain the American form of government, and try to persuade your reader to put aside any misconceptions.

Like many persuasive essays, the following example takes a strong stand on a controversial set of topics.

59 Marya Mannes in "Who Am I?"

[1] Your parents, I would imagine, consider your generation incomprehensible, sometimes frightening, and certainly unconventional. Everything you wear, grow on your face or head, think, believe, do, is way out of their norm.

[2] Except marriage. In a world of undreamed-of scope and opportunity and choice, most of you do exactly what your parents did in a much more limited world. You rush to the altar to tie the legal tie from the age of eighteen onward to a girl no older. Here you are in the full flower of body and mind (and I speak of both sexes) and with the only pure freedom of action you will ever know again, and you tie yourself to one mate and one hearth before you know who you are.

[3] If you're lucky, you will find yourselves *through* each other—the ideal nature of love, the true—and rare—blessing of marriage.

[4] If you're not lucky—and the evidence would call you a majority—you will be two half-persons, half-grown, prematurely bound, inhibiting each other's growth, choking up the road to your full development as a human being.

[5] Many of our laws and institutions, as you well

know, have not yet caught up with reality . . . the fact that men and women cannot be codified. So long as we do others no harm, how we choose to live is our own affair, and ours alone. How *you* choose to live is yours alone. And if you are able to bring about an intelligent society—I avoid the word "great"—one of the most important things you will have to do is remove the senseless stigmas that still prevail against single men or single women . . . .

[6] One of your great influences already is that in your new sense of community—in part forced upon you by isolation from your elders—you have managed to blur already many of the lines of demarcation—between races, between sexes, between thought and feeling, between feeling and action—which have trapped the former generations in patterns of sterility. The best of you have not only discovered your conscience, but are living it.

[7] But apart from the terrible issues of the day—to which the best of you address your conscience—war in Vietnam, the brutal war in the streets—how much are you living it as individuals, how much in group conformity?

[8] How brave, how independent are you when you are alone? I ask this chiefly of my own sex, for I wonder whether girls now really know and want the chance and choices that are open to them, or whether they have been so conditioned by history and habit that they slip back into the old patterns of their mothers the minute they graduate. Oddly enough, this supposed choice between marriage and a career never bothered my generation as much as it seems to have bothered the postwar ones. And I lay the blame for it on a mass media—mainly television, advertising, and women's magazines—which maintain the fiction that the only valid goal for women is marriage and children and domesticity (with a little community work thrown in), and that women who demand and seek more than this from life are at best unfulfilled and at worst unfeminine. It is about time

that we realized that many women make better teachers than mothers, better actresses than wives, better diplomats than cooks. Just as many men are better dreamers than providers. We have lost a great deal of talent and wasted a great many lives in the perpetuation of these myths that are called "the role of men" or "the role of women." And just as you have managed to dissipate some of them in your dress, I hope you will dissipate others in your lives. The only thing you need to aspire to, the only ultimate identity you must discover, is that of a human being. The sex, believe it or not, is secondary.

[9] But in the search for this human identity, I urge you to remember one thing. I said before that our first recognition of it comes when we know we are not like anybody else, that we are unique. That is so.

[10] But we did not spring into this world through galactic explosion—we did not even burst from the head of Zeus.

[11] We came from somewhere. Not just the womb of our mothers and the seeds of our fathers but from a long, long procession of identities—whose genes we possess.

[12] Whether we like it or not, we bear the past inside us. Good or bad, it cannot be excised, it cannot be rejected, . . . it should not be. Humanity is a continuous process, and without a past there is no future.

[13] In your worship of Now, in your fierce insistence that only the present exists, that you are new on the face of the earth, owing nothing to history—you are cheating yourself. You are not only denying evolution but limiting your future.

[14] You may say you have nothing in common with the preceding generation, you may lay the blame for the present entirely on their shoulders and on the mistakes of the past. But what of the others who came before? What of the great rebels, the great innovators, the great voices without which no light,

no truth would ever have prevailed? Much of what poets and philosophers and artists and scientists said ten centuries ago is as valid now as it was then. Where would you be, where would we be, without them?

[15] On a much humbler level, I remember the photograph albums so many families kept when I was a child. There, in our own, were these strange faces and strange clothes of the dead who preceded me: the tall, gaunt old baker in Poland, the opera singer in Germany, the immigrant furniture dealer in New York, the violinist in Breslau, the General near Kiel, the incredible web of cells and genes contained in my own self.

[16] It took me more than twenty years to realize that they lived in me, that I was part of them, and that in spite of distance, time, and difference, I was part of them. I was not, in short, alone.

[17] And neither are you. I suppose what I am asking for here is that, along with your pride of generation, you somehow maintain compassion for those who preceded you as well as for those who will come after you.

[18] If you will, this is a community just as important as any living community of your own age and time, and if you deny your connection with it, you deny evolution, you deny the human race.

[19] Don't play it too cool. The ultimate pattern of life is immense, there are other worlds in other galaxies that may have far transcended ours, and if you aren't turned on more by a shower of meteors than by any electric circus, you're half dead already.

[20] You won't find yourself in a crowded room. You may find yourself under the crowded sky of night, where—if you attach yourself to a single star— you will discover that you are one of many millions, but still—One.

[21] Listen to your own drum and march to it. You may fall on your face—but then, anybody who never does is—Nobody!

The Writer's Craft

1. In Model 58, Mortimer J. Adler asks readers to change their way of reading. What does Marya Mannes ask her readers to change? Which writer has a more difficult task? Account for your reasoning.

2. Adler wants his readers to copy his example, to do what he does, when it comes to reading books. Mannes, in her sixties, exhorts readers, in their teens, to think for themselves, to be individuals, but she refers to her own development as an individual only briefly, in paragraphs 15 and 16. Adler, in other words, is preaching what he does; Mannes is preaching what she has already done. Do you find one technique more effective than the other in a persuasive essay, or do you think there's time and place for both methods of persuasion? Explain.

3. In paragraphs 2–5, Mannes makes her position very clear: she is against young marriages and upset with the stigma attached to unmarried adults in our society. At the end of paragraph 6, she commends young people for living according to their consciences, but in paragraphs 7 and 8, she asks hard, direct questions that challenge her readers. How did you find yourself reacting to the challenges?

4. In the middle of paragraph 8, Mannes softens her challenges by writing

It is about time that *we* realized that many women make better teachers than mothers . . . . *We* have lost a great deal . . . .

What relationship between writer and reader do the italicized pronouns suggest? Why is the use of the first-person plural pronoun an effective persuasive technique here?

5. In paragraph 9, Mannes expands the idea stated at the end of paragraph 8: each person's search for his or her unique identity as a human being is primary. Then in paragraphs 10–18, Mannes develops another theme. What point do those paragraphs make? As you know, in an effective persuasive essay, the writer makes clear what the readers are to do. Does Mannes do so in paragraphs 10–18?

6. Taking paragraphs 19–21 together as the conclusion to the essay, would you say it ends on a positive or a negative note? Explain. What overall effect does the essay have on you?

Now You Try It

Marya Mannes chose a topic about which she had strong feelings. Select an issue about which you have strong feelings and write an essay in which you attempt to persuade readers to think and feel about that issue as you do.

LESSON **27**

Tone in Essays of Opinion and Persuasion

Tone of voice, which reflects your mood and attitude, helps indicate what you mean by the words you speak. The expression "That's all right," for instance, can mean very different things, depending in part on whether the tone in which you speak it is sympathetic, sarcastic, resigned, exasperated, or matter of fact.

Tone in writing is similar to tone in speaking. The writer's attitude toward the audience and toward the subject determines tone by affecting the selection of words and details, as well as the structure of the sentences and the organization of the paragraphs. In reading the following persuasive essay, see how long it takes you to recognize the attitude that the author is taking toward his topic. In other words, how soon are you able to recognize his tone?

60   **Chris Welles in "Music to Acquire Couth By"**

If you're anything like me, you probably have a rough time keeping up with all the culture that everybody who is anybody just *has* to know about. That's why I was glad a few years ago when they started putting out condensations of all the important books on the best-seller lists. Now there are all kinds of other

Helpful Devices: capsule outlines of history, quickie guides to famous art, "instant" language instruction courses. You can get abridged, edited, condensed, excerpted versions of just about anything.

Until recently, there was one great big exception: classical music. But I'm happy to tell you they've finally licked the problem of editing a full-blown, hour-long symphony. Something called RTV Sales, Inc. has come up with a two-volume package called *50 Great Moments in Music*, which squeezes big pieces with status like Rachmaninoff's *Second Piano Concerto* and Beethoven's *Ninth Symphony* down into bite-sized bits.

". . . Own the Best Parts of Nearly Forty Other Records," say the ads. "Saves you hours of unfamiliar listening."

It's always been all that listening that's bothered me about classical music. Just imagine what it would be like to sit through 40 long albums. It would take *a day and a half*.

The ad goes on: "You can give your family a priceless shortcut to broad musical knowledge . . . let your children build a rich musical heritage." "Heritage," "shortcut" — those are my kind of words.

True to its promise, all the moments are there. Schubert's *Eighth Symphony*, even though he never finished it, meanders along for 25 long minutes in its original form. The Great Moments people have really unfinished it, right down to a compact 78-second moment where the cellos come in with that pretty tune. (But the Great Moments people let me down here. They repeat that tune four times.) The best shortcut is the job done on Beethoven's *Ninth Symphony*. It saves you a whole hour of unfamiliar listening by bringing you a 41-second moment from the last movement — the big booming part with the horns.

I felt a little guilty about skipping all those unfamiliar parts, but an accompanying brochure cleared my conscience. "Every one of these great composers," it begins, "may accurately be called a genius." But, and here's the point, "great musical geniuses are much

like other men in many ways. Like writers who in their
entire lifetime will produce only one great master-
piece . . . like athletes who rise to one great feat . . .
a great composer will, in his entire lifetime, produce
one or two great moments that rise above everything
else he has written . . . a moment that is breathtakingly beautiful."

So why feel guilty? If all those hours of unwanted
listening were composed while the composers were
writing just like ordinary men, I mean, who really
needs it? Besides, I think it will be a kind of cultural
plus at your next party when you hear the hi-fi playing and can remark, "Oh, I see they're playing the
Great Moment from Rachmaninoff's *Second Piano
Concerto*." That ought to impress all your brainy
friends. And if they start getting smart with one of
the unfamiliar parts, you can just come right back
and say, "Well, not only are those parts unfamiliar,
they aren't even breathtakingly beautiful."

Or you could call their attention to the one piece in
the album that is played in its entirety — Chopin's
Minute Waltz. I think it was pretty brave to include it.
After all, if there were more composers as succinct as
Chopin, the Great Moments people wouldn't be in
business.

The Writer's Craft

1. What opinion does the essay express? How does the author feel about *50 Great Moments in Music* and other such short-
cuts to culture?

2. The tone of the essay is in part ironical; that is, the author
is saying something quite different from what he means. While
pretending to approve of the records he is describing, he is actually expressing strong disapproval of them. Which expressions
in the first paragraph convey the irony? Is the ironical tone maintained throughout the essay?

3. Another aspect of the tone of this essay is its conversational quality; the author seems to be chatting with the reader.
Explain how that casual tone is established and maintained.

4. Do you think a chatty, ironical tone is an effective persuasive technique? Explain why or why not. In answering, consider that the tone of the essay might appropriately have been indignant or even outraged. Would an indignant essay have been more or less effective than the casual, ironical essay that Welles wrote? Discuss.

Here is another essay in which tone helps convey the author's opinion — in this essay, an opinion about "training aids for writers."

61   E. B. White in "Calculating Machine"

A publisher in Chicago has sent us a pocket calculating machine by which we may test our writing to see whether it is intelligible. The calculator was developed by General Motors, who, not satisfied with giving the world a Cadillac, now dream of bringing perfect understanding to men. The machine (it is simply a celluloid card with a dial) is called the Reading-Ease Calculator and shows four grades of "reading ease" — Very Easy, Easy, Hard, Very Hard. You count your words and syllables, set the dial, and an indicator lets you know whether anybody is going to understand what you have written. An instruction book came with it, and after mastering the simple rules, we lost no time in running a test on the instruction book itself, to see how *that* writer was doing. The poor fellow! His leading essay, the one on the front cover, tested Very Hard.

Our next step was to study the first phrase on the face of the calculator: "How to test Reading-Ease of written matter." There is, of course, no such thing as reading ease of written matter. There is the ease with which matter can be read, but that is a condition of the reader, not of the matter. Thus the inventors and distributors of this calculator got off to a poor start, with a Very Hard instruction book and a slovenly phrase.

Already they have one foot caught in the brier patch of English usage.

Not only did the author of the instruction book score badly on the front cover, but inside the book he used the word *personalize* in an essay on how to improve one's writing. A man who likes the word *personalize* is entitled to his choice, but we wonder whether he should be in the business of giving advice to writers. "Whenever possible," he wrote, "personalize your writing by directing it to the reader." As for us, we should as lief * Simonize our grandmother as personalize our writing.

In the same envelope with the calculator, we received another training aid for writers — a booklet called "How to Write Better," by Rudolf Flesch. This, too, we studied, and it quickly demonstrated the broncolike ability of the English language to throw whoever leaps cocksurely into the saddle. The language not only can toss a rider but knows a thousand tricks for tossing him, each one more gay than the last. Dr. Flesch stayed in the saddle only a moment or two. Under the heading "Think Before You Write," he wrote, "The main thing to consider is your *purpose* in writing. Why are you sitting down to write?" And Echo answered: Because, sir, it is more comfortable than standing up.

Communication by the written word is a subtler (and more beautiful) thing than Dr. Flesch and General Motors imagine. They contend that the "average reader" is capable of reading only what tests Easy, and that the writer should write at or below this level. This is a presumptuous and degrading idea. There is no average reader, and to reach down toward this mythical character is to deny that each of us is on the way up, is ascending. ("Ascending," by the way, is a word Dr. Flesch advises writers to stay away from. Too unusual.)

It is our belief that no writer can improve his work until he discards the dulcet notion that the reader is

* **lief:** willingly, gladly.

feeble-minded, for writing is an act of faith, not a trick of grammar. Ascent is at the heart of the matter. A country whose writers are following a calculating machine downstairs is not ascending — if you will pardon the expression — and a writer who questions the capacity of the person at the other end of the line is not a writer at all, merely a schemer. The movies long ago decided that a wider communication could be achieved by a deliberate descent to a lower level, and they walked proudly down until they reached the cellar. Now they are groping for the light switch, hoping to find the way out.

We have studied Dr. Flesch's instructions diligently, but we return for guidance in these matters to an earlier American, who wrote with more patience, more confidence. "I fear chiefly," he wrote, "lest my expression may not be *extravagant* enough, may not wander far enough beyond the narrow limits of my daily experience, so as to be adequate to the truth of which I have been convinced. . . . Why level downward to our dullest perception always, and praise that as common sense? The commonest sense is the sense of men asleep, which they express by snoring." *

Run that through your calculator! It may come out Hard, it may come out Easy. But it will come out whole, and it will last forever.

* Henry David Thoreau writing in *Walden*.

The Writer's Craft

1. In a sentence, state E. B. White's opinion of the pocket calculating machine. At what point in the essay are you certain of his opinion? What is the author's opinion of the booklet entitled "How to Write Better"? Where are you first certain of that opinion? Explain how you know the author's opinion of each product.

2. Point to specific words, phrases, and sentences that contribute effectively to setting the tone of the essay.

3. Compare the tone of Model 61 with that of Model 60. Are they similar or different? Explain.

Now You Try It

Select one of the following:

1. Below is a list of items that have both good and bad features. Choose one you want to criticize or defend, then write a composition in which you use an appropriate tone to reinforce your opinion. There is, of course, a whole range of tones from which to choose, but some possibilities are enthusiasm, delight, affection, ridicule, indignation, irritation, sarcasm, and anger. Throughout the essay, maintain whatever tone you assume, and specify that tone at the top of your paper.

    a. A very expensive new car
    b. Plastic model kits
    c. Home permanent kits
    d. Color television sets
    e. Luxury motels
    f. Extras on new cars
    g. French poodles
    h. Photographic gadgets
    i. Report cards
    j. Book condensations

2. Write a composition in which you try to persuade readers that a certain trend, product, issue, or popular idea is ridiculous. Use irony as one of your persuasive techniques.

> The following reflective essay is concerned not with an immediate problem or a transient commercial product but with a question of human behavior and attitudes. Although it is entertainingly written, its tone nonetheless indicates the author's serious intent.

62   Jan Struther in "One of the Best"

> An uncle of mine who had a quite fantastically ugly housekeeper was in the habit of reproving his wife when, in her impulsive way, she referred to some moderately plain person as "the most hideous woman in the world." "Steady on, my dear," he would say. "That leaves one nothing for Mrs. Mackillop."

I was reminded of this yesterday by hearing two men in a bus discussing a third.

"And what about George?" said the first.

"George?" the other echoed. "Oh, George is one of the best. Not much of a talker, of course, but the sort of chap who'd never let you down." I held my breath, fascinated, making an inward bet; and sure enough, he added in a second or two, "Children and animals absolutely worship him, and I always think that's the biggest test."

It was a complete portrait of George in three strokes. I could see him, pipe and all, in my mind's eye: the sort of man who looks his best in mackintosh. A good fellow, certainly, but not — and this is the point — one of the best.

True, he may be the average Englishman's idea of the best. But the trouble with the English is that their standards have been lowered by too much tolerance. Tolerance is their outstanding characteristic, making allowance — at any rate for their own fellow countrymen — the most flourishing industry they possess. But a mind can become so broad as to be practically shapeless; and the danger of a charitable outlook is that it so often leads to the glorification of the mediocre. It begins with not thinking the worse of a man because he is not clever, and ends with thinking the better of him because he is stupid. It begins by excusing his lack of eloquence, and ends by making a virtue of his taciturnity. It begins with forgiving him for being unreliable, and ends with calling him a fine fellow for keeping his word. It begins with observing that even a criminal may retain the affection of his child and his dog, and ends with believing that children and animals are infallible dowsers * of excellence.

Which (to take the last point first) they are not. One of the chief trials and disillusionments of dog-owning or parenthood is the utterly appalling people that the cherished creatures make friends with: the toughs on beaches, the oicks ° in buses, the bores and

* **dowsers:** diviners, those who foretell.
° **oicks:** people who spit.

ne'er-do-wells among your own acquaintance upon whom they fling their person, their affection, and their respect. "And yet," you muse, "they seem to be fond of *me*, too. Am I like that? Or worse still, do they wish that I was?" A thought so unendurable demands instant comfort: you find it in the reflection that children and animals are charming immaturities, lacking in judgment, devoid of discrimination, swayed by trifles; and that winning their approval is a matter, not of mental or spiritual worth, but of a willingness to throw sticks into the sea or an ability to draw elephants with a single line.

As to the second point which has been put forward in George's favor, namely, that "he would never let you down": I grant that this is a virtue; but not so rare a one surely as to be singled out for such emphatic comment. Civilized human beings do not, on the whole, let one another down. Benevolence is a stronger instinct than malice, cooperation than hostility. Chronologically, both in the history of the race and in the life of the individual, love comes before hate. Crooks and murderers are rare in comparison with the uncounted hordes of honest and amiable men; and it is the exception rather than the rule to be robbed by an absconding partner or to have your secrets betrayed by a confidant. This being so, why should George receive such a thumping pat on the back? To refrain from letting people down is something, but it is not enough. Does he, I should be interested to know, ever lift people up? Does he kindle them to action by his vitality, quicken them to laughter by his humor, or inspire them to creation by his intelligence? If he does none of these things, then he is still not "one of the best," though he never broke a promise in his life.

And now for the other remark, the first and most telling stroke in the Portrait of George. "Not much of a talker." The words were deprecating enough, but the tone in which they were uttered belied them. It was heavy with the flotsam and jetsam of age-old prejudices and half-digested copybook maxims. Still waters, it implied, run deep; least said is soonest mended; speech is silver, but silence is golden; and the French are filthy frogs and jabber your head off.

Things have come to a pretty pass, I must say, if men are to be blamed for exercising the power which is said to distinguish them from the beasts — a point of view that reaches its pinnacle of absurdity in Carlyle's famous dictum that "No speech ever uttered or utterable is worth comparison with silence." (Jane * must have got a lot of quiet enjoyment out of that.) Was any statement ever so demonstrably untrue? Certainly, speech may sometimes do harm; but so may silence, and a worse harm at that. No offered insult ever caused so deep a wound as a tenderness expected and withheld; and no spoken indiscretion was ever so bitterly regretted as the words that one did not speak. Moreover, the injuries done by speech can usually be cured by speech; whereas those caused by silence are merely aggravated and deepened by further silence, and must come at last to words for their healing.

So much for the debit side. As for the credit — what good does silence do in the world? At the best, it may help you to catch a fish, save you from betraying your ignorance, or allow somebody else to get off to sleep. But these are small benefits compared with those of speech. If silence is really golden, which I quarrel with, then speech is the purest platinum inlaid with diamonds. It spreads wisdom, dispels ignorance, ventilates grievances, stimulates curiosity, lightens the spirits, and lessens the fundamental loneliness of the soul.

But fighting proverbs with reasonable arguments is uphill work. Quicker, perhaps, and surer, to bring up a battery of counter-proverbs. "A lame tongue gets nowt ° " is a good one; and here is an older and a better: "From a cholerick man withdraw a little; from him that saies nothing, forever." And when it comes to

* Jane: Thomas Carlyle's wife.
° nowt: nothing.

quotations, there are many that one might marshal against Carlyle's piece of didactic folly. "Oh! have a care of natures that are mute," says Meredith * in *Modern Love*. And no less reputable a person than Keble ° assures us that "Strong men delight in forceful speech."

Strong men, mark you. In other words, Georges. But that, alas! was a hundred years ago. Nowadays, it seems, we are expected to choose between the S.S.M.† and the voluble decadent — the former complacently inarticulate, and the latter arrogantly wordy; between the Hearty Man, who (on that hackneyed and hypothetical desert island so dear to amateur psychologists) would build you a hut in twenty-four hours but bore you to death in a week, and the Arty Man, who would talk to you quite brilliantly while you died of starvation and mosquito bites.

But there are a few exceptions; a few who are loved, not only by children and animals, but by discerning adults as well; who not only never let you down but are constantly buoying you up; and who, into the bargain, are capable of wise and witty conversation. They are rare, it is true, but they exist; and if people in buses are to be allowed to refer to George as "one of the best" — well, what, so to speak, is there left for Mrs. Mackillop?

* **Meredith,** George: English poet and novelist (1828–1909).
° **Keble,** John: English clergyman and poet (1792–1866).
† **S.S.M.:** Strong Silent Man.

The Writer's Craft

1. The organizational pattern of an essay sometimes suggests the tone. A light, informal essay is often rather loosely organized; the author may digress occasionally, much as one would in conversation. A more formal essay, on the other hand, is likely to have an organizational plan from which the author does not deviate. As for Jan Struther's essay, although it is informal, it does show

careful organization — for example, the reference in the last sentence of the essay to the anecdote in the first paragraph. Are George's three traits treated point by point? Does such organization create the impression of careful planning and, therefore, serious intent?

2. Word choice and sentence structure often work together to determine tone. Contrast the following sentences from the three essays in this lesson:

> *Welles:* "It's always been all that listening that's bothered me about classical music."
>
> *White:* "Already they have one foot caught in the brier patch of English usage."
>
> *Struther:* "No offered insult ever caused so deep a wound as a tenderness expected and withheld; and no spoken indiscretion was ever so bitterly regretted as the words that one did not speak."

The tone of the first two sentences seems almost playful. But in the third sentence, the language and sentence structure are formal. Welles's sentence sounds like ordinary conversation; White's sounds a bit less like conversation, mainly because of the "brier patch" allusion and the position of *Already*. Does Jan Struther's sentence sound at all like ordinary conversation? Explain.

3. The tone of Model 62 is harder to categorize than the tone of Models 60 and 61. Jan Struther is writing about a serious subject; yet one could hardly say that the tone of her essay is wholly solemn. Point to words and phrases that make her writing sound *less* serious than the sentence quoted in item 2 above might indicate. Would you be willing to say, however, that the overall tone of the Struther essay is *more* serious than the tone of the preceding two? Discuss.

Now You Try It

The appropriate tone for a composition is determined to some extent by the audience for which it is intended. Choose one of the topics listed in the left-hand column at the top of the following page, and write a persuasive letter to a person listed in the right-hand column. Specify the kind of reader for whom the letter is intended, and be sure the tone is appropriate for that reader.

a. A proposal for (or against) shorter Presidential terms

b. A proposal outlawing cars in business sections of cities

c. A defense (or criticism) of the merit of certain courses taught in your high school

(1) A member of Congress who opposes your views

(2) A member of Congress who favors your views

(3) The editor of your school or local newspaper (a letter you hope will be printed)

(4) A friend, or a member of your family

Sentence Skills

56 Gilbert Highet in "History on the Silver Screen" (pages 203–10)

Usually modifiers that function as adverbs can be moved from one place to another within a sentence. The Sentence Skills section on pages 194–95 demonstrates that a one-word adverb is often movable. A prepositional phrase used as an adverb can generally be moved, too; so can an adverb clause.

In the following sentence from Model 56, the italicized prepositional phrase, which modifies the verb *charge*, functions as an adverb.

Up the deadly slope they charge, with rebel yells almost drowned by the thunder of Federal cannon.

The phrase could have been placed after the verb:

They charge *up the deadly slope*, with rebel yells almost drowned by the thunder of Federal cannon.

Whether an adverb phrase should be moved from one place to another is primarily a question of style, not grammar. By placing the phrase at the beginning of the sentence, Highet emphasizes it. Do you find the emphasis different in the rewritten sentence? Explain.

Like phrases functioning as adverbs, adverb clauses can usually be moved from one place to another within the sentence. The adverb clause is italicized in the following sentence from Model 56:

Just at the summit, *as the lines are about to meet*, up spring the defending Federal troops.

The clause might have been placed in one of two other positions in the sentence:

As the lines are about to meet, just at the summit, up spring the defending Federal troops.

Up spring the defending Federal troops, just at the summit, *as the lines are about to meet.*

Which of the two rewritten sentences sounds better to you? Why?

In revising compositions, you will find it worthwhile to ask yourself if some of the adverb phrases or clauses might sound better in a different position. If you are like most writers, you will have a tendency to "tack on" such phrases and clauses to the ends of sentences, more or less as afterthoughts. For that reason, by reading your compositions carefully during revision you are likely to find that some clauses and phrases would be more effective at the beginning of a sentence, or even in a position between the subject and the verb.

■ **EXERCISE** Rewrite the following paragraph, moving each italicized phrase or clause to a different position in the sentence in which it appears. Some rewording may be necessary. Your rewritten version should sound much better than the original.

Television news correspondents are expected and, indeed, required to interpret the news, *although they are not permitted to editorialize.* These interpretations are *in a free society* certain to arouse controversy. A correspondent's interpretation of the news will differ, *even though the correspondent aims at absolute impartiality,* from that of many of the viewers. You may regard, *if you are a liberal Democrat,* the interpretation as too conservative. You may regard the interpretation, *if you are a conservative Republican,* as too liberal. Correspondents cannot be entirely free from their own backgrounds, opinions, and prejudices, *no matter how hard they try.* Correspondents cannot help having views on events and personalities, *because they live daily with the news.* These judgments, *once they have made judgments,* inevitably become a part of what they report. Thus, you should realize that, *when you listen to a television news correspondent,* you are hearing an interpretation of the news. *By a trained and conscientious professional* the interpretation has been made, but it is an interpretation nonetheless.

57 H. L. Mencken in "The Libido for the Ugly"
(pages 212–15)

As a rule, good writing is concise. There are times, though, when repetition of words and phrases helps the writer achieve a desired emphasis, as in the following extract from Model 57:

> *Here was* the very heart of industrial America, the center of its most lucrative and characteristic activity, the boast and pride of the richest and grandest nation ever seen on earth — and *here was* a scene so dreadfully hideous, so intolerably bleak and forlorn that it reduced the whole aspiration of man to a macabre and depressing joke. *Here was* wealth beyond computation, almost beyond imagination — and *here were* human habitations so abominable that they would have disgraced a race of alley cats.

The passage contrasts the vast wealth of a region with its wretched appearance. The repeated use of *here was* serves to emphasize not only the phrase itself but the elements of contrast that follow each use of the phrase. In other words, repetition underscores the contrast. Notice that other repetitive patterns occur within this basic pattern:

> *so* dreadfully hideous
> *so* intolerably bleak and forlorn
> *so* abominable
>
> *beyond* computation
> *beyond* imagination

How do those repetitions also help emphasize the point the passage is making?

Consider another passage from the Mencken selection. What is emphasized by the repetition?

> *There was not a* single decent house within eye range from the Pittsburgh suburbs to the Greensburg yards. *There was not one* that was not misshapen, and *there was not one* that was not shabby.

■ **EXERCISE** Write a brief, well-constructed paragraph in which you repeat one of the phrases below several times for emphasis. The use of parallel grammatical constructions

should help emphasize the elements following your repeated uses of the phrase.

    a. I have never seen . . .
    b. I can still hear . . .
    c. You feel . . .
    d. We fear . . .
    e. I love . . .
    f. I believe . . .
    g. Here was . . .

INFORMAL AND FORMAL STYLES

61 E. B. White in "Calculating Machine"
(pages 235–37)

There are styles of writing, as there are styles of dress.
The "right" style of dress, formal or informal, depends on
the period in which we live, the people we expect to be
with, and the occasion for which we dress. Similarly, the
"right" style in prose depends on the times, the audience,
and the occasion. In addition, the subject matter of a composition can have a bearing on whether a formal or informal
style is appropriate.

Although a writer's style is always an expression of personality, we can be sure that the informal style of Model
61 is to some extent determined by the subject matter
and by the fact that it was written in the 1950's for
The New Yorker magazine. Here is a paragraph from E. B.
White's essay:

> Not only did the author of the instruction book score
> badly on the front cover, but inside the book he used
> the word *personalize* in an essay on how to improve
> one's writing. A man who likes the word *personalize*
> is entitled to his choice, but we wonder whether he
> should be in the business of giving advice to writers.
> "Whenever possible," he wrote, "personalize your writ-
> ing by directing it to the reader." As for us, we should
> as lief Simonize our grandmother as personalize our
> writing.

Contrast the style of that paragraph with the style of the
following passage from George Santayana's philosophical
essay "Tipperary," published in 1922.

As it is, we live experimentally, moodily, in the dark; each generation breaks its eggshell with the same haste and assurance as the last, pecks at the same indigestible pebbles, dreams the same dreams, or others just as absurd, and if it hears anything of what former men have learned by experience, it corrects their maxims by its first impressions, and rushes down any untrodden path which it finds alluring, to die in its own way, or become wise too late and to no purpose. These young men [veterans of World War I] are no rustics, they are no fools; and yet they have seen the mad heart of this world riven and unmasked, they have had long vigils before battle, long nights tossing with pain, in which to meditate on the spectacle; and yet they have learned nothing. The young barbarians want to be again at play.

It is easier to recognize differences between an informal and a formal style than it is to explain them. However, the following factors are involved:

Sentence length. The sentences in White's passage contain 33, 27, 13, and 14 words. The first two sentences in Santayana's passage contain 85 and 49 words. An 85-word sentence, or even a 49-word one, is long. Very long sentences, occasionally relieved by a short sentence, are characteristic of formal style. Notice, however, that the Santayana passage could be broken into ten sentences by punctuating it differently. Not that such reduction in the length of the sentences would alone make Santayana's style informal, for their are other elements in the passage that help account for its formality.

Word choice. For the most part, informal writing contains words in everyday, conversational use. The only unusual word in the White passage is the archaic *lief*, used for humorous effect. The Santayana passage, on the other hand, contains a number of words not commonly used in conversation: *untrodden, rustics, riven, vigils,* and others. A second point concerning word choice is that informal writing is likely to contain fewer abstract words than formal writing does.

Figurative language. Figurative language is probably used as frequently in informal as in formal writing; the differences that exist are to be found in the kind of figurative expressions used. White writes, "we should as lief Simonize our grandmother as personalize our writing." Santayana writes, "each generation breaks its eggshell with the same haste and assurance as the last." The former comparison is down-to-earth and amusing; the latter is more serious.

Sentence structure. A good conversationalist might have spoken White's sentences just as they are written. Although they are not simple ones grammatically, they are typical of sentences people actually use in speaking. Santayana's sentences are different. They are consciously "composed"; no one, either today or in the 1920's, would have used Santayana's elaborate and eloquent sentences in ordinary conversation.

In general, the difference between the informal and formal styles is the difference between incisive conversation and "literary" writing, or writing consciously crafted for rhetorical effect. The modern trend is toward informal writing, even in business letters, research papers, and quality-magazine articles. Both the informal and the formal style have their uses, but you will probably find that the informal style, having the advantages of directness and simplicity, is more useful than the formal in most of what you write.

■ **EXERCISE** The following passage, from a nineteenth-century manual of model letters, is written in a style typical of the era. Rewrite the passage so that it has an informal style more appropriate for today.

My dear friend,

It is with the greatest reluctance that I feel I must terminate our relationship. Recent events, of which we both are painfully aware, have indicated to me in clear and compelling terms that our natures are essentially incompatible and our viewpoints on many crucial issues too completely dissimilar. While your companionship in the past has brought me moments of joy which I shall treasure eternally, I feel it would be injudicious on both our parts to prolong a relationship, which, it has become increasingly clear, is not based on mutual trust and respect. Please extend to your dear mother my best wishes for a speedy and quick recovery from her untimely accident.

Sincerely,
Alberta

Writing About Literature

LESSON **28**

Writing About a Short Story

The subject of a composition about literature is the literary work itself — a short story, novel, play, or poem. Your reading of the subject should yield a topic — some interesting general statement about an aspect of the work. Then, using specific details from the selection, you develop the topic into a well-organized composition, which may vary in length from one to several paragraphs, but which should exhibit all the characteristics of effective exposition: unity, coherence, appropriate emphasis, clarity, and interest. What you write should also resemble a good essay of opinion in presenting convincing evidence to support the topic you have chosen.

This lesson guides you through the preliminary steps in writing a composition about a short story — specifically, about Graham Greene's "I Spy." First read the story attentively, responding to its plot, characterizations, setting, point of view, and theme. A number of appropriate topics may emerge from considering any one of those aspects of the story.

I Spy

GRAHAM GREENE

Charlie Stowe waited until he heard his mother snore before he got out of bed. Even then he moved with caution and tiptoed to the window. The front of the house was irregular,

so that it was possible to see a light burning in his mother's
room. But now all the windows were dark. A searchlight ⁵
passed across the sky, lighting the banks of cloud and probing
the dark deep spaces between, seeking enemy airships. The
wind blew from the sea, and Charlie Stowe could hear behind
his mother's snores the beating of the waves. A draught
through the cracks in the window-frame stirred his nightshirt. ¹⁰
Charlie Stowe was frightened.

But the thought of the tobacconist's shop which his father
kept down a dozen wooden stairs drew him on. He was
twelve years old, and already boys at the County School
mocked him because he had never smoked a cigarette. The ¹⁵
packets were piled twelve deep below, Gold Flake and Players,
De Reszke, Abdulla, Woodbines, and the little shop lay under a thin haze of stale smoke which would completely disguise his crime. That it was a crime to steal some of his father's stock Charlie Stowe had no doubt, but he did not love ²⁰
his father; his father was unreal to him, a wraith, pale, thin,
and indefinite, who noticed him only spasmodically and left
even punishment to his mother. For his mother he felt a pas-
sionate demonstrative love; her large boisterous presence and
her noisy charity filled the world for him; from her speech ²⁵
he judged her the friend of everyone, from the rector's wife
to the "dear Queen," except the "Huns," the monsters who
lurked in Zeppelins in the clouds. But his father's affection and
dislike were as indefinite as his movements. Tonight he had
said he would be in Norwich, and yet you never knew. ³⁰
Charlie Stowe had no sense of safety as he crept down the
wooden stairs. When they creaked he clenched his fingers on
the collar of his nightshirt.

At the bottom of the stairs he came out quite suddenly
into the little shop. It was too dark to see his way, and he ³⁵
did not dare touch the switch. For half a minute he sat in
despair on the bottom step with his chin cupped in his hands.
Then the regular movement of the searchlight was reflected
through an upper window and the boy had time to fix in
memory the pile of cigarettes, the counter, and the small hole ⁴⁰
under it. The footsteps of a policeman on the pavement made

him grab the first packet to his hand and dive for the hole. A light shone along the floor and a hand tried the door, then the footsteps passed on, and Charlie cowered in the darkness.

At last he got his courage back by telling himself in his [45] curiously adult way that if he were caught now there was nothing to be done about it, and he might as well have his smoke. He put a cigarette in his mouth and then remembered that he had no matches. For a while he dared not move. Three times the searchlight lit the shop, while he muttered taunts [50] and encouragements. "May as well be hung for a sheep," "Cowardy, cowardy custard," grown-up and childish exhortations oddly mixed.

But as he moved he heard footfalls in the street, the sound of several men walking rapidly. Charlie Stowe was old enough [55] to feel surprised that anybody was about. The footsteps came nearer, stopped; a key was turned in the shop door, a voice said, "Let him in," and then he heard his father, "If you wouldn't mind being quiet, gentlemen. I don't want to wake up the family." There was a note unfamiliar to Charlie in the [60] undecided voice. A torch * flashed and the electric globe burst into blue light. The boy held his breath; he wondered whether his father would hear his heart beating, and he clutched his nightshirt tightly and prayed, "O God, don't let me be caught." Through a crack in the counter he could see [65] his father where he stood, one hand held to his high stiff collar, between two men in bowler hats and belted mackintoshes. They were strangers.

"Have a cigarette," his father said in a voice dry as a biscuit. One of the men shook his head. "It wouldn't do, not [70] when we are on duty. Thank you all the same." He spoke gently, but without kindness; Charlie Stowe thought his father must be ill.

"Mind if I put a few in my pocket?" Mr. Stowe asked, and when the man nodded he lifted a pile of Gold Flake and [75] Players from a shelf and caressed the packets with the tips of his fingers.

* torch: flashlight.

"Well," he said, "there's nothing to be done about it, and I may as well have my smokes." For a moment Charlie Stowe feared discovery, his father stared round the shop so thor- [80] oughly; he might have been seeing it for the first time. "It's a good little business," he said, "for those that like it. The wife will sell out, I suppose. Else the neighbors'll be wrecking it. Well, you want to be off. A stitch in time. I'll get my coat."

"One of us'll come with you, if you don't mind," said the [85] stranger gently.

"You needn't trouble. It's on the peg here. There, I'm all ready."

The other man said in an embarrassed way: "Don't you want to speak to your wife?" The thin voice was decided. "Not [90] me. Never do today what you can put off till tomorrow. She'll have her chance later, won't she?"

"Yes, yes," one of the strangers said and he became very cheerful and encouraging. "Don't you worry too much. While there's life . . ." And suddenly his father tried to laugh. [95]

When the door had closed Charlie Stowe tiptoed upstairs and got into bed. He wondered why his father had left the house again so late at night and who the strangers were. Surprise and awe kept him for a little while awake. It was as if a familiar photograph had stepped from the frame to reproach [100] him with neglect. He remembered how his father had held tight to his collar and fortified himself with proverbs, and he thought for the first time that, while his mother was boisterous and kindly, his father was very like himself, doing things in the dark which frightened him. It would have pleased him to [105] go down to his father and tell him that he loved him, but he could hear through the window the quick steps going away. He was alone in the house with his mother, and he fell asleep.

Writing About "I Spy"

Appreciating a story is usually a matter of understanding how well all the aspects — character, setting, plot, point of view, tone, theme — work together; but in analyzing the story in a relatively brief composition, you will need to separate one aspect from the others in order to focus on it. Not that the other aspects mustn't be mentioned; rather, they should be subordinated to the central concern of the essay.

Before deciding what that central concern, or topic, will be in this instance, make sure you have the main points of Graham Greene's story clear. The setting is England. (How do you know?) It is wartime, and the enemy are the Germans. (What details in the story support those inferences?) Near the end of the story the father is revealed as having committed some crime against his neighbors so grievous that they will "be wrecking" his shop when they find out what he has done (line 83). Considering the time of the story, what might that crime have been? Could he have had dealings with the Germans — the monstrous "Huns" whom Charlie's mother despises? Who are the two men in mackintoshes accompanying Charlie's father? Why, at the end, has Mr. Stowe "left the house again so late at night"?

When you feel you understand what "I Spy" reveals and implies, decide on an interesting topic to develop. One impression you may have is that the story defines the character and changing attitudes of a twelve-year-old in a world he imperfectly understands. If a rereading confirms the impression that grasping the character of Charlie Stowe is essential to appreciating the story, you may want to make the boy's character the topic of a composition. Accordingly, to phrase a general statement, you should look back at the story in order to note what Charlie does and thinks. No two readers will arrive at exactly the same general statement (some, in fact, may disagree about the validity of yours), but here is one possibility:

> In "I Spy," a boy comes to understand how closely he resembles his father, whom he had thought he did not love.

With that generalization in mind, you might list details that support it: descriptions, interpretations by the author, actions, lines of dialogue, anything in the story that will support the insight. Here are a number of points pertaining to Charlie and his father that indicate what sort of material should prove useful:

1. Twelve-year-old Charlie sneaks down to the tobacco shop in darkness to commit what he has no doubt is a "crime" (lines 12–20).
2. His father at the start of the story is "unreal to him, a wraith, pale, thin, and indefinite, who [notices] him only

spasmodically and [leaves] even punishment to his mother" (lines 21–23).

3. In performing his crime, the boy bolsters his courage by "telling himself in his curiously adult way that if he were caught now there was nothing to be done about it . . ." (lines 45–47).

4. In the midst of his crime, he fortifies himself with other proverbs to keep up his courage: "May as well be hung for a sheep [as a lamb]," etc. (lines 51–52).

5. When Charlie's father first speaks, his voice is undecided (lines 60–61), as hesitant as Charlie himself has been; and he clutches his collar just the way his son clutches his nightshirt.

6. "O God, don't let me be caught," Charlie prays, even as his father may have prayed a short time earlier. (lines 64–65)

7. Charlie's father, like his son a moment earlier, takes cigarettes from the counter (lines 75–76).

8. What the father says to the strangers indicates that he has been caught committing some serious crime, but he tries to console himself with proverbs; compare Charlie's ". . . there was nothing to be done about it, and he might as well have his smoke" (lines 46–48) with the father's "there's nothing to be done about it, and I may as well have my smokes" (lines 78–79).

9. After his father's departure, Charlie realizes "for the first time that, while his mother was boisterous and kindly, his father was very like himself, doing things in the dark which frightened him" (lines 103–05).

10. But at the end Charlie still doesn't understand what he has seen; he falls asleep, wishing he could tell his father that he loves him.

These details are listed simply as examples, to suggest the kind of material you can use in developing a composition on literature. Probably you would not use all the listed details in your composition, and you certainly would not present them in the order they appear here, which is simply the order of their occurrence in the story. Your task is to find an effective organizational plan, then present relevant details with interpretative statements about aspects of Charlie's character as compared with his father's. In doing so, you should make clear to the reader the relationship between details cited from the story and the topic they serve to support. Appropriate transitional expressions should connect your interpretations and references to the story. And, finally, you should undertake whatever revising and rewriting will be necessary (and some is always necessary) to achieve a polished composition.

Now You Try It

1. Write a composition about "I Spy" based on one of the topics suggested below or an appropriate topic of your own. Use details from the story to support the general statement that serves as the topic, as well as to support any of the subpoints you make in developing the composition.

   a. The wartime setting of "I Spy" is an indispensable ingredient in making the story meaningful and effective.
   b. The plot of "I Spy" moves economically through the conventional pattern, from exposition through complication to climax and dénouement.
   c. One theme of "I Spy" concerns the nature of the criminal act: why people commit it, how they react to it, and what they learn — or fail to learn — from it.
   d. Dialogue in "I Spy" helps reveal Mr. Stowe's character and feelings, so that the reader finally comes to understand him remarkably well.
   e. The use of dialogue in "I Spy" is kept to a minimum — for very good reasons.
   f. The situation revealed in "I Spy" is one that is filled with irony.
   g. "I Spy" gains force from being so compressed; within a brief space, three lives are revealed comprehensively, so that the reader finds himself extending those lives into the future that will occur after the story ends.

2. Write a composition of 300 to 500 words about the short story on pages 265–79 or some other short story you know well. Concentrate on a specific aspect of the story: theme, plot, characters, setting, tone, or point of view. And don't begin with your opinion of the story; rather, let your opinion emerge from the specific observations you make about it.

LESSON **29**

Writing About a Poem

Perhaps the principal difference between writing about poems and writing about short stories lies in the number of readings you have to give a poem before understanding it well enough to organize a composition; as a rule, a poem requires more readings and a closer analysis of structure and individual words than does a story.

Accordingly, to write about a poem, you should first read and analyze it until you understand its meaning and the way special poetic devices contribute to the total effect it creates. Then you are ready to consider a topic for your composition. The general statement that serves as the topic may concern the overall meaning of the poem or the picture or feeling it conveys. Or it may be about the use in the poem of one or more poetic devices or elements: rhythm, rhyme, figurative language, imagery, diction.

After selecting the topic, look back at the poem to be sure you can support it with specific details, which should then be listed. Include in the list quotations of words, phrases, and whole lines, for you will want to make specific references in the composition. After you have listed the details, you will probably find it helpful to make an outline that shows which details you intend to use and the order in which you plan to present them. Finally, make a clear, concise statement of the topic; in other words, phrase the general statement that you will use to begin the composition.

This lesson illustrates how to form a general statement about a poem and then develop it into a composition. Begin by reading and rereading Emily Dickinson's "I Like to See It Lap the Miles" until you are sure you understand it.

I Like to See It Lap the Miles

EMILY DICKINSON

I like to see it lap the miles,
And lick the valleys up,
And stop to feed itself at tanks;
And then, prodigious, step

Around a pile of mountains,   5
And, supercilious, peer
In shanties by the sides of roads;
And then a quarry pare

To fit its ribs, and crawl between,
Complaining all the while   10
In horrid, hooting stanza;
Then chase itself down hill

And neigh like Boanerges;
Then, punctual as a star,
Stop — docile and omnipotent —   15
At its own stable door.

In reading any poem, make sure first of all that you know
what the words mean and how they are used. What is *prodigious?*
What does *supercilious* mean? What part of speech is *pare* in
line 8? What does it mean? What or who is *Boanerges?* Give a
synonym for *docile.*

One interesting fact about this poem is the vivid impression
of an object it creates without ever mentioning the object by
name. A train is being described, but in terms normally used to
describe the behavior of a horse. The comparison of a train to a
horse is, as you know, a metaphor, and because the comparison
runs throughout the poem, it is called an extended metaphor. If
you chose to make the metaphor the topic of a composition about
the poem, you might phrase a general statement something like
the following:

> "I Like to See It Lap the Miles" makes use of an extended
> metaphor to create a vivid impression of a train.

A list of details supporting that statement might include the following observations:

1. The first stanza depicts the movement of the train in terms that refer to the way a horse eats. The train laps the miles, licks the valleys up, and stops to feed itself at tanks.
2. The train's journey through the countryside is depicted in terms that refer to actions of a horse: it steps around a pile of mountains, peers in shanties by the sides of roads, crawls between the walls of a quarry, and chases itself downhill.
3. The sounds of the train are compared to a horse's. It complains in horrid, hooting stanza as it crawls through the quarry, and it neighs.
4. The train's arrival at its destination is compared to the end of a horse's journey. It stops — docile and omnipotent — at its own stable door.

To write a composition, you would begin with the general statement and then develop it by citing and interpreting details from the list, being careful to show the relationship of each detail to the topic of the composition.

Now You Try It

Write a brief composition, developing one of the following general statements about "I Like to See It Lap the Miles":

1. The word choice in Emily Dickinson's poem adds a great deal to the impression of the train it creates. (In developing the topic, you may want to discuss such words as *prodigious, supercilious, docile,* and *omnipotent,* as well as some of the words that have already been cited in the list of supporting details above.)

2. In "I Like to See It Lap the Miles," rhythm and rhyme are effective and appropriate. (Notice, for example, the run-on lines at the ends of stanzas. How do they contribute to the overall impression of the train? How do the inexact, or slant, rhymes contribute to the total effect of the poem? How many sentences does the poem contain, and what is the effect of that attribute?)

Emily Dickinson's poem presents a picture. Accordingly, your writing about it is concerned with the picture or impression it makes. But in writing about other poems, your main task may be to understand and then discuss the insight it presents, rather than the picture it describes. Read the following poem with that consideration in mind.

To an Athlete Dying Young

A. E. HOUSMAN

The time you won your town the race
We chaired you through the market-place;
Man and boy stood cheering by,
And home we brought you shoulder-high.

To-day, the road all runners come,   5
Shoulder-high we bring you home,
And set you at your threshold down,
Townsman of a stiller town.

Smart lad, to slip betimes away
From fields where glory does not stay,   10
And early though the laurel grows
It withers quicker than the rose.

Eyes the shady night has shut
Cannot see the record cut,
And silence sounds no worse than cheers   15
After earth has stopped the ears.

Now you will not swell the rout
Of lads that wore their honors out,
Runners whom renown outran
And the name died before the man.   20

So set, before its echoes fade,
The fleet foot on the sill of shade,
And hold to the low lintel up
The still-defended challenge-cup.

And round that early-laurelled head   25
Will flock to gaze the strengthless dead,
And find unwithered on its curls
The garland briefer than a girl's.

What does *chaired* mean, and what picture does line 2 create in your mind? Give a synonym for *betimes*. What are the connotations of *laurel;* that is, with what is it associated? What is a *lintel?*

After reading the poem carefully, if you decide that it expresses the insight that there are advantages in a young athlete's dying early, you might frame a general statement like the following:

> "To an Athlete Dying Young" views death as a victory.

Rereading the poem with that idea in mind, you might note the following details:

1. The lad is smart, the poet says, to slip away early from fields where glory does not stay.
2. In death his eyes cannot see his record cut, or broken, and his ears cannot tell the difference between the cheers and the silence.
3. The athlete who has died young will not join the ranks of those who "wore their honors out," whose names died before they did.
4. The young athlete takes his honors, the laurel, and the still-defended cup into death, where they will last forever.

This general statement and these details could then be developed into a composition.

Now You Try It

1. Develop into a composition one of the following general statements about "To an Athlete Dying Young":

   a. "To an Athlete Dying Young" is about a pathetic event, but the poet's tone and imagery keep the poem from being sentimental.
   b. Housman's citing of the advantages of early death serves to underscore the sadness of the event.
   c. The poem gains force through irony, which suggests meanings different from the expected ones.

2. Following the steps outlined in this lesson, write a composition about one of the poems on pages 280–83.

Selections to Write About

Here are a short story and several poems that will serve as subjects for compositions about literature. To write about any one of the selections, follow the steps outlined in the preceding lessons: read and analyze the selection carefully, choose a topic, and use specific details to develop the topic into a well-organized, coherent essay.

Taste

ROALD DAHL

There were six of us to dinner that night at Mike Schofield's house in London: Mike and his wife and daughter, my wife and I, and a man called Richard Pratt.

Richard Pratt was a famous gourmet. He was president of a small society known as the Epicures, and each month he circulated privately to its members a pamphlet on food and wines. He organized dinners where sumptuous dishes and rare wines were served. He refused to smoke for fear of harming his palate, and when discussing a wine, he had a curious, rather droll habit of referring to it as though it were a living being. "A prudent wine," he would say, "rather diffident and evasive, but quite prudent." Or, "a good-humored wine, benevolent and cheerful — slightly obscene, perhaps, but nonetheless good-humored."

I had been to dinner at Mike's twice before when Richard Pratt was there, and on each occasion Mike and his wife had gone out of their way to produce a special meal for the famous gourmet. And this one, clearly, was to be no exception. The moment we entered the dining room, I could see that the table was laid for a feast. The tall candles, the yellow roses, the quantity of shining silver, the three wineglasses to each person, and above all, the faint scent of roasting meat from the kitchen brought the first warm oozings of saliva to my mouth.

As we sat down, I remembered that on both Richard Pratt's previous visits Mike had played a little betting game with him over the claret, challenging him to name its breed and its vintage. Pratt had replied that that should not be too difficult provided it was one of the great years. Mike had then bet him a case of the wine in question that he could not do it. Pratt had accepted, and had won both times. Tonight I felt sure that the little game would be played over again, for Mike was quite willing to lose the bet in order to prove that his wine was good enough to be recognized, and Pratt, for his part, seemed to take a grave, restrained pleasure in displaying his knowledge.

The meal began with a plate of whitebait, fried very crisp in butter, and to go with it there was a Moselle. Mike got up and poured the wine himself, and when he sat down again, I could see that he was watching Richard Pratt. He had set the bottle in front of me so that I could read the label. It said, "Geierslay Ohligsberg, 1945." He leaned over and whispered to me that Geierslay was a tiny village in the Moselle, almost unknown outside Germany. He said that this wine we were drinking was something unusual, that the output of the vineyard was so small that it was almost impossible for a stranger to get any of it. He had visited Geierslay personally the previous summer in order to obtain the few dozen bottles that they had finally allowed him to have.

"I doubt anyone else in the country has any of it at the moment," he said. I saw him glance again at Richard Pratt. "Great thing about Moselle," he continued, raising his voice, "it's the perfect wine to serve before a claret. A lot of people serve a Rhine wine instead, but that's because they don't know any better. A Rhine wine will kill a delicate claret, you know that? It's barbaric to serve a Rhine before a claret. But a Moselle — ah! — a Moselle is exactly right."

Mike Schofield was an amiable, middle-aged man. But he was a stockbroker. To be precise, he was a jobber in the stock market, and like a number of his kind, he seemed to be somewhat embarrassed, almost ashamed to find that he had made so much money with so slight a talent. In his heart he knew that he was not really much more than a bookmaker — an unctuous, infinitely respectable, secretly unscrupulous bookmaker — and he knew that his friends knew it, too. So he was seeking now to become a man of culture, to cultivate a literary and aesthetic taste, to collect paintings, music, books, and all the rest of it. His little sermon about Rhine wine and Moselle was a part of this thing, this culture that he sought.

"A charming little wine, don't you think?" he said. He was still watching Richard Pratt. I could see him give a rapid furtive glance down the table each time he dropped his head to take a mouthful of whitebait. I could almost *feel* him waiting for the moment when Pratt would take his first sip, and look up from his glass with a smile of pleasure, of astonishment, perhaps even of wonder, and then there would be a discussion and Mike would tell him about the village of Geierslay.

But Richard Pratt did not taste his wine. He was completely engrossed in conversation with Mike's eighteen-year-old daughter, Louise. He was half turned toward her, smiling at her, telling her, so far as I could gather, some story about a chef in a Paris restaurant. As he spoke, he leaned closer and closer to her, seeming in his eagerness almost to impinge upon her, and the poor girl leaned as far as she could away from him, nodding politely, rather desperately, and looking not at his face but at the topmost button of his dinner jacket.

We finished our fish, and the maid came around removing the plates. When she came to Pratt, she saw that he had not yet touched his food, so she hesitated, and Pratt noticed her. He waved her away, broke off his conversation, and quickly began to eat, popping the little crisp brown fish quickly into his mouth with rapid jabbing movements of his fork. Then, when he had finished, he reached for his glass, and in two short swallows he tipped the wine down his throat and turned immediately to resume his conversation with Louise Schofield.

Mike saw it all. I was conscious of him sitting there, very still, containing himself, looking at his guest. His round jovial face seemed to loosen slightly and to sag, but he contained himself and was still and said nothing.

Soon the maid came forward with the second course. This was a large roast of beef. She placed it on the table in front of Mike who stood up and carved it, cutting the slices very thin, laying them gently on the plates for the maid to take around. When he had served everyone, including himself, he put down the carving knife and leaned forward with both hands on the edge of the table.

"Now," he said, speaking to all of us but looking at Richard Pratt. "Now for the claret. I must go and fetch the claret, if you'll excuse me."

"You go and fetch it, Mike?" I said. "Where is it?"

"In my study, with the cork out — breathing."

"Why the study?"

"Acquiring room temperature, of course. It's been there twenty-four hours."

"But why the study?"

"It's the best place in the house. Richard helped me choose it last time he was here."

At the sound of his name, Pratt looked around.

"That's right, isn't it?" Mike said.

"Yes," Pratt answered, nodding gravely. "That's right."

"On top of the green filing cabinet in my study," Mike said. "That's the place we chose. A good draft-free spot in a room with an even temperature. Excuse me now, will you, while I fetch it."

The thought of another wine to play with had restored his humor, and he hurried out the door, to return a minute later more slowly, walking softly, holding in both hands a wine basket in which a dark bottle lay. The label was out of sight, facing downward. "Now!" he cried as he came toward the table. "What about this one, Richard? You'll never name this one!"

Richard Pratt turned slowly and looked up at Mike; then his eyes traveled down to the bottle nestling in its small wicker basket, and he raised his eyebrows, a slight, supercilious arching of the brows, and with it a pushing outward of the wet lower lip, suddenly imperious and ugly.

"You'll never get it," Mike said. "Not in a hundred years."

"A claret?" Richard Pratt asked, condescending.

"Of course."

"I assume, then, that it's from one of the smaller vineyards?"

"Maybe it is, Richard. And then again, maybe it isn't."

"But it's a good year? One of the great years?"

"Yes, I guarantee that."

"Then it shouldn't be too difficult," Richard Pratt said, drawling his words, looking exceedingly bored. Except that, to me, there was something strange about his drawling and his boredom: between the eyes a shadow of something evil, and in his bearing an intentness that gave me a faint sense of uneasiness as I watched him.

"This one is really rather difficult," Mike said, "I won't force you to bet on this one."

"Indeed. And why not?" Again the slow arching of the brows, the cool, intent look.

"Because it's difficult."

"That's not very complimentary to me, you know."

"My dear man," Mike said, "I'll bet you with pleasure, if that's what you wish."

"It shouldn't be too hard to name it."

"You mean you want to bet?"

"I'm perfectly willing to bet," Richard Pratt said.

"All right, then, we'll have the usual. A case of the wine itself."

"You don't think I'll be able to name it, do you?"

"As a matter of fact, and with all due respect, I don't," Mike said. He was making some effort to remain polite, but Pratt was not bothering overmuch to conceal his contempt for the whole proceeding. And yet, curiously, his next question seemed to betray a certain interest.

"You like to increase the bet?"

"No, Richard. A case is plenty."

"Would you like to bet fifty cases?"

"That would be silly."

Mike stood very still behind his chair at the head of the table, carefully holding the bottle in its ridiculous wicker basket. There was a trace of whiteness around his nostrils now, and his mouth was shut very tight.

Pratt was lolling back in his chair, looking up at him, the eyebrows raised, the eyes half closed, a little smile touching the corners of his lips. And again I saw, or thought I saw, something distinctly disturbing about the man's face, that shadow of intentness between the eyes, and in the eyes themselves, right in their centers where it was black, a small slow spark of shrewdness, hiding.

"So you don't want to increase the bet?"

"As far as I'm concerned, old man, I don't give a damn," Mike said. "I'll bet you anything you like."

The three women and I sat quietly, watching the two men. Mike's wife was becoming annoyed; her mouth had gone sour and I felt that at any moment she was going to interrupt. Our roast beef lay before us on our plates, slowly steaming.

"So you'll bet me anything I like?"

"That's what I told you. I'll bet you anything you damn well please, if you want to make an issue out of it."

"Even ten thousand pounds?"

"Certainly I will, if that's the way you want it." Mike was more confident now. He knew quite well that he could call any sum Pratt cared to mention.

"So you say I can name the bet?" Pratt asked again.

"That's what I said."

There was a pause while Pratt looked slowly around the table, first at me, then at the three women, each in turn. He appeared to be reminding us that we were witness to the offer.

"Mike!" Mrs. Schofield said. "Mike, why don't we stop this nonsense and eat our food. It's getting cold."

"But it isn't nonsense," Pratt told her evenly. "We're making a little bet."

I noticed the maid standing in the background holding a dish of vegetables, wondering whether to come forward with them or not.

"All right, then," Pratt said. "I'll tell you what I want you to bet."

"Come on, then," Mike said, rather reckless. "I don't care what it is — you're on."

Pratt nodded, and again the little smile moved the corners of his lips, and then, quite slowly, looking at Mike all the time, he said, "I want you to bet me the hand of your daughter in marriage."

Louise Schofield gave a jump. "Hey!" she cried. "No! That's not funny! Look here, Daddy, that's not funny at all."

"No, dear," her mother said. "They're only joking."

"I'm not joking," Richard Pratt said.

"It's ridiculous," Mike said. He was off balance again now.

"You said you'd bet anything I liked."

"I meant money."

"You didn't *say* money."

"That's what I meant."

"Then it's a pity you didn't say it. But anyway, if you wish to go back on your offer, that's quite all right with me."

"It's not a question of going back on my offer, old man. It's a no-bet anyway, because you can't match the stake. You yourself don't happen to have a daughter to put up against mine in case you lose. And if you had, I wouldn't want to marry her."

"I'm glad of that, dear," his wife said.

"I'll put up anything you like," Pratt announced. "My house, for example. How about my house?"

"Which one?" Mike asked, joking now.

"The country one."

"Why not the other one as well?"

"All right then, if you wish it. Both my houses."

At that point I saw Mike pause. He took a step forward and placed the bottle in its basket gently down on the table. He moved the saltcellar to one side, then the pepper, and then he picked up his knife, studied the blade thoughtfully for a moment, and put it down again. His daughter, too, had seen him pause.

"Now, Daddy!" she cried. "Don't be *absurd!* It's *too* silly for words. I refuse to be betted on like this."

"Quite right, dear," her mother said. "Stop it at once, Mike, and sit down and eat your food."

Mike ignored her. He looked over at his daughter and he smiled, a slow, fatherly, protective smile. But in his eyes, suddenly, there glimmered a little triumph. "You know," he said, smiling as he spoke. "You know, Louise, we ought to think about this a bit."

"Now, stop it, Daddy! I refuse even to listen to you! Why, I've never heard anything so ridiculous in my life!"

"No, seriously, my dear. Just wait a moment and hear what I have to say."

"But I don't *want* to hear it."

"Louise! Please! It's like this. Richard, here, has offered us a serious bet. He is the one who wants to make it, not me. And if he loses, he will have to hand over a considerable amount of property. Now, wait a minute, my dear, don't interrupt. The point is this. *He cannot possibly win.*"

"He seems to think he can."

"Now listen to me, because I know what I'm talking about. The expert, when tasting a claret — so long as it is not one of the famous great wines like Lafite or Latour — can only get a certain way toward naming the vineyard. He can, of course, tell you the Bordeaux district from which the wine comes, whether it is from St. Emilion, Pomerol, Graves, or Médoc. But then each district has several communes, little counties, and each county has many, many small vineyards. It is impossible for a man to differentiate between them all by taste and smell alone. I don't mind telling you that this one I've got here is a wine from a small vineyard that is surrounded by many other small vineyards, and he'll never get it. It's impossible."

"You can't be sure of that," his daughter said.

"I'm telling you I can. Though I say it myself, I understand quite a bit about this wine business, you know. And anyway, heavens alive, girl, I'm your father and you don't think I'd let you in for — for something you didn't want, do you? I'm trying to make you some money."

"Mike!" his wife said sharply. "Stop it now, Mike, please!"

Again he ignored her. "If you will take this bet," he said to his daughter, "in ten minutes you will be the owner of two large houses."

"But I don't want two large houses, Daddy."

"Then sell them. Sell them back to him on the spot. I'll arrange all that for you. And then, just think of it, my dear, you'll be rich! You'll be independent for the rest of your life!"

"Oh, Daddy, I don't like it. I think it's silly."

"So do I," the mother said. She jerked her head briskly up and down as she spoke, like a hen. "You ought to be ashamed of yourself, Michael, ever suggesting such a thing! Your own daughter, too!"

Mike didn't even look at her. "Take it!" he said eagerly, staring hard at the girl. "Take it, quick! I'll guarantee you won't lose."

"But I don't like it, Daddy."

"Come on, girl. Take it!"

Mike was pushing her hard. He was leaning toward her, fixing her with two hard bright eyes, and it was not easy for the daughter to resist him.

"But what if I lose?"

"I keep telling you, you can't lose. I'll guarantee it."

"Oh, Daddy, must I?"

"I'm making you a fortune. So come on now. What do you say, Louise? All right?"

For the last time, she hesitated. Then she gave a helpless little shrug of the shoulders and said, "Oh, all right, then. Just so long as you swear there's no danger of losing."

"Good!" Mike cried. "That's fine! Then it's a bet!"

"Yes," Richard Pratt said, looking at the girl. "It's a bet."

Immediately, Mike picked up the wine, tipped the first thimbleful into his own glass, then skipped excitedly around the table filling up the others. Now everyone was watching Richard Pratt, watching his face as he reached slowly for his glass with his right hand and lifted it to his nose. The man was about fifty years old and he did not have a pleasant face. Somehow, it was all mouth — mouth and lips — the full, wet lips of the professional gourmet, the lower lip hanging downward in the center, a pendulous, permanently open taster's lip, shaped open to receive the rim of a glass or a morsel of food. Like a keyhole, I thought, watching it; his mouth is like a large wet keyhole.

Slowly he lifted the glass to his nose. The point of the nose entered the glass and moved over the surface of the wine, delicately sniffing. He swirled the wine gently around in the glass to receive the bouquet. His concentration was intense. He had closed his eyes, and now the whole top half of his body, the head and neck and chest, seemed to become a kind of huge sensitive smelling-machine, receiving, filtering, analyzing the message from the sniffing nose.

Mike, I noticed, was lounging in his chair, apparently unconcerned, but he was watching every move. Mrs. Schofield, the wife, sat prim and upright at the other end of the table, looking straight ahead, her face tight with disapproval. The daughter, Louise, had shifted her chair away a little, and sidewise, facing the gourmet, and she, like her father, was watching closely.

For at least a minute, the smelling process continued; then, without opening his eyes or moving his head, Pratt lowered the glass to his mouth and tipped in almost half the contents. He paused, his mouth full of wine, getting the first taste; then he permitted some of it to trickle down his throat and I saw his Adam's apple move as it passed by. But most of it he retained in his mouth. And now, without swallowing again, he drew in through his lips a thin breath of air which mingled with the fumes of the wine in the mouth and passed on down into his lungs. He held the breath, blew it out through his nose, and finally began to roll the wine around under the tongue, and chewed it, actually chewed it with his teeth as though it were bread.

It was a solemn, impressive performance, and I must say he did it well.

"Um," he said, putting down the glass, running a pink tongue over his lips. "Um — yes. A very interesting little wine — gentle and gracious, almost feminine in the aftertaste."

There was an excess of saliva in his mouth, and as he spoke he spat an occasional bright speck of it onto the table.

"Now we can start to eliminate," he said. "You will pardon me for doing this carefully, but there is much at stake. Normally I would perhaps take a bit of a chance, leaping forward quickly and landing right in the middle of the vineyard of my choice. But this time — I must move cautiously this time, must I not?" He looked up at Mike and he smiled, a thick-lipped, wet-lipped smile. Mike did not smile back.

"First, then, which district in Bordeaux does this wine come from? That is not too difficult to guess. It is far too light in the body to be either from St. Emilion or Graves. It is obviously a Médoc. There's no doubt about *that*.

"Now — from which commune in Médoc does it come? That also, by elimination, should not be too difficult to decide. Margaux? No. It cannot be Margaux. It has not the violent bouquet of a Margaux. Pauillac? It cannot be Pauillac, either. It is too tender, too gentle and wistful for a Pauillac. The wine of Pauillac has a character that is almost imperious in its taste. And also, to me, a Pauillac contains just a little pith, a curious, dusty, pithy flavor that the grape acquires from the soil of the district. No, no. This — this is a very gentle wine, demure and bashful in the first taste, emerging shyly but quite graciously in the second. A little arch, perhaps, in the second taste, and a little naughty also, teasing the tongue with a trace, just a trace, of tannin. Then, in the aftertaste, delightful — consoling and feminine, with a certain blithely generous quality that one associates only with the wines of the commune of St. Julien. Unmistakably this is a St. Julien."

He leaned back in his chair, held his hands up level with his chest, and placed the fingertips carefully together. He was becoming ridiculously pompous, but I thought that some of it was deliberate, simply to mock his host. I found myself waiting rather tensely for him to go on. The girl Louise was lighting a cigarette. Pratt heard the match strike and he turned on her, flaring suddenly with real anger. "Please!" he said. "Please don't do that! It's a disgusting habit, to smoke at table!"

She looked up at him, still holding the burning match in one hand, the big slow eyes settling on his face, resting there a moment, moving away again, slow and contemptuous. She bent her head and blew out the match, but continued to hold the unlighted cigarette in her fingers.

"I'm sorry, my dear," Pratt said, "but I simply cannot have smoking at table."

She didn't look at him again.

"Now, let me see — where were we?" he said. "Ah, yes. This wine is from Bordeaux, from the commune of St. Julien, in the district of Médoc. So far, so good. But now we come to the more difficult part — the name of the vineyard itself. For in St. Julien there are many vineyards, and as our host so rightly remarked earlier on, there is often not much difference between the wine of one and the wine of another. But we shall see."

He paused again, closing his eyes. "I am trying to establish the 'growth,' " he said. "If I can do that, it will be half the battle. Now, let me see. This wine is obviously not from a first-growth vineyard — nor even a second. It is not a great wine. The quality, the — the — what do you call it? — the radiance, the power, is lacking. But a third growth — that it could be. And yet I doubt it. We know it is a good year — our host has said so — and this is probably flattering it a little bit. I must be careful. I must be very careful here."

He picked up his glass and took another small sip.

"Yes," he said, sucking his lips, "I was right. It is a fourth growth. Now I am sure of it. A fourth growth from a very good year — from a great year, in fact. And that's what made it taste for a moment like a third — or even a second-growth wine. Good! That's better! Now we are closing in! What are the fourth-growth vineyards in the commune of St. Julien?"

Again he paused, took up his glass, and held the rim against that sagging, pendulous lower lip of his. Then I saw the tongue shoot out, pink and narrow, the tip of it dipping into the wine, withdrawing swiftly again — a repulsive sight. When he lowered the glass, his eyes remained closed, the face concentrated, only the lips moving, sliding over each other like two pieces of wet, spongy rubber.

"There it is again!" he cried. "Tannin in the middle taste, and the quick astringent squeeze upon the tongue. Yes, yes, of course! Now I have it! This wine comes from one of those small vineyards around Beychevelle. I remember now. The Beychevelle district, and the river and the little harbor that has silted up so the wine ships can no longer use it. Beychevelle . . . could it actually be a Beychevelle itself? No, I don't think so. Not quite. But it is somewhere very close. Château Talbot? Could it be Talbot? Yes, it could. Wait one moment."

He sipped the wine again, and out of the side of my eye I noticed Mike Schofield and how he was leaning farther and farther forward over the table, his mouth slightly open, his small eyes fixed upon Richard Pratt.

"No. I was wrong. It was not a Talbot. A Talbot comes forward to you just a little quicker than this one; the fruit is nearer to the surface. If it is a '34, which I believe it is, then it couldn't be Talbot. Well, well. Let me think. It is not a Beychevelle and it is not a Talbot, and yet — yet it is so close to both of them, so close, that the vineyard must be almost in between. Now, which could that be?"

He hesitated, and we waited, watching his face. Everyone, even Mike's wife, was watching him now. I heard the maid put down the dish of vegetables on the sideboard behind me, gently, so as not to disturb the silence.

"Ah!" he cried. "I have it! Yes, I think I have it!"

For the last time, he sipped the wine. Then, still holding the glass up near his mouth, he turned to Mike and he smiled, a slow, silky smile, and he said, "You know what this is? This is the little Château Branaire-Ducru."

Mike sat tight, not moving.

"And the year, 1934."

We all looked at Mike, waiting for him to turn the bottle around in its basket and show the label.

"Is that your final answer?" Mike said.

"Yes, I think so."

"Well, is it or isn't it?"

"Yes, it is."

"What was the name again?"

"Château Branaire-Ducru. Pretty little vineyard. Lovely old château. Know it quite well. Can't think why I didn't recognize it at once."

"Come on, Daddy," the girl said. "Turn it round and let's have a peek. I want my two houses."

"Just a minute," Mike said. "Wait just a minute." He was sitting very quiet, bewildered-looking, and his face was becoming puffy and pale, as though all the force was draining slowly out of him.

"Michael!" his wife called sharply from the other end of the table. "What's the matter?"

"Keep out of this, Margaret, will you please."

Richard Pratt was looking at Mike, smiling with his mouth, his eyes small and bright. Mike was not looking at anyone.

"Daddy!" the daughter cried, agonized. "But, Daddy, you don't mean to say he's guessed it right!"

"Now, stop worrying, my dear," Mike said. "There's nothing to worry about."

I think it was more to get away from his family than anything else that Mike then turned to Richard Pratt and said, "I'll tell you what, Richard. I think you and I better slip off into the next room and have a little chat?"

"I don't want a little chat," Pratt said. "All I want is to see the label on that bottle." He knew he was a winner now; he had the bearing, the quiet arrogance of a winner, and I could see that he was prepared to become thoroughly nasty if there was any trouble. "What are you waiting for?" he said to Mike. "Go on and turn it round."

Then this happened: The maid, the tiny, erect figure of the maid in her white-and-black uniform, was standing beside Richard Pratt, holding something out in her hand. "I believe these are yours, sir," she said.

Pratt glanced around, saw the pair of thin horn-rimmed spectacles that she held out to him, and for a moment he hesitated. "Are they? Perhaps they are. I don't know."

"Yes sir, they're yours." The maid was an elderly woman — nearer seventy than sixty — a faithful family retainer of many years' standing. She put the spectacles down on the table beside him.

Without thanking her, Pratt took them up and slipped them into his top pocket, behind the white handkerchief.

But the maid didn't go away. She remained standing beside and slightly behind Richard Pratt, and there was something so unusual in her manner and in the way she stood there, small, motionless, and erect, that I for one found myself watching her with a sudden apprehension. Her old gray face had a frosty, determined look, the lips were compressed, the little chin was out, and the hands were clasped together tight before her. The curious cap on her head and the flash of white down the front of her uniform made her seem like some tiny, ruffled, white-breasted bird.

"You left them in Mr. Schofield's study," she said. Her voice was unnaturally, deliberately polite. "On top of the green filing cabinet in his study, sir, when you happened to go in there by yourself before dinner."

It took a few moments for the full meaning of her words to penetrate, and in the silence that followed I became aware of Mike and how he was slowly drawing himself up in his chair, and the color coming to his face, and the eyes opening wide, and the curl of the mouth, and the dangerous little patch of whiteness beginning to spread around the area of the nostrils.

"Now, Michael!" his wife said. "Keep calm now, Michael, dear! Keep calm!"

A Narrow Fellow in the Grass

EMILY DICKINSON

A narrow fellow in the grass
Occasionally rides.
You may have met him — did you not?
His notice sudden is.

The grass divides as with a comb;   5
A spotted shaft is seen,
And then it closes at your feet
And opens further on.

He likes a boggy acre,
A floor too cool for corn —   10
Yet when a boy, and barefoot,
I more than once at noon

Have passed, I thought, a whiplash
Unbraiding in the sun;
When, stooping to secure it,   15
It wrinkled, and was gone.

Several of Nature's people
I know, and they know me.
I feel for them a transport
Of cordiality,   20

But never met this fellow,
Attended or alone,
Without a tighter breathing
And zero at the bone.

The Onset

ROBERT FROST

Always the same, when on a fated night
At last the gathered snow lets down as white
As may be in dark woods, and with a song
It shall not make again all winter long
Of hissing on the yet uncovered ground,   5
I almost stumble looking up and round,
As one who overtaken by the end
Gives up his errand, and lets death descend
Upon him where he is, with nothing done
To evil, no important triumph won,   10
More than if life had never been begun.

Yet all the precedent is on my side:
I know that winter death has never tried
The earth but it has failed: the snow may heap
In long storms an undrifted four feet deep   15
As measured against maple, birch, and oak,
It cannot check the peeper's silver croak;
And I shall see the snow all go down hill
In water of a slender April rill
That flashes tail through last year's withered brake   20
And dead weeds, like a disappearing snake.
Nothing will be left white but here a birch,
And there a clump of houses with a church.

The Writer

RICHARD WILBUR

In her room at the prow of the house
Where light breaks, and the windows are tossed with linden,
My daughter is writing a story.

I pause in the stairwell, hearing
From her shut door a commotion of typewriter-keys   5
Like a chain hauled over a gunwale.

Young as she is, the stuff
Of her life is a great cargo, and some of it heavy:
I wish her a lucky passage.

But now it is she who pauses,   10
As if to reject my thought and its easy figure.
A stillness greatens, in which

The whole house seems to be thinking,
And then she is at it again with a bunched clamor
Of strokes, and again is silent.   15

I remember the dazed starling
Which was trapped in that very room, two years ago;
How we stole in, lifted a sash

And retreated, not to affright it;
And how for a helpless hour, through the crack of the door, 20
We watched the sleek, wild, dark

And iridescent creature
Batter against the brilliance, drop like a glove
To the hard floor, or the desk-top,

And wait then, humped and bloody,   25
For the wits to try it again; and how our spirits
Rose when, suddenly sure,

It lifted off from a chair-back,
Beating a smooth course for the right window
And clearing the sill of the world.   30

It is always a matter, my darling,
Of life or death, as I had forgotten. I wish
What I wished you before, but harder.

Breaking Camp

DAVID WAGONER

Having spent a hard-earned sleep, you must break camp in
    the mountains
At the break of day, pulling up stakes and packing,
Scattering your ashes,
And burying everything human you can't carry. Lifting
Your world now on your shoulders, you should turn   5
To look back once
At a place as welcoming to a later dead-tired stranger
As it was to your eyes only the other evening,
As the place you've never seen
But must hope for now at the end of a day's rough journey: 10
You must head for another campsite, maybe no nearer
Wherever you're going
Than where you've already been, but deeply, starkly appealing
Like a lost home: with water, the wind lying down
On a stretch of level earth,   15
And the makings of a fire to flicker against the night
Which you, traveling light, can't bring along
But must always search for.

The Secret

DENISE LEVERTOV

Two girls discover
the secret of life
in a sudden line of
poetry.

I who don't know the   5
secret wrote
the line. They
told me

(through a third person)
they had found it   10
but not what it was,
not even

what line it was. No doubt
by now, more than a week
later, they have forgotten   15
the secret,

the line, the name of
the poem, I love them
for finding what
I can't find,   20

and for loving me
for the line I wrote,
and for forgetting it
so that

a thousand times, till death   25
finds them, they may
discover it again, in other
lines,

in other
happenings. And for   30
wanting to know it,
for

assuming there is
such a secret, yes,
for that   35
most of all.

Index of Writers

Index of Writing Skills

D
E
F
G
H
I
J